# A HISTORY OF
## *Sevier County*

# A HISTORY OF

## *Sevier County*

M. Guy Bishop

1997
Utah State Historical Society
Sevier County Commission

Copyright © 1997 by Sevier County Commission
All rights reserved

ISBN 0-913738-07-7
Library of Congress Catalog Card Number 96-60163
Map by Automated Geographic Reference Center—State of Utah
Printed in the United States of America

Utah State Historical Society
300 Rio Grande
Salt Lake City, Utah 84101-1182

*Dedicated to my parents,*
*George O. and Bernice F. Bishop,*
*for their constant encouragement and support.*

# Contents

# *Acknowledgments*

I would like to thank Kent Powell and Craig Fuller of the Utah State Historical Society, who have been the best support team an author could ever ask for. Their editorial input has been invaluable throughout the writing of this project. Many residents and officials of Sevior County also have been very supportive. My local readers, La Rue Larsen, Max E. Robinson, and former county commissioner T. Merlin Ashman, provided a great deal of help, often clarifying local issues for me. The professional historians who read the entire manuscript, Sevier County native Jeff Johnson of the Utah State Archives and Professor Wayne Hinton of Southern Utah University, offered sound comments which, I believe, improved the finished work. Any errors that remain are unintentional and are mine alone. My heartfelt gratitude goes out to my wife, Kathy, and our nine children, who have lived with this history probably a lot longer than they would have wished. Finally, as the dedication page indicates, this book is for my parents, who have always been there for me.

M. Guy Bishop

## General Introduction

When Utah was granted statehood on 4 January 1896, twenty-seven counties comprised the nation's new forty-fifth state. Subsequently two counties, Duchesne in 1914 and Daggett in 1917, were created. These twenty-nine counties have been the stage on which much of the history of Utah has been played.

Recognizing the importance of Utah's counties, the Utah State Legislature established in 1991 a Centennial History Project to write and publish county histories as part of Utah's statehood centennial commemoration. The Division of State History was given the assignment to administer the project. The county commissioners, or their designees, were responsible for selecting the author or authors for their individual histories, and funds were provided by the state legislature to cover most research and writing costs as well as to provide each public school and library with a copy of each history. Writers worked under general guidelines provided by the Division of State History and in cooperation with county history committees. The counties also established a Utah Centennial County History Council to help develop policies for distribution of state-appropriated funds and plans for publication.

Each volume in the series reflects the scholarship and interpretation of the individual author. The general guidelines provided by the Utah State Legislature included coverage of five broad themes encompassing the economic, religious, educational, social, and political history of the county. Authors were encouraged to cover a vast period of time stretching from geologic and prehistoric times to the present. Since Utah's statehood centennial celebration falls just four years before the arrival of the twenty-first century, authors were encouraged to give particular attention to the history of their respective counties during the twentieth century.

Still, each history is at best a brief synopsis of what has transpired within the political boundaries of each county. No history can do justice to every theme or event or individual that is part of an area's past. Readers are asked to consider these volumes as an introduction to the history of the county, for it is expected that other researchers and writers will extend beyond the limits of time, space, and detail imposed on this volume to add to the wealth of knowledge about the county and its people. In understanding the history of our counties, we come to understand better the history of our state, our nation, our world, and ourselves.

In addition to the authors, local history committee members, and county commissioners, who deserve praise for their outstanding efforts and important contributions, special recognition is given to Joseph Francis, chairman of the Morgan County Historical Society, for his role in conceiving the idea of the centennial county history project and for his energetic efforts in working with the Utah State Legislature and State of Utah officials to make the project a reality. Mr. Francis is proof that one person does make a difference.

ALLAN KENT POWELL
CRAIG FULLER
GENERAL EDITORS

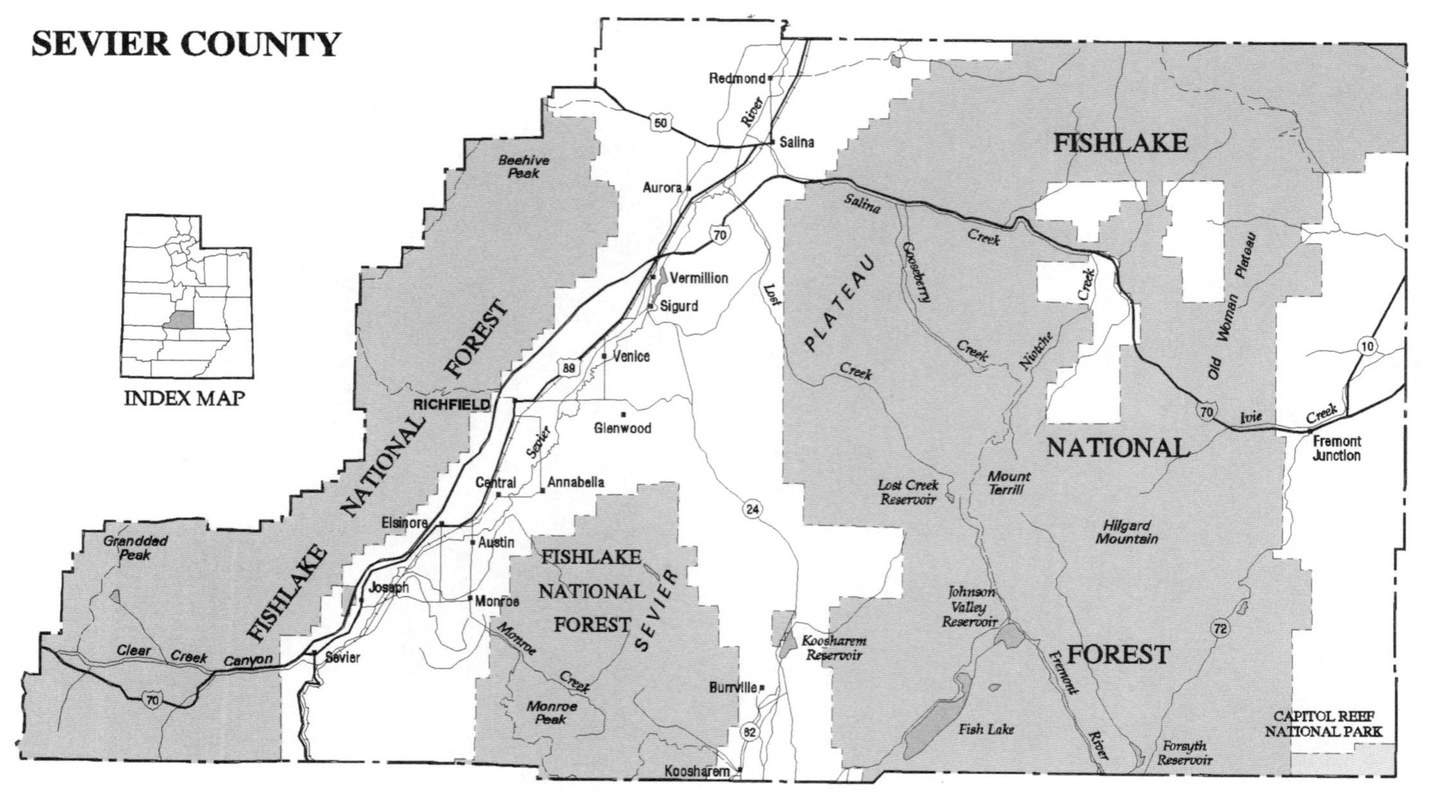

SEVIER COUNTY
INDEX MAP
FISHLAKE
NATIONAL
FOREST
CAPITOL REEF NATIONAL PARK
Redmond
Salina
Beehive Peak
Aurora
Vermillion
Sigurd
Venice
Glenwood
Annabella
Central
Austin
Elsinore
Joseph
Monroe
Sevier
Plateau
Salina Creek
Gooseberry Creek
Niotche Creek
Old Woman Plateau
Ivie Creek
Fremont Junction
Lost Creek Reservoir
Mount Terill
Hilgard Mountain
Johnson Valley Reservoir
Koosharem Reservoir
Fish Lake
Fremont River
Forsyth Reservoir
RICHFIELD
FISHLAKE NATIONAL FOREST
Grandad Peak
Clear Creek Canyon
FISHLAKE NATIONAL FOREST
SEVIER
Monroe Peak
Monroe Creek
Burrville
Koosharem

# A Harsh Land

Geographer Richard H. Jackson has described much of the state of Utah as a "harsh land." In fact, Jackson points out that it is part of Utah Mormon folklore that the entire state was a desert when it was first settled by the Mormon pioneers.[1] He finds it useful to classify Utah into harsh and fertile lands, and, although others may not divide the state as Jackson has done, harsh or, at best, inhospitable, seems to be an accurate adjective for describing much of the Sevier County landscape.

Not only does the directly observed landscape of the county offer a seemingly inhospitable scene to the human eye, the more hidden aspects of nature also add to the uncharitable nature of the county. Given the region's unstable geological history, shaped by volcanos and earthquakes, life in Sevier County also can be potentially hazardous. Seismological history shows that the region was shaken by noticeable earth tremors at least twenty-nine times during the last one hundred years.[2] All of these earthquakes occurred along the Tushar Fault, which stretches from the southwest to the northeast portion of the county.

Main street in Richfield about 1900. (Utah State Historical Society)

On 29 December 1876 a "slight but distinct" earthquake was felt at Richfield shortly after ten o'clock at night. According to local reports, it "felt like two shocks in quick succession." Three days later, on 1 January 1877, a quake of moderate intensity again struck Richfield. The seismic activity was not yet through, however. Two weeks later (15 January 1877), the *Deseret News* noted, "Sevier County was visited, at five o'clock this morning by two more earthquake shocks."[3]

Nearly twenty-four years later, on 13 November 1901, the Richfield area withstood an even larger quake, which was felt in a 50,000-square-mile area. This tremor struck in the early morning hours and reportedly lasted at least ten seconds. The intense shaking caused local residents to flee outdoors seeking safety. Brick buildings in the Richfield vicinity suffered considerable damage. The newly constructed Sevier LDS Stake Tabernacle was severely damaged. Chimneys toppled over, cracks were noticed in the ground east of Richfield, and rockslides in the nearby canyons rendered them almost impassable for several weeks afterward. The epicenter of this earthquake was near Marysvale in Piute County. Modern seismologists have estimated the intensity of the quake to have been 6.0 or greater on the Richter scale. It was felt more than two hundred miles away at Salt Lake City.[4]

In 1880 U. S. Army Captain Clarence E. Dutton published a geological survey, *Report of the Geology of the High Plateaus of Utah, With Atlas,* which might well have served notice to local residents of the unstable nature of the county's unstable land.

Seismographic technician Steve Bellon of the University of Utah has observed that "quakes are not uncommon in this area . . . but generally [are] never felt by residents."[5] During the first half of the twentieth century, the county experienced earth tremors about every twenty years or so. Some were notable occurrences, others were not. For example, on the night of 20 February 1906 the farming village of Elsinore was shaken by a small quake, but little damage was done. Unfortunately, such was not always the case. Fifteen years later, between 13 September and 20 December 1921, the Tushar Fault was active once again as tremors were felt at Richfield, Elsinore, and Joseph. The quake which struck Elsinore on 1 October was the most severe. Brick and stone buildings were rendered uninhabitable by the damage. At nearby Monroe, the city hall was "shattered." By this date scientists were coming to believe that "the whole Sevier Valley was a fault zone."[6] So, although more recent residents of Sevier County might not have experienced major earth movement, the ground in the region is constantly shifting, sometimes quite dramatically and at other times much less noticeably. Sporadic earthquakes have always been a part of the county's natural history.

This has been more recently borne out. At 3:21 a. m. on Monday 3 January 1972, county residents were roused from bed by a sharp earthquake which was felt from Richfield and Glenwood on the north to as far south as Joseph. Fortunately, no major damage occurred. This quake was measured at 3.7 Richter scale magnitude by the area's University of Utah seismograph station—making it relatively small when compared with earlier tremors. The epicenter was judged to be about seventeen miles southeast of Richfield.[7]

Elsinore, Monroe, and Joseph were the hardest hit. Law enforcement offices received several reports of cracked walls and ceilings and broken dishes and light fixtures around the county. This quake was the third major tremor to be felt in the Richfield area since 1968, according to the *Richfield Reaper*.

The people of Sevier County have often been reminded of nature's power. Along with earthquakes, water can be both a godsend and a curse, and the county has historically experienced frequent serious flooding. Flash flooding, while always fearsome, is an even greater concern in agricultural communities. Raging torrents pouring out of mountain canyons often disrupted life in isolated rural communities and in a short period of time ruined a season's hard work.

During the summer of 1896 several devastating floods roared through Sevier County communities. From 11 July to 17 July, waters from Otter Creek inundated Koosharem. Local runoff also flooded Annabella, Elsinore, Joseph, Monroe, Richfield, Sevier, and Sigurd between 14 July and 28 August 1896, submerging adjacent cropland. On Monday, 18 July, a deluge heavily damaged Richfield.[8] Five years later, on 3 August 1901, high water from Cottonwood Creek struck Richfield again. "A cloudburst in the canyon caused a mud and debris-laden stream to pour forth," noted a local report.[9]

County residents who were facing recurring natural calamity wisely moved to try to confine ravaging floodwater by means of the construction of flood canals. At first, however, their efforts proved fruitless. Part of the flow was diverted from Richfield by a large canal, but it was soon filled to overflowing and much additional damage resulted.[10] Try as they might, the citizens of the county seemed powerless to control nature's might.

On 25 August 1905, according to local reports, Richfield suffered again, this time from one of the most destructive floods known in years, as a "huge body of water emerged from [Cottonwood and Willow Creek] canyons and spread over the valley." The Sevier Valley Canal quickly filled with mud and rocks. Fields were covered, shocks of grain were submerged in water or mud, and many fields were washed away. Main Street was flooded and nine head of cattle were washed away and drowned.[11]

Monroe was especially hard hit between 1896 and 1929, as thirteen floods swamped the village. On 18 July 1896 the community

An early road and bridge in Sevier County. (Utah State Historical Society)

reported "Thunder, lightning and damaging floods." In 1922 Monroe suffered from a cloudburst in the hills which caused "considerable damage" to gardens and crops in the town. As so often happened, "Mud and debris were deposited eight to ten inches deep" near the village.[12]

Thirty-three years later, on 27 August 1929, Cottonwood Creek again flooded Richfield; that same day, waters from Denmark Wash gushed into Aurora. During the intervening years, over thirty other recorded floods had occurred within the county.[13] Natural forces continued to be prominently featured in the history of this harsh land.

In 1992, county residents were reminded again of the county's yet-untamed natural environment. This time, rather than shaking ground or raging waters, the disturber was millions of Mormon crickets from the Pahvant Mountains.[14] The result was what the local newspaper termed a "war." It must have reminded many of the stories of the battle more than one hundred years before between the Mormon pioneers of the Great Salt Lake Valley and a similar insect army. Legend says that seagulls providentially saved these early settlers from disaster in their moment of need. It was modern pesticides rather than the fortuitous descent of gulls which rescued Sevier County's harvest. According to Greg Abbott of the Utah Department of Agriculture, carbaryl bran bait was used to stem the infestation.[15]

One year earlier, crickets had swarmed out of the same mountains crossing west of Interstate 15 to inundate fields and several residential areas. In 1992 the infestation resulted in a concentrated effort on the part of the Richfield city government led by Mayor Jay Anderson to halt the march of the crickets. Earthquakes, floods, and insect infestations have all contributed to what makes Sevier County a harsh land.

Former Sevier County Commissioner T. Merlin Ashman, a farmer by profession, identified yet another aspect of the harshness of the county's land. He used the word "arid" to describe Sevier County.[16] Aridity and the accompanying need for water is a key to understanding much of the county's history. It is a complex situation: sometimes moisture is the most precious commodity to be found; at other times the rain pours from the sky in cloudbursts that cause devastating floods. The human tenacity required to remain in such a place is enormous.

It has been said that irrigation is the human response to drought. This has been true in Sevier County, where nature often presents people with an inhospitable, harsh environment. County residents have set about to conquer their surroundings. In the nineteenth century, Mormon settlers of the county dug miles of ditches to bring water to their thirsty crops. By the next century irrigation efforts were expanded and improved, and the county also considered and employed modern technology (for example, cloud-seeding) to bring moisture to the parched land. The silver iodide smoke dispersed from ground-based generators may have worked too well at times—at least, there was sometimes too much rain. Destructive cloudbursts, perhaps brought on by cloud-seeding, became frequent hindrances to county prosperity.

Contemporary with the cloud-seeding project was an ongoing project from 1957 to 1972 conducted at the request of the Sevier River Water Users Association to measure any changes in water yield

Looking south to the community of Glenwood with Glenwood Mountain in the background. (Allan Kent Powell)

from the river. Max Robinson of the Forest Service spearheaded the study, known as the Sheep Creek Water Evaluation Project, which, it was hoped, might determine whether the runoff water yield could be increased through changing the type of vegetation in the Fishlake National Forest.[17]

Vegetation conservation in the Sheep Creek area was found to increase water yield from 463 acre-feet to 621 acre-feet.[18] While cloud-seeding was the most spectacular (and controversial) means tried to increase the water supply in Sevier County, the vegetation conservation fostered by the Forest Service quietly increased the local water supply. Also, the flooding which sometimes accompanied cloud-seeding was absent with the Forest Service's type of water management.

The human touch has tempered the land somewhat, making it less brutal. Through the prudent manipulation of water by irrigation, Sevier County had become by 1995 a fertile agricultural region. The Mormon pioneers who came to the Sevier River Valley in 1864 must have taken very seriously the biblical injunction to "subdue" the earth (Genesis 1:28). Not only did they subdue or tame, at least to a degree, the harsh land but they also prospered there.

The sense or feel of a place as it relates to the human experience there is intimately linked with the environment. What, we might well ask, characterizes Sevier County and its people? The obvious answer is that the land is harsh but its inhabitants have always proved hardy.

Regarding the harsh, arid nature of the land, let us recall the words of an early explorer and of a nineteenth-century resident of the region. In the early 1870s U. S. Army Captain Clarence E. Dutton, who surveyed the geology of south-central Utah, found the area marked by the remnants of "old volcanic piles worn down by ages of decay." A harsh scene, to say the least. Some fifteen years later, another observer wrote in the records of the LDS Sevier Stake how the Sevier River Valley appeared "never to have been soaked with water."[19] Yet, following the development of irrigation techniques bringing much-needed water to the soil, by the twentieth century this harsh land had fallen under human control, as distribution ditches brought priceless water to county farmers. Recently, sprinkler irrigation employing water on-call from local reservoirs has rendered county agriculture productive beyond anything ever imagined by preceding generations of farmers.

The Sevier County story is one of humankind succeeding in an unfriendly land. The people who have flourished here are a strong and dedicated lot. While the county's environment can be a demanding one, its people have generally proven equal to the task. In an agricultural county like this, it can truly be said that "the land on which we live is the major source of wealth and economic growth."[20]

This rich land is beautiful and undulating. But with this beauty lies the potential for great destruction. Earthquakes, floods, and pestilence have served to test the mettle of the people of Sevier County throughout its history. Yet, it must be remembered that the county's history is not only one of natural disasters but also of human triumphs. People and nature are intimately intertwined in Sevier County.

## ENDNOTES

1. Richard H. Jackson, "Utah's Harsh Lands, Hearth of Greatness," *Utah Historical Quarterly* 49 (Winter 1981): 5.

2. J. Stewart Williams and Mary L. Tapper, "Earthquake History of Utah, 1850–1953," *Bulletin of the Seismological Society of America* 43 (July 1953): 193; *Richfield Reaper,* 6 January 1972, 1.

3. Williams and Tapper, "Earthquake History of Utah," 197.

4. Ibid., 202.

5. *Richfield Reaper,* 6 January 1972, 1.

6. Williams and Tapper, "Earthquake History of Utah," 209–10.

7. *Richfield Reaper,* 6 January 1972, 1.

8. United States Department of Agriculture, "Sevier River Basin Floods," Appendix VII (September 1971), 27, 28, 30, 33, 35, 40, 47, copy available at the Utah State Historical Society, Salt Lake City.

9. Ibid., 30.

10. Ibid., 56.

11. Ibid., 59.

12. Ibid., 48, 71.

13. Ibid., 23–33.

14. *Richfield Reaper,* 19 August 1992, 3-A.

15. Ibid.

16. T. Merlin Ashman, interview with the author, 23 March 1995.

17. *Deseret News,* 13 January 1967.

18. Max E. Robinson, "Sheep Creek Water Evaluation Project, Fishlake

National Forest," abridged by Delpha M. Noble (Ogden, UT: United States Department of Agriculture, 1973).

19. Clarence Dutton, *Report of the Geology of the High Plateaus of Utah* (Washington, D.C.: Government Printing Office, 1880), 226; Sevier Stake Historical Records and Minutes, 14 April 1886, Archives, Church of Jesus Christ of Latter-day Saints, Salt Lake City (hereafter cited as LDS Archives).

20. Robert D. Nielsen, "Land Use in Utah," in "The Future of Utah's Environment," edited by Michael Treshow and C. M. Gilmour, proceedings of a conference held at the University of Utah, 17–18 October 1968, 44, typescript, copy at the Utah State Historical Society Library.

1

# The Natural History of Sevier County

South-central Utah's Sevier County is a moderately populated county of 15,431, according to the 1990 U.S. Census. This ranks Sevier fourteenth in inhabitants out of twenty-nine counties in the state, just behind Summit County (15,518) and nearly three thousand people more than Duchesne (12,645) following.

Sevier County is part of a huge expanse. Like a great deal of Utah and the Intermountain West, it is an arid land. Anyone who has driven across modern-day Sevier County discerns its stern and demanding character. But at the same time the county offers a rough beauty which in many ways is moving and inspiring.

Eighteenth-century white explorers of the area helped create fantastic legends about the lands which they saw or had heard about. The Spanish friars Francisco Atanasio Domínguez and Silvestre Vélez de Escalante traversed some of what is today is south-central Utah in 1776, reporting on "a combined lake [with] an outlet to the sea."[1] Domínguez and Escalante's task was to find a route to California from Santa Fe, New Mexico.

They may have thought they had found just such a water-born

Cattle graze in Plateau Valley with the Fishlake Hightop Plateau in the background. (Allan Kent Powell)

highway when they first crossed the Green River and later when they encountered the Sevier River. They had heard from the Indians of a mythical river which ran west to the ocean, a river they called the Rio

Buenaventura. The Sevier River, however, drained into Sevier Lake. The diary of their journey in 1776 reveals that these Catholic clerics were the first Europeans known to have visited central Utah, traveling from Utah Lake through the Sevier Desert west of present-day Sevier County to southwestern Utah and then east back to Santa Fe.

After Domínguez and Escalante, neither the Catholic church nor government officials from Spain returned to colonize and settle Utah. However, some five decades later, Spanish traders and men of commerce did visit the territory frequently, traveling by horse and mule caravans through central Utah and Sevier County on the Old Spanish Trail between Santa Fe and the Spanish colonies in California.

Seventy-five years after the Spanish clerics visited the area, Utah's most famous pioneer, Brigham Young, thanked the Lord in a 7 June 1857 address for bringing his people to the unwanted Salt Lake Valley. Young began his sermon listing for his Latter-day Saint listeners the follies which might have befallen them had they settled elsewhere, as some Mormons had wanted. He reminded them that they were favored to live in the "happiest situation of any people in the world."[2] Young went on to express his gratitude that "the Lord has brought us to these barren valleys, to these sterile mountains, to this desolate waste, where only Saints can or would live, to a region that is not desired by another class of people on the earth." Surely early settlers of Sevier County felt they were fulfilling Brigham Young's fondest hopes in this regard when they later were sent by the church leader to colonize the area.

Sevier County is the southern portion of an even larger area of what is often considered "inhospitable land"—the Great Basin. The Great Basin stretches from southeastern Oregon into Nevada and southern California, extending east through Nevada into central and northwestern Utah. It is a unique land marked by an interior drainage of its rivers and streams; that is, water falling in the Great Basin has no outlet to the ocean. Scientists believe the Great Basin dates back some 75,000 years. The eastern (or Utah) portion of the basin was submerged under ancient Lake Bonneville, a huge freshwater lake, of which the present Great Salt Lake is but a remnant.[3]

The Sevier Valley is believed to have been above and beyond the expanse of this primeval sea, but it is possible to imagine the waters of that substantial lake lapping at portions of the Sevier Valley. In fact, there is some evidence of shorelines low on the base of the Pavant and Tushar mountains in this vicinity.[4]

The county's western border is the Pavant Plateau, described by one explorer as a "bleak and windy plain."[5] However, Pavant is a Paiute term thought to mean "water people." The Pavant Plateau, which runs from northeast to southwest, begins at Scipio Valley in northern Millard County and terminates when it intersects the Tushar Mountains at the Clear Creek drainage at the extreme southwest section of Sevier County. The Tushars are the highest range in southern Utah, attaining an elevation in places of more than 12,000 feet.[6] There are several peaks in the Pavant Plateau which exceed 10,000 feet, including White Pine Peak west of Sigurd and Mount Catherine and Jacks Peak, both located in Millard County east of Fillmore. The Pavant Plateau and the Tushar Mountains to the south serve as natural boundaries for the Sevier River Valley along with the Sevier Plateau, which serves the same purpose to the east. Mount Marvine—named for noted geologist Archibald R. Marvine and member of the 1873 Hayden geological survey in the West—is the highest peak in the county, with an elevation of more than 11,600 feet.

These plateaus and mountains were formed during the late Cretaceous era (over 100 million years ago) when a major geological disturbance occurred in south-central Utah. This natural phenomenon is known as the Sevier Orogeny. An orogeny is literally the process by which mountains are formed. Over geological time, compressive forces have bent and folded the land, fracturing and elevating it in places along thrust faults. Later, these portions often slide under the pull of gravity from higher to lower positions. For example, in central Utah, the Charleston-Nebo Thrust Plate clearly originated at a higher elevation than its present setting.

Geologists believe that Mount Timpanogos in Utah County was carved from an over-riding slice of the Charleston-Nebo Thrust, which came to rest at its present location on the Wasatch Mountain line.[7] Similarly, the Sevier Orogeny resulted in massive deposits in the Indianola Conglomerate stretching southward from the vicinity of Gunnison in Sanpete County through the High Plateau regions of both Sanpete and Sevier counties. Signs of this geologic activity can be seen in the coarse sediments found in both counties.[8] The Pavant Plateau is a result of great thrust faults occurring during the Sevier Orogeny of the older Cambrian period (about 570 million years ago) and the Silurian period (about 440 million years ago), rocks from the west having moved eastward across rocks to the east.

Sevier County is located in what seismologists call the Intermountain Seismic Belt, which stretches from the northwestern corner of Montana to the north-central section of Arizona. Active surface displacement continues in the county from four seismic faults which parallel each other. The Tushar Fault, which begins near Sigurd and terminates west of Junction in Piute County, runs through the Pavant Plateau. The Hurricane Fault is found farther west of the Tushar Fault, and it extends from about Scipio to northern Arizona, paralleling Interstate 15. Extending from Mayfield in Sanpete County to northern Arizona is the Sevier Fault. It generally parallels U.S. Highway 89 and is located east of the highway. The fourth significant fault is the shorter Elsinore Fault, which runs north and south of Elsinore.

These faults have spawned a significant number of earthquakes since the settlement of the county in the mid-1860s. In this century, earthquakes have jolted the county with some regularity, as was noted in the introduction to this book. In the pre-dawn hours of 13 November 1901 a powerful earthquake on the Tushar Fault hit the county. It was felt over a 50,000-square-mile area of Utah. Damage to buildings occurred as far south as St. George and Kanab; the quake was felt in Milford to the west, and property damage was experienced in Elsinore, Richfield, Monroe, and other communities in the county.[9] Two earthquakes hit the county on 10 and 11 January 1910, both originating along the Tushar Fault. The first resulted in the closing of some of the schools in the county.[10]

The year 1921 was a particularly active year for earthquakes in central Utah. At least a dozen earthquakes rumbled through various parts of the county from September to December. The 1 October earthquake was particularly severe. Dr. Frederick J. Pack, head of the Department of Geology at the University of Utah, was in Sevier County investigating earlier earthquakes. He was at a public meeting in Elsinore to discuss recent numerous earthquakes in the county; however, the people of Elsinore refused to meet in the local ward meetinghouse to hear his report. Pack was forced to address the frightened people of Elsinore from the steps of the meetinghouse. Very early the next morning, Dr. Pack and the people of the county experienced a large earthquake which rocked the county. Pack reported that "the walls of even the more substantial buildings swayed back and forth in such a manner as to topple or otherwise destroy practically every chimney in the city." The falling trees and the collapse of various buildings from the earthquake created a great amount of dust, which in certain locations in the county "was so dense that one could see only a few rods away," Pack reported to the *Deseret News.* [11] That night, many of the people of Monroe slept "in haystacks" fearing more shocks and greater damage to buildings in town. The city hall in Monroe, which was built of rock, "was badly shattered," the *Salt Lake Tribune* reported.

What of the lay of Sevier County's land? The renowned western explorer Major John Wesley Powell wrote in his *Lands of the Arid Region of the United States:* "The road leading southward from Gunnison up the valley of the Sevier River lies along a smooth plain between the Pavant Range on the west and the monoclinal on the east. . . . Far to the south-southeast is seen a portion of the Tushar, the main mass being hidden by a very obtuse salient of the Pavant."[12] Volcanic eruptions between 35 and 22 million years ago were responsible for raising the land and leaving the massive debris which resulted in the Tushar Mountains.

Glacial erosion, water, and wind during the past 15 million years have largely removed the distinctive volcanic shape from the Tushars. But the yellow color of many peaks on the east (Sevier County) side of the range attests to the volcanic activity which gave birth to these mountains. At the southwestern tip of the Tushar Mountains near Circleville in Piute County the mountains and the Sevier Plateau draw close together, almost confining the Sevier River.

The geological backbone of central Utah is the high plateaus, which includes the Pavant Plateau, Tushar Mountains, and the Sevier Plateau. The high plateaus were surveyed in the 1870s by Captain Clarence E. Dutton of the United States Geological Survey.[13] Dutton's monumental report, the words of which have been said paint "romantic pictures" of Utah's high plateau country, serves as a geological guide to Sevier County's natural history.[14] And it is the county's mountains and plateaus that provide the most distinguishing aspects of the landscape.

Dutton's surveys, undertaken during the summers of 1875, 1876, and 1877, were done under the direction of Major John Wesley Powell, soon-to-be head of the U.S. Geological Survey. In 1871 Dutton was stationed in Washington, D.C., where he found himself attracted to the local philosophical society's meetings. At one of these gatherings he made the acquaintance of Powell. At that time, Powell was preparing for his second descent through the canyons of the Green and Colorado rivers, and he was reportedly "besieged" by adventurous men eager to accompany him.

As destiny would have it, Captain Dutton became a member of Powell's 1871–72 exploration of the Colorado Plateau country of southern Utah and northern Arizona.[15] A graduate of Yale, Dutton became one of the nation's premier nineteenth-century scientists. Major Powell proposed to Dutton as early as 1874 that the captain survey "the large volcanic tract in the Territory of Utah."[16] Clarence Dutton later wrote: "The High Plateaus are in the chief part of a great volcanic area, in which eruptions have occurred upon a grand scale." Scientists like Powell and Dutton had long hypothesized that repeated volcanic explosions spread ash northward across the southeast corner of the Pavant Range to the present area of Richfield. The 1880 publication of Dutton's *The High Plateaus of Utah* enhanced earlier observations made by Powell. Twentieth-century scientists have tended to concur. Sevier County is a land born of the cataclysms of nature.

Dutton's writings on the high plateaus first brought the region to national attention. During the mid-1870s he surveyed the plateau country which today makes up Sevier County. With the exactness of a topographical engineer, Clarence Dutton described the Sevier Plateau as "a long and rather narrow uplift, having a fault along its western base and inclining to the eastward; at first very gently, then with a stronger slope, which grades rapidly down into Grass Valley."[17]

Drawing upon his earlier experiences with the Powell surveys of the Colorado Plateau, Dutton likened the Sevier Plateau to a "tabular mass" resembling "the Kaibab region to the southward." Of the south-central Utah region, he wrote:

> Standing in the Sevier Valley and looking at this barrier there are many stretches which appear along its western front which appear quite like a common mountain range. Profound gorges, V-shaped, heading far back in its mass, have cut the table from summit to base and open magnificent gateways into the valley.[18]

Staying with the volcanic-derivation interpretive theme which both he and later geographers have applied to this region of Utah, Dutton observed that the summit of the Sevier Plateau was marked by the "remnants of old volcanic piles worn down and obliterated by long ages of decay." These volcanoes, he conjectured, belonged to the middle epoch of the Middle Miocene geological period (approximately 15 to 20 million years ago).

The Tushar Mountains of extreme southern Sevier County have a significant amount of mineral wealth, which includes deposits of gold, silver, lead, zinc, uranium, and alunite. The Marysvale mining region encompassing Sevier and Piute counties contains the most concentrated and varied assemblage of igneous rocks within the state. Several major groups of these rocks have been identified in this district.[19] Piute County's famed Big Rock Candy Mountain is located within the Marysvale region. While this landmark is not actually in Sevier County, its relationship to the county and its natural history is nonetheless worthy of note.

The Big Rock Candy Mountain appears almost out of nowhere around a bend in Marysvale Canyon twenty-one miles south of Richfield. The mountain's vivid bright-yellow color presents a stark contrast to the typical drab grey hills of south-central Utah's desert country. Like much of Sevier County's geological landscape, this popular mountain resulted from volcanic activity eons ago. Its yellowish color is derived from the minerals found in the mountain—potassium, iron, aluminum, sulfate, and sulfide.[20] These same minerals are found in abundance throughout the high plateau country of the county, including the Sevier, Awapa, and Fish Lake plateaus.[21]

The Sevier Plateau shapes the topography of the eastern half of

The Big Rock Candy Mountain with the Sevier River in the foreground in southern Sevier County. (Utah State Historical Society)

the county. It is more than seventy miles long and varies in width from ten to twenty miles. The northern end, which is not well defined, begins near Salina. It extends south, terminating in northern Garfield County, where it joins the Paunsaugunt Plateau. Located on the eastern flank of the Sevier Plateau is Fishlake Plateau, where the beautiful alpine Fish Lake is located. The lake lies at an elevation of about 8,000 feet and occupies a small graben or rift valley, formed as a depression between two blocks of earth bounded by faults. The north end of the lake is dammed by a glacial moraine, or rock deposited from the grinding and scouring action of glacier ice. The lake is the mother of the Fremont River, which is part of the Colorado River drainage system. The average depth of the lake is about eighty-five feet, with a maximum depth of more than 115 feet.[22] The lake drainage is about forty square miles.

Fish Lake was probably well known by Mexican and other traders using the Spanish Trail and its variants. One of the first known

Boaters on Fish Lake. (Utah State Historical Society)

recorded visits was by Lieutenant George D. Brewerton, who in 1848 accompanied Christopher "Kit" Carson from Los Angeles, California, to Taos, New Mexico, using the Old Spanish Trail to deliver mail. The party traveled east carrying word of the discovery of gold in California.

In June the small company of about twenty men reached Sevier County and Fish Lake. "We camped one evening upon a beautiful little lake situated in a hollow among the mountains," wrote Brewerton, "but at so great an elevation that it was, even in summer, surrounded by snow, and partially covered with ice."[23] Soon after making camp at Fish Lake, Brewerton and Carson learned of the abundance of fish found in the lake and its small tributary streams. One Ute method for fishing was to spear the fish as they began to spawn in the small streams. Brewerton tried his hand using the Utes' method. "For my own part, with an old bayonet fastened to a stick, I caught five dozen," he later recalled.[24] Brewerton and the Utes fished for the two native fish species, cutthroat trout and Colorado mottled sculpin.[25] With this kind of plentiful catch in a very short time, it is assumed that the Indians living in the area must have fished the lake extensively; they also hunted the mountains for game and collected berries in season.

Frands Peterson, who lived in Grass Valley near Koosharem at the turn of the century, recalled the abundance of cutthroat trout in Seven Mile Creek and Fish Lake: "Cutthroat trout didn't depend on just streams that flowed into Fish Lake in which to spawn. I have seen thousands of them migrate down out of the lake and swim up Seven Mile Creek where the big spawning beds for this fine trout were found. After the spawning season, the fish came back down Seven Mile Creek and up into Fish Lake."[26]

The Sevier Plateau contains significant deposits of gypsum which was formed during the Jurassic period when Sevier County was covered with saline water. Gypsum is used in the manufacturing of construction wallboard, and the Jumbo Plaster and Cement Company began manufacturing gypsum on a large scale about 1908 near Sigurd.[27] Since the turn of the century, the mining of gypsum and the manufacturing of gypsum wallboard has added significantly to the economy of the county.

Underlying parts of the eastern Sevier Plateau in the northeastern corner of the county are several significant deposits of coal. The Salina Canyon District extends westward from near the Sevier-Emery county line in an oblong configuration along Interstate 70 to within several miles of Salina. Immediately north and east of the Salina Canyon Coal District are the Wasatch Plateau and Castle Valley fields. The Wasatch Plateau Field is sandwiched between the Castle Valley Field to the east and the Salina Canyon District to the west. Both large coal fields run in a northeast-to-southwest direction, with the vast majority of the coal deposits located in Emery County. The Wasatch Plateau Field extends south and west to Mount Hilgard. These beds of coal were formed more than 60 million years ago during the Cretaceous period. The majority of coal mined in the county has been extracted since the outbreak of World War II. During the twenty-year period between 1942 and 1963 at least one million tons of coal were mined in the county, which represents only about .046 percent of the estimated coal reserves in the county.[28] Coal mining and the transportation of coal has added to the county's overall economy, especially the northern part of the county and the community of Salina.

An outstanding natural resource of Sevier County is the forest and grazing land of the high plateaus, including the Pavant Plateau. Forested and grazing lands on these plateaus surrounding the county were first designated a forest reserve in February 1897 by President Grover Cleveland. The Fishlake Reserve, as originally constituted, embraced land from Sevier, Piute, and Wayne counties. The establishment of forest reserves, beginning in 1891 nationally, grew out of concern for the general deterioration of forested lands in the West. In the 1890s Sevier County and central Utah in general experienced growing numbers of sheep and cattle on the area mountains. In northern Sevier County and southern Sanpete County, transient stock and migratory and trail herds were inflicting severe damage to the watersheds. Concerned with this growing problem of transient herds devastating their watersheds and the heavy grazing of their traditional summer grazing grounds, residents of the Sevier Valley petitioned the federal government to create the Fishlake Forest Reserve in July 1896.[29]

Six year later, in the summer and fall of 1902, an extensive survey of the forested lands of Utah was conducted by forester Albert Potter, a former Arizona livestockman, for the purpose of expanding existing forest reserves and creating new ones. Meeting with townspeople and ranchers alike, he found mixed reactions in central Utah and in Sevier County to any proposed enlargement or creation of new forest reserves. During his summer survey, Potter found some of the land in northeastern Sevier County near Salina and Clear creeks being "overgrazed and trampled by sheep," the grass "all eaten off very close."[30] As a result of his findings and continued interest by some residents of the county and elsewhere in central Utah, the Fishlake Reserve was enlarged.

Then, by the summer of 1906, other forest reserves were created by presidential decrees in the central part of the state including the Fillmore and the Beaver forest reserves, which extended from Scipio, Millard County, on the north to Bear Valley near Circleville in Piute County on the south. At about the same time, the Nebo Forest Reserve, also in Millard County, was created. A few years later the

Sheep on the Fish Lake National Forest in Sevier County, November 1916. (Utah State Historical Society)

Nebo Reserve was joined with what was by then known as the Fillmore National Forest. In 1907 the name "national forest" was adopted for all forest reserves.

Later, on 4 September 1923, the Fillmore National Forest and the Fishlake National Forest were combined as the Fishlake National Forest.[31] The current (1997) Fishlake National Forest encompasses a gross area (public and private) of slightly more than 1,540,000 acres and spans nine counties in central Utah. Fishlake National Forest was originally (1908) headquartered at Salina, while the Fillmore National Forest was administered from Beaver (south) and Nephi (north).[32]

The Sevier River Valley, which begins near the present town of Joseph in the county's southwestern corner and extends in a north-easterly direction for forty-five miles to the community of Gunnison in neighboring Sanpete County, has been described as "good farming land."[33] The valley is quite narrow in the southwest near Joseph and widens gradually, reaching its maximum width, about five miles,

United States Forest Service Experiment Station near Salina in July 1917. (Utah State Historical Society)

in the Gunnison area. The altitude of Sevier Valley varies from about 5,300 feet at Joseph to 5,000 feet at Gunnison. At Richfield the altitude is 5,270 feet, with an average of 113 frost-free days, which limits the kind of farm crops which can be grown in the county.[34] The livestock industry in conjunction with forage crops for beef and milch cattle as well as sheep have constituted the main elements of agriculture in the county.[35]

Water, or the lack thereof, is a pivotal aspect of Sevier County's natural and human history. Water provides the lifeblood of the county. It brings forth the agricultural crops which, to a large extent, sustain the economy and human life of the county. Whether among the aboriginal tribesmen or the modern peoples of the region, adequate moisture always separates a good year from a bad one.

Historian Leonard J. Arrington had called the Sevier a "turbulent" river.[36] The Sevier River was named the *Rio Severo* (Severe) by Spanish fur trappers working out of Taos, New Mexico, in 1813. By the 1840s, however, the name had been Anglicized by American trappers who began to refer to it as the "Sevier." Reflecting his American bias, famed Western American explorer John C. Frémont inaccurately noted upon entering the Sevier Valley from the north: "May 23, 1844. We reached Sevier River. . . . The name of this river and lake was an indication of our approach to regions of which our people had been the explorers. It was probably named after some American trapper or hunter."[37]

The county's agricultural prosperity is largely dependent upon local snowfall, which can vary dramatically from year to year, and upon the Sevier River. In 1886, a nameless clerk of the Sevier Stake of the Church of Jesus Christ of Latter-day Saints (LDS or Mormon) headquartered at Richfield offered a telling but perhaps a little over-stated summation of factors influencing the valley's water conditions: "Naturaly [sic] Sevier Valley is perhaps the driest part of Utah. Much of the soil there appears never to have been soaked with water; . . . but little snow falls in the valley and the frost is seldom severe."[38]

The Sevier River's main stem begins in the Pink Cliffs of northern Kane County. Additional water is added to this main stream from the Markagunt Plateau of eastern Iron and western Garfield counties. Small streams from the east slopes of the Hurricane Cliffs and the west face of the Sevier Plateau add to the Sevier River as it flows northward through Garfield County. Near Junction in Piute County, the East Fork of the Sevier joins the main stem. The East Fork of the Sevier begins in the Paunsaugunt Plateau in northern Kane County. It passes through Johns Valley in Garfield County, where it is fed from various small streams from the Escalante Mountains and the Aquarius Plateau. In the southeast corner of Piute County, the East Fork makes a sharp departure from its flow north to a westerly direction. At the most severe bend of the East Fork, Otter Creek (which drains the east side of the Sevier Plateau and Parker Mountain to the east, and flows south) joins the East Fork of the Sevier. Otter Creek's headwaters originate on the west face of Mount Terrill in east-central Sevier County.

From Junction in Piute County, the Sevier River rushes northward to Sevier County. The Sevier River exits the county north of Redmond. From there the Sevier River begins to make a slight bend to the northwest after having being joined by the San Pitch River. In

Mills Valley in Juab County the Sevier River makes a sharp curve to the west, flowing through Sevier Canyon. In Leamington Canyon in extreme northern Millard County the wandering Sevier River turns south to die with a whimper in the Sevier Desert in central Millard County.

In all, the Sevier River Basin is about 170 miles long and 100 miles wide, or about 16,000 square miles of central and south-central Utah. According to hydraulic studies made in 1969, the annual stream flow near the Piute-Sevier county line is 137,300 acre feet. Water is both added to and diverted from the Sevier River in Sevier County, and when it leaves the county, as measured near Sigurd, the river's flow averages 57,500 acre feet annually. Farther downstream, stream inflows and diversions add to and subtract from the Sevier River, making it "one of the most completely consumed rivers in the United States."[39]

The Sevier River and its tributaries which provide the source of life also cause destruction in the county. Situated within both the Colorado Plateau region and on the easternmost edge of the Great Basin, the Sevier River drainage system is a unique ecosystem unto itself. The elevation differences within the Sevier River Basin are great. The lofty Tushar Mountains reach over 12,000 feet, towering over the valley by more than 7,000 feet. Due to the steep gradients of the river basin, it has been a somewhat unsatisfactory watershed, rendering the Sevier River Valley prone to flooding. Where the Sevier Plateau faces the valley, it presents a greatly eroded fault scarp some seventy miles in length. Near Monroe, for example, this scarp has 5,700 feet of relief, with streams traversing this elevation for a distance of five miles.[40] Due to this condition, Monroe Creek, Thompson Creek, Mill Creek Canyon, Water Canyon, and other streams within the southwest portion of the county have recorded frequent flooding.

Since 1894 there have been over 150 incidents of flooding in Sevier County.[41] Most of these disasters were spawned by the many rain-swollen creeks cascading out of the mountains to join with the Sevier River. In July 1896, for example, a summer cloudburst caused a "severe flood" of Otter Creek near Koosharem. That same month, an unidentified village a short distance south of Monroe was flooded, with "great damage" being done to farms, orchards, roads, and bridges. At Richfield, "waters rushed on into town, submerging the streets, covering fields and gardens with mud and debris."[42]

Fifty years later, flooding of the Sevier River near Redmond was the subject of a report issued by the Army Corps of Engineers (the federal entity in charge of flood control). A letter seeking authorization for a survey of the Sevier River near Redmond, Utah, was submitted to the Secretary of War by the chief of engineers in April 1944. "Between Salina and the San Pitch River," the letter noted, "sediments carried [by flooding] from the steeper upstream areas and deposited in the valley section have raised the stream bed about 10 feet during the past 40 years." This change was reported to have reduced the flow of the river from 2,600 cubic feet per second to a "bankfull capacity" of 400 cubic feet per second.[43] In the past the Sevier River certainly possessed a much swifter flow than is witnessed today.

The natural result of this reduced river flow was flooding "3 times every 5 years." Simply put, the engineers found the river to be "clogging." They proposed that the Sevier River be deepened and widened to alleviate the problem. Such actions by the Army Corps of Engineers and later by the Bureau of Reclamation were quite common during the 1930s and 1940s.[44]

A "hidden" water source still waiting to be fully tapped in Sevier County is underground water. The county's underground water, known since at least 1900, is derived from the rain and snow that fall on the drainage areas. According to a 1907 United States Geological Survey report, of this cumulative natural moisture, "part evaporates, part flows off in streams, and part sinks into the ground."[45] Whether surface or underground, free flowing or manipulated for the uses of humankind, water plays a very important part in the daily life of Sevier County residents.

The high mineral content of the county's water, which at the Monroe Hot Springs is highly valued for its health benefits, has tended to be a curse to some who farm Sevier County's soil. As is the case with much of the American West, Sevier County has a problem with alkali. In fact, in some areas the county's soils have historically been sufficiently crusted with salt to significantly restrict agricultural production.[46]

Monroe Mountain, a landmark on the east side of Sevier Valley. (Allan Kent Powell)

A natural hot spring lies near Monroe at the base of Monroe Mountain in the southern portion of the county. The Monroe Hot Springs is the only non-sulphurous body of hot water in the state. It is of such high quality that if located near a larger metropolis it perhaps would be worth a large fortune. From this spring nearly 200 gallons of water flows each minute. With a temperature of 168 degrees Fahrenheit when it emerges from the depths of the earth, the water is allowed to cool to a comfortable temperature of 68 degrees for the bathers who come to enjoy its wonderful therapeutic qualities. The water is lightly laced with salt, magnesium, potash, and soda. Local residents claim it has remarkable healing powers. These hot springs add uniqueness to the county's natural features.

In Sevier County water truly is the key to human settlement. Without access to sufficient moisture, the agricultural pursuits of many of the county's people would be destined to dismal failure. In Sevier County, as throughout the American West, water allocation and management has had an incredibly complex cultural history. Water technology, or the manipulation of the resource to serve human ends, was a significant tool of growth in the American West. Simply, in an agricultural society, he who controls the water controls the productive capability. And, in this regard, the Mormon pattern of sharing water resources provided an excellent means of making the most of the limited resource.[47]

A soil survey of the Sevier Valley conducted at the turn of the twentieth century tells much about the agricultural potential of the valley at that time. The native flora of the Sevier Valley is dominated by such salt-loving species as greasewood, shadscale, rabbitbrush, saltgrass, foxtail, and a few other varieties. Sagebrush is found on the foothills and in the mountains, but rarely is found in the valley. The very character of the indigenous vegetation found within the Sevier Valley bears an intimate relation to the kind of soil and water available. For example, both saltgrass and foxtail require plenty of surface moisture while greasewood is indicative of dry land containing considerable salt.[48]

The native wildlife of the region was noted by the fur trappers, or mountain men, who roamed the Sevier Valley in the late 1820s. Jedediah Smith, fur trapper and explorer of the West, observed, "On Ashley's River [Sevier River] . . . I found no more signs of buffalo; there are a few antelope and mountain sheep, and an abundance of *black tailed hares*." Smith's fellow mountain man Daniel Potts was also impressed by the hares. In fact, he referred to the Sevier River as "Rabbit river" because of the "great number of large black tail rabbits or hares found in the vicinity." Twentieth-century archaeology has borne out the accuracy of Smith's and Potts's observations, as rabbit bones have consistently been recovered from Indian sites in Sevier County.[49]

The Pavant Plateau and the other physical elements of the high plateau country have significantly influenced the travel of people and commerce and the settlement of Sevier County and central Utah from the time of prehistoric Indians to the location and completion of Interstate 70 in the modern era. The high plateaus shunted the intrepid Spanish explorers fathers Domínguez and Escalante westward as they traveled from Utah Lake south. Later, using Indian trails, Spanish, Mexican, and American explorers and travelers broke through the high plateau country using Salina and Clear canyons. Add to this mix the Sevier River and other water sources, the altitude of the county, and the mineral resources found in various parts of the county, and we have the setting for human occupancy of the region, which extends back thousands of years.

## ENDNOTES

1. See Dale L. Morgan, *Jedediah Smith and the Opening of the West* (Lincoln: University of Nebraska Press, 1967), 163.

2. See *Journal of Discourses,* 26 vols. (Liverpool: S.W. Richards, 1854–86), 4:343–44.

3. On this ancient body of water see Samuel G. Houghton, *A Trace of Desert Water: The Great Basin Story* (Salt Lake City: Howe Brothers, 1986), 18–22; and S. George Ellsworth, *Utah's Heritage* (Salt Lake City: Peregrine Smith, Inc., 1972), 18–19.

4. Frank D. Gardner and Charles A. Jensen, *Soil Survey in the Sevier Valley, Utah* (Washington, D.C.: U.S. Department of Agriculture, 1900), 244.

5. See Leonard J. Arrington, "Taming the Turbulent Sevier: A Story of Mormon Desert Conquest," *Western Humanities Review* 5 (Autumn 1951): 393.

6. For basic information regarding the Tushar Mountains see M. Biddle, *Fishlake National Forest: Backcountry Guide* (Salt Lake City: Wasatch Publishers, Inc., 1993), 73–74; and Lawrence Reyer and Michael J. Dalton,

*Land Use in Utah Canyon Country: Tourism, Interstate 70, and the San Rafael Swell* (Washington, D.C.: U.S. Department of Agriculture, June 1972), copy located in Frank E. Moss Papers, box 637, Special Collections, Marriott Library, University of Utah, Salt Lake City.

7. William Lee Stokes, *Geology of Utah* (Salt Lake City: Utah Museum of Natural History and Utah Geological and Mineral Survey, 1986), 21–22.

8. Ibid., 145.

9. J. Stewart Williams and Mary L. Tapper, "Earthquake History of Utah, 1850–1949," *Bulletin of the Seismological Society of America* 43 (July 1953): 202.

10. Ibid., 205.

11. *Deseret News,* 3 October 1921.

12. J. W. Powell, *Lands of the Arid Region of the United States with a More Detailed Account of the Lands of Utah* (Washington, D.C.: Government Printing Office, 1879), 169.

13. See Clarence E. Dutton, *Report of the Geology of the High Plateaus of Utah, with Atlas,* (Washington, D.C.: Government Printing Office, 1880). For a brief biography of Dutton see Wallace E. Stegner, *Clarence Edward Dutton: An Appraisal* (Salt Lake City: University of Utah Press, c. 1936).

14. William H. Goetzman, *Exploration and Empire: The Explorer and the Scientist in Winning of the American West* (New York: Alfred A. Knopf, 1966), 568.

15. See Frederick S. Dellenbaugh, *The Romance of the Colorado River* (New York and London: G.P. Putnam's Sons, 1902), v, 42.

16. Dutton, *High Plateaus,* xv.

17. Ibid., 225.

18. Ibid., 226.

19. Stokes, *Geology of Utah,* 176.

20. See F. B. Salisbury, "The Big Rock Candy Mountain," *Utah Science* 46 (Winter 1985): 112–18.

21. Stokes, *Geology of Utah,* 177.

22. William F. Sigler, "The Rainbow Trout in Relation to the Other Fish in Fish Lake," *Agricultural Experiment Station Bulletin 358,* Utah State Agricultural College, Logan, 1953, 5.

23. George D. Brewerton, *A Ride with Kit Carson Across the Great American Desert and Through the Rocky Mountains* (Palo Alto, CA: Lewis Osborne, 1969), 76.

24. Ibid., 78.

25. See Sigler, "The Rainbow Trout," 7. Sigler indicates that earlier in the century there were reports of thousands of cutthroat trout which swam

the streams to spawn each spring. In 1953 the number of cutthroat trout accounted for only a very small percentage of fish caught from the lake.

26. "Stories of Old Timers: Frands Peterson," *Utah Fish and Game Bulletin* (December 1955): 4–5.

27. Jeanne Dastrup, "The Sigurd Story," research paper, Dixie College, 1971, photocopy at Utah State Historical Society Library.

28. Robert E. Maurer, "Review of the Coal Deposits of Eastern Sevier County, Utah," *Utah Geological and Mineralogical Survey, Special Studies 15* (May 1966): 4, 8.

29. For further study of the development of national forest system in central Utah see Thomas G. Alexander, *The Rise of Multiple-Use Management in the Intermountain West: A History of Region 4 of the Forest Service* (Washington, D.C.: United States Department of Agriculture, 1987), 29–85.

30. Quoted in Alexander, *The Rise of Multiple-Use Management*, 22.

31. *Fishlake National Forest Utah* (Washington, D.C.: Department of Agriculture, 1932), 3–4.

32. See Alexander, *The Rise of Multiple-Use Management*, 35, 38.

33. Gardner and Jensen, *Soil Survey in the Sevier Valley, Utah*, 243.

34. R. Clayton Brough et al., *Utah's Comprehensive Weather Almanac* (Salt Lake City: n.p., 1987), 20.

35. In 1900, Sevier County produced 33,547 tons of forage, which included wild-, salt-, and prairie grass; alfalfa and lucerne; clover hay; and cultivated grains for livestock. *Twelfth Census of the United States, 1900*, vol. 6, *Agriculture*, part II, various pages. In 1910 farmers and ranchers in Sevier County raised 23,753 head of dairy and beef cattle and 77,453 head of sheep. *Thirteenth Census of the United States, 1910*, vol. 7, *Agriculture*, various pages.

36. Arrington, "Taming the Turbulent Sevier," 393.

37. Quoted in Rufus Wood Leigh, "Naming the Green, Sevier and Virgin Rivers," *Utah Historical Quarterly* 29 (Spring 1961): 142.

38. Sevier Stake Historical Records and Minutes, 14 April 1886, Archives, Church of Jesus Christ of Latter-day Saints, Salt Lake City, Utah (hereafter LDS Archives).

39. "Irrigation Water Management Sevier River Basin, Utah," Appendix III (Washington, D.C.: United States Department of Agriculture, 1976), map 9, p. 3.

40. U.S. Department of Agriculture, *Sevier River Basin Floods, Appendix VII*, (Washington, D.C.: United States Department of Agriculture, 1976), 11.

41. Ibid., 23–36.

42. Ibid., 47, 48.

43. *Sevier River Near Redmond, Utah* (Washington, D.C.: United States Government Printing Office, 1944), 1, copy at Utah State Historical Society Library.

44. See, for example, John A. Adams, Jr., *Damming the Colorado: The Rise of the Lower Colorado River Authority, 1933–39* (College Station: Texas A&M University Press, 1990).

45. G.B. Richardson, *Underground Water in Sanpete and Central Sevier Valleys, Utah* (Washington, D.C.: Government Printing Office, 1907), 14, copy at Utah State Historical Society Library.

46. Frank D. Gardner and Charles A. Jensen, *Soil Survey in the Sevier Valley, Utah* (Washington, D.C.: U.S. Department of Agriculture, 1900), 280.

47. See Donald Worster, *An Unsettled Country: Changing Landscapes of the American West* (Albuquerque: University of New Mexico Press, 1994), 31; and Donald Worster, "The Kingdom, the Power, and the Water," in *Great Basin Kingdom Revisited: Contemporary Perspectives,* ed. Thomas G. Alexander (Logan: Utah State University Press, 1991), 27.

48. Gardner and Jensen, *Soil Survey,* 248.

49. Quoted in Morgan, *Jedediah Smith,* 226, 334. See also Duncan Metcalfe, "Gooseberry Archeological Project: 1093," University of Utah Archeological Center, 1984, 123, copy at Utah State Historical Society.

2

# THE NATIVE PEOPLES OF SEVIER COUNTY

In south-central Utah the bridge between pre-history and recorded history was crossed in October 1776 when Europeans made contact with native peoples near the Sevier River in today's Millard County. Catholic priests Francisco Atanasio Domínguez and Silvestre Vélez de Escalante instantly struck fear in the Indian women and all but two successfully fled.[1] These women were Southern Paiutes.

The Southern Paiutes were not, however, the earliest native inhabitants of central Utah and today's Sevier County. They were preceded much earlier by other prehistoric Indians identified by anthropologists as Paleo-Indians (10000 B.C. to 7500 B.C.), followed by the western Archaic culture (7500 B.C. to A.D. 500), and then the Fremont culture (A.D. 500 to about A.D. 1300).

The first physical evidence of Paleo-Indians living in the county was the discovery of a weapon point identified as a Clovis fluted point found near Accord Lake in northeastern Sevier County.[2] Prehistoric Indians used such points to hunt mammoths. In the 1980s a large mammoth skelton was found high in the mountains between Emery and Sanpete counties. Clovis fluted points have been

34

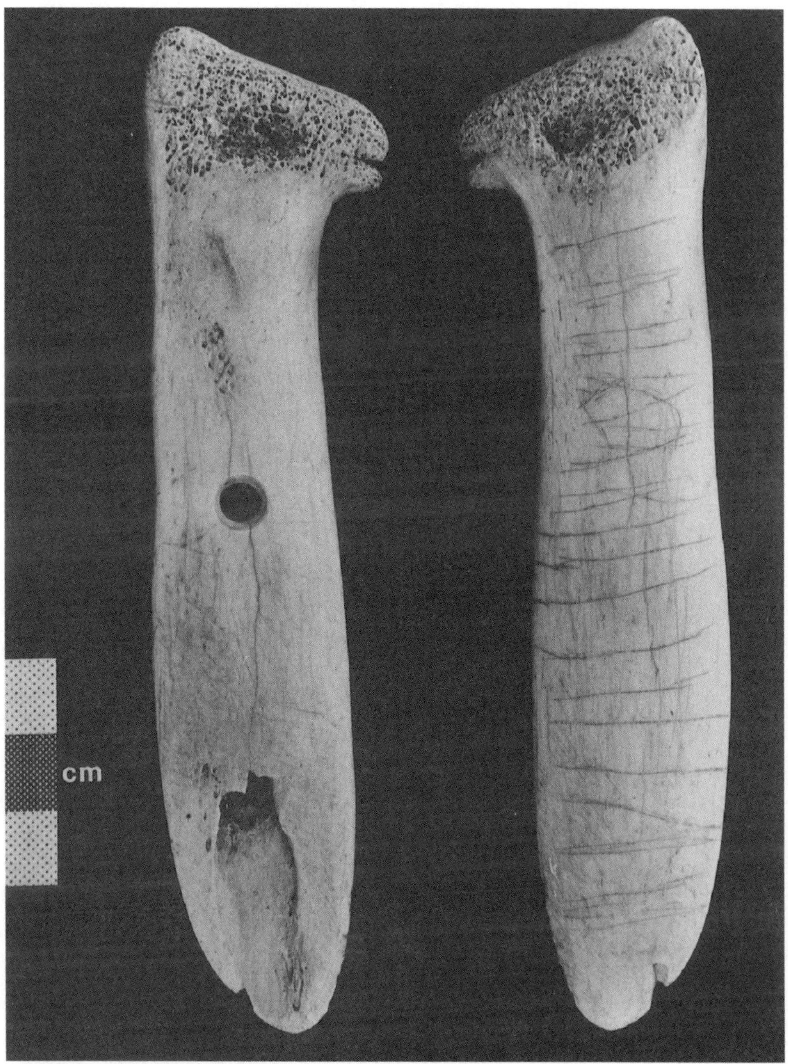

Fremont Indian bone awl implements excavated at the Backhoe Village in Richfield. (Utah State Historical Society)

found widely throughout the Great Basin, generally associated near Pleistocene lakes and marshes. The Paleo-Indians attached the crudely notched points to spears and used the weapons to hunt big game which lived near ancient lakes and marshes such as ancient Accord Lake.

Several anthropologists have theorized that the Paleo-Indians who used the Clovis points lived in the eastern Great Basin during a period of transition. Archaeologists identify this new culture as the Western Desert Archaic culture. These prehistoric Indians shifted their food and clothing sources from big game to smaller game such as mule deer and bighorn sheep because of the demise of the larger mammals. They used more sophisticated devices such as traps and snares to hunt jackrabbits, squirrels, mice, sage hens, California gulls, and magpies. They also gathered seeds and other plant materials from the wetlands and shorelines of lakes for their food and clothing. Near these rich resources, the Desert Archaic people lived in caves and rock shelters. They made tools from wood, bone, and stone; and from various plants they fashioned sandals and wove clothing as well as making baskets and trays to harvest, carry, and store seeds and other edible plants. There is some archaeological evidence of Desert Archaic people living in the county, and it is at least to be expected that the hunter-gatherers periodically traveled through portions of the future county with its rich resources of mountains, canyons, and river valleys.

Beginning at about the start of the Christian era, the Desert Archaic people were replaced by a new group of people whom archaeologists identify as the Fremont culture. This people occupied most of Utah, including Sevier County. The Fremont culture was first identified in 1931 from archaeological sites found along the Fremont River in Wayne County near Capitol Reef National Monument. The Fremont, as a group, were dispersed throughout the western fringe of the Colorado Plateau and the eastern part of the Great Basin region of Utah. The Fremont culture flourished in the county and other parts of the state until about A.D. 1300 when, like their predecessors, the Fremont people disappeared and either were absorbed or replaced by Numic-speaking Indians from the American Southwest.

There are several theories regarding the origin of the Fremont culture. Some archaeologists suggest that they migrated from the southwestern part of the United States to the eastern Great Basin and the northern Colorado Plateau country. Others suggest they were speakers of the Athapaskan language group who migrated from the northwestern Great Plains to the eastern Great Basin. A third theory is that the Fremont developed *in situ,* or in place, in Utah from the earlier Archaic culture people.[3] Whatever their origins, there is much physical evidence of the Fremont culture in Sevier County, and their legacy is preserved at several important sites in the county. Fremont dwellings and food-storage structures, showing where the people lived in relation to the physical environment, the tools they used, societal artifacts, and their artwork provide trained archaeologists and other scientists with windows by which to study these early inhabitants of Sevier County and Utah.

Anthropologist David B. Madsen has observed of these ancient people that "'Fremont' is really a generic label for a people who, like the land in which they lived, are not easily described or classified."[4] For the purpose of study and inquiry, archaeologists have divided the Fremont culture into several variants, identified by the type of clay pottery they made, their geographical location, their ways and means of constructing dwellings and storage buildings, and the adoption of maize (corn) horticulture, as well as other criteria. The Sevier variant of the Fremont culture occupied generally the west-central part of the state, with what was to become Sevier County being the center of their activity.

The Fremont were quite dependent upon nature.[5] They literally lived in and from the environment. The Fremont culture is characterized by the utilization of small constructed permanent buildings, the making of clay pottery, improved stone and bone implements from those of their predecessors, the development of the bow and arrow, and in some instances the adoption of maize horticulture. It is this practice of maize agriculture that is perhaps the single most determining feature of Fremont culture. This is what archaeologists feel "most clearly sets off the Anasazi, Fremont and their contemporary native cultures from the earlier Archaic cultures."[6] The Sevier Fremont culture variant is known also for its rock art pictographs (paintings on canyon walls) and petroglyphs (chipped or chiseled etchings on rock walls). Some are located in Clear Creek Canyon and preserved at Fremont Indian State Park near the community of Sevier.

As of 1984, along Sevier County's Gooseberry Creek on the northern slope of the Fishlake Plateau east of present Salina, some thirty-nine recorded Fremont sites had been uncovered, some thor-

Archaeological excavation at Backhoe Village in Richfield. (Utah State Historical Society)

oughly researched. Archaeologists are convinced, based upon the types of artifacts recovered, that these ancient villagers had a subsistence economy based upon a broad array of plants and animals. Corn, beans, and squash were grown, while small and medium-sized animals were used to supplement the people's diet.[7]

Nawthis Village in Gooseberry Valley has yielded much information about the Fremont culture. Of particular interest to archaeologists is the location of this early prehistoric Indian agricultural settlement. Located away from marshland at an altitude of over 6,500 feet, it appears that the Fremont living in this village were more dependent on corn agriculture than were other Fremont people living in the county.[8]

One of the earliest Fremont sites studied was the Sudden Shelter site, located along Ivie Creek in the northeastern corner of the county. First discovered in the mid-1950s, it wasn't until the mid-1970s when road construction in the area pressed archaeologists that they made a thorough study of the shelter. Based on projectile points found at the site, the shelter was used by Archaic Indians more than

6,000 years ago. As one might presume, over time the occupants of this shelter developed more sophisticated tools and gathered over twenty types of plants for food, medicine, and other uses. They hunted mule deer, cottontail rabbits, porcupine, and bighorn sheep for food, and they used the hides for clothing and the bones for various tools. Their utilization of the flora and fauna changed as the environment of northeastern Sevier County gradually changed.[9]

A very important site was discovered in 1976 when construction work began on the Sevier Valley Trade Technical College building in Richfield. Archaeologists soon realized that what had been discovered by construction workers was much more than a site—it was a village of the Fremont culture. Identified as the "Backhoe Village" due to its modern means of discovery, the Fremont village yielded substantial more information about the Sevier Fremont culture than what had been gathered from other sites in the county, and it helped to substantiate certain theories and presumptions about the Sevier Fremont Indians.

The people at Backhoe Village relied on a mixed subsistence economy based on agriculture, particularly corn, heavily supplemented with the collection and processing of wild flora, especially plants associated with a marsh environment, and fauna found in the valley. The people living at Backhoe Village did not need to hunt for food as much as did some of their contemporaries because of their successful harvest of plants associated with a marsh environment and their annual cultivated agricultural yields. This kind of economy allowed for a more sedentary life for the people of the village. At the same time, the success of their agricultural endeavors and the rich nearby wetlands provided the people of the village time and means to trade with people at some distance from Sevier County. The presence of olivella shell and obsidian in the village indicates that the village inhabitants were part of a fairly extensive trade network.

Archaeologists have found that the pit dwellings and adobe storage structures found at Backhoe Village were similar to other Fremont-built structures in central Utah. They also discovered that the walls of some of the structures at Backhoe Village had been plastered.[10]

Clear Creek Canyon has proven to be a fruitful area for studying the Fremont culture. The extensive study of Clear Creek Canyon by archaeologists and others was a result of the construction of Interstate 70 in the early 1980s. Field surveys of sections of the canyon were conducted in 1979. That survey located the Workshop Knoll site on the northern flank of the Tushar Mountains. This site, which was an open campsite and lithic (rock) processing site, is immediately adjacent to the confluence of Mill Creek and Clear Creek. The Workshop Knoll site is dominated by pinyon pine and Utah juniper. At lower elevations the area features scrub oak, bitterbrush, and squawbush. Given the more mountainous character of this site, the Fremont here likely supplemented their maize diet with deer and elk.[11]

Other sites were identifed in the canyon in 1979, including the historical cabin of Joe Lott. Excavation of one of the sites was undertaken by Brigham Young University archaeologists in the fall of 1983. As field work progressed, students from the county were invited to witness an archaeological dig. One of the students reported his experience in Clear Creek to his parents. The father of the student then remembered what he had noticed at an earlier time on a nearby ridge and notified the archaeologists at the excavation site. This lead to the discovery of the Five Fingers Ridge Fremont village and other sites in the canyon. Archaeological work was expanded, and the yield of artifacts and information about the Fremont culture was extensive. Five Finger Village contained 102 recognizable architectual features which included at least forty habitation structures. The findings of the archaeologists suggest that Clear Creek Canyon area has been used for the last 4,000 years and that, like today, the canyon was a significant route used by prehistoric Indians.[12]

The knowledge gleaned from the extensive archaeological work in Clear Creek Canyon, the preservation of artifacts, and the location and preservation of area rock art spawned a much broader interest in the canyon by the people of the county and drew statewide attention. In 1985 the Utah State Legislature established the Fremont Indian State Park in Clear Creek Canyon to preserve the canyon's rock art and archaeological sites. The Fremont Indian State Park is operated by the Utah Division of State Parks and is one of the more visited state parks in the state. It includes some eighty residential

Fremont Indian petroglyphs in Clear Creek Canyon. (Utah State Historical Society)

structures and pithouses as well as many storage granaries. To date (1997) some seven tons of cultural material including pottery, implements, and projectile points have been recovered from the park site by archaeologists.

Recognized as having been at least marginally dependent upon agriculture, the natives of the region cultivated maize (corn), beans, and squash through dry-farming methods and limited irrigation during the spring and summer months.[13] The Fremont people and those who preceeded them lived where the environment provided them with food, clothing, and shelter. The county a thousand years ago seemed to have had the flora, fauna and water resources to make the Fremont culture successful for several centuries.

The practice of agriculture was one of the things which distinguished the Fremont people from earlier cultures. The legacy of the Fremont is found today in their rock art and other artifacts of their culture, including basketry and pottery, the distinctive trapezoidal art style manifest in Fremont clay figurines and necklaces, and in unique moccasins constructed from the hock of a deer or a mountain sheep leg.[14] One of five major variant styles of Fremont pottery is known as Sevier gray, and the name Sevier Fremont is also used by some anthropologists as a classification of the people in the central Utah area. The extant material culture of these ancient inhabitants provides current residents tangible links with Sevier County's prehistoric past.

As a recognizable group, however, the Fremont seem to have begun to vanish from the entire region by about A.D. 1250. Why they vanished or what happened to them remains a mystery. Historically speaking, they faded as elusively as they had earlier appeared. It has been suggested that a general climate change or extended period of severe drought may have reduced their ability to grow corn, squash, and beans, forcing them to rely on wild foods to a greater extent. The Anasazi to the south also mysteriously disappeared from the archaeological record at about this same time. Either or both great cultures may have simply died out, they may have been forced to move on by more forceful and aggressive immigrants to the area, or they may have become integrated with and absorbed by the newly arriving Numic-speaking peoples. "No one can quite agree on what happened to them," writes David B. Madsen, who personally believes that the Fremont were simply forced to move on by more powerful newcomers to the region.[15]

By A.D. 1500 the Fremont people of the county and central Utah had been essentially replaced by Numic-speaking people who were much more dependent upon hunting and gathering techniques for their survival than they were upon horticulture as practiced by the less aggressive and more sedentary Fremont people. This linguistic group of Indians was divided into various tribes, including the Southern Paiutes and Utes, who came to occupy much of Sevier County at the time of the first incursion of Euro-Americans into the area.

The Southern Paiute Indians, who came to the area after the Fremont vanished, were accomplished hunter-gatherers who in historic time were able to survive in lands considered inhospitable if not actually uninhabitable by immigrating whites. There is also some evi-

Excavation of Backhoe Village, a Fremont Indian village in Richfield. (Utah State Historical Society)

dence, however, of the Paiutes practicing some forms of horticulture to supplement their hunting and gathering activities well before the Mormon arrival in the Sevier River Valley in the 1860s. In fact, historical investigation suggests that the Southern Paiutes farmed the valley utilizing a number of quite sophisticated land-management techniques, including burning the grasslands to stimulate new growth and deliberately propagating some natural plants to foster soil conservation.[16] Their farming methods, including limited flood irrigation, were insufficient to precipitate salts and bicarbonates to the soil surface. Not until the Mormon colonists came to the area would irrigation be used extensively enough to begin the "mineralization" and degradation of the soil. Only through the careful application of water and the installation of drainage systems were salts and bicarbonates kept from the roots of most plants.[17]

The Southern Paiutes occupied certain portions of southern California, southern Nevada, southern Utah, and northern Arizona. Their economy was based upon hunting and gathering, with agriculture being practiced only on a very limited scale. Milt Daily, a Southern Paiute from the Cedar City area, labeled his people as historically being "very poor," at least by white men's standards.[18] Certainly the coming of whites to the area definitely impoverished all the territory's Native Americans through the usurpation of much of the finest land and the killing of many game animals. The Southern Paiutes did raise some crops. They reportedly secured squash and corn seeds from the Hopis.[19] It has been estimated that the Southern Paiute population in the mid-nineteenth century numbered 2,000 to 3,000 persons.[20]

People of the Southern Paiute tribe have historically considered most of today's Sevier County to be within their traditional use area. This territory straddles the boundary between the physiographic regions of the Great Basin and the high plateaus to the east and south. It is largely a semi-desert realm of sagebrush, greasewood, and juniper. Such a land required a population with specialized skills, and this specialization was achieved by the Southern Paiutes. Rather than traveling in large bands, the natives avoided clustering in favor of dispersal in small groups which could be supported by the land's limited resources.[21] More nomadic Ute bands also utilized the more arid areas of the county from time to time. Many of the Utes had adopted the horse as a means of locomotion, which allowed them to be more mobile and even to prey upon the Paiutes in historic time, seeking women and children to trade into slavery to the Spanish colonialists to the southeast and west. Utes also presumably made more use of the mountainous areas of the future county. It was the Southern Paiutes who called the valley and desert region home prior to the coming of the Mormons in the mid-nineteenth century. The Paiutes' relationship with the Utes was ambivalent, the two groups sometimes coexisting peacefully and at other times more aggressively competing for the area's resources.

The early Spanish priests and missionaries as well as some Anglo-American explorers who later encountered the Southern Paiutes almost universally characterized them as "peaceful" or "timid."[22] As late as the nineteenth century, the Southern Paiutes were armed only with bows and arrows, were totally lacking in horses, and lived what was considered to be a primitive existence in a harsh country. Because of their non-aggressive nature and weak defenses, the Southern Paiutes were frequently victimized by their stronger, mounted neighbors. The Utes often conducted raiding parties during the eighteenth and nineteenth centuries to steal Southern Paiute women and children to trade into slavery.[23]

As ethnohistorian Ronald L. Holt has observed, "Suffering has not been a stranger to the Southern Paiutes of Utah." Whether it be the loss of loved ones to slave traders or to death, loss of the lands to white encroachment, or the benevolent paternalism of the Mormons in the mid-nineteenth-century, the Southern Paiute people have consistently been forced into the role of victim or dependent.[24] The Utes victimized them, as did also the Mormons and the federal government, which sought to place them in the role of a dependent. The greatest irony of Southern Paiute history is that, although the avowed purpose of both federal and Mormon policy was to make the Paiutes independent, "the actual results of these policies," writes Holt, "have been to create and maintain a situation of insidious dependence on outside help." So complete were early Mormon efforts to work with the local natives that scholars have deemed the Southern Paiutes by the early 1870s to have been under "some form of direct and sustained contact with [white] settlers for at least a decade."[25]

While Brigham Young generally demonstrated what some have called "quite favorable" policies toward Utah Indians, including his oft-quoted maxim that it was better to feed the Indians than fight them, individual Mormon settlers in Sevier County and elsewhere held varying opinions about the region's Native Americans. Often the common white stereotypes regarding Native Americans, such as that they were shiftless, thieving, and lazy, were applied to Sevier County Indians. Institutionally speaking, the Mormon church theologically held all aboriginal peoples of the Americas (whom they termed Lamanites) to descend from a Book of Mormon figure named Lehi who was of the House of Israel, God's chosen people of the Old Testament.[26] In actual practice, however, the Mormon attitude toward the Indians was often more paternalistic or antagonistic than it was brotherly. The Indians of Utah generally have been relegated to dependent status and have not had the opportunities and benefits accorded white citizens.

In 1963, for example, the average level of education among the Southern Paiutes of Sevier County was only 4.4 years. The head of the family was employed only 54 percent of the time among Southern Paiutes in the Richfield area. As Ronald L. Holt has written, "The Utah Paiutes remained on the periphery of the Anglo world."[27] A general lack of education, widespread poverty, discrimination, and association with an impoverished and scattered regional reservation system tends to breed hopelessness and despair. The average annual income per family for a Sevier County Paiute as of 1968 was $1,940.[28] Comparatively, the per capita family income for the county in 1960 was $15,355. The Southern Paiute yearly family income in the late 1960s was at least $14,000 less per year than the county average, which was about $16,300. By 1970 this figure had risen to $23,437.[29] In 1968 the average monthly wage in Sevier County was $381. For a Southern Paiute able to find work it was about $161.[30]

In 1970 the Native American population of Sevier County numbered eighty-six persons, a distant second to the white population of 9,990. Two decades later, the Native American population had increased to 318 and the white population had reached 14,982.[31] The humble and peaceful people encountered by Domínguez and Escalante over two hundred years ago had by the late twentieth century become a people who are struggling to maintain their very existence. There is hope that as the county's economy continues to grow the Southern Paiutes may become more fully integrated socially, politically, and economically. "The LDS Church is still the major non-governmental force in the Paiutes lives and Mormon paternalism still seeks to mold their lives 'for their own good,'" writes Ronald Holt.[32] Many Southern Paiutes now dress, live, and act like white people generally and Mormons more particularly.

Another Sevier County band, the Koosharem, are remnants of the Fish Lake Utes; but they really represent a variation of the Ute and the Paiute cultures. Anthropologists have found the Koosharem band to be more closely akin to the horseless society of the Great Basin than to the nomadic mounted raiders who came to characterize the Utes of the nineteenth century.

In the 1860s, following earlier Indian-white difficulties in northern and central Utah over mounting demands on limited natural resources, Utah Superintendent of Indian Affairs Oliver H. Irish negotiated with the Utes and other Indian bands and tribes of the territory to relinquish their lands and move to the newly established Uintah Valley Indian Reservation in northeastern Utah. However, the Spanish Fork Treaty made in 1865 and signed in good faith by several of the Ute and Paiute chiefs was never ratified by Congress. Some Utes resisted removal. Others like the very small band of Fish Lake Utes—a mixed band of Paiutes and Utes—living on the Fish Lake Plateau, were overlooked or ignored by Indian officials. Other Paiutes of central and southern Utah resisted the "trail of tears" to the Uinta Basin reservation. In the 1870s an attempt to remove the Fish Lake Utes to the Moapa Reservation in eastern Nevada also met with resistence.

For the remainder of the nineteenth century, the Koosharem Indians of the county made do the best they could, increasingly relying on the good will of the settlers of the county and the Mormon church for their needs. Near the turn of the century, the scattered Paiute Indians living in central Utah were encouraged to relocate to the Shivwits Reservation in Washington County, even though it

An early automobile passes through Clear Creek Canyon along a route that was an important transportation corridor for Utah's prehistoric peoples. (Utah State Historical Society)

wasn't officially designated a reservation until 1903. Not all of the several small scattered bands of Paiutes agreed to move. A dozen or so Paiute and Ute Indians living in the county chose to stay. The federal Indian censuses for the decades 1890, 1900, and 1910 indicate that fewer than five Indians resided in the county although one must suspect that the census takers did not travel outside the settled areas to count the area's Native Americans. The official number slowly increased to thirty-five "Utes" when the Koosharem Reservation was established in 1928.[33]

The Paiute and Ute Indians of Sevier County continued to suffer from the lack of federal assistance, interest, and concern. The federal government felt no obligation to assist Indians who were not living on reservations. Most of the Indians living in the county were able to eke out a living raising some grain and hay, and some hired out as seasonal laborers to work in the sugar beet fields in the county, earning two dollars a day to supplement their meager incomes.[34] As seasonal laborers, the Koosharem Indians were dependent upon the farmers around Richfield. Ignored by Bureau of Indian Affairs (BIA) officials, and with the state taking no responsibility, the Koosharem Indians essentially fell under the control of the local Mormon church (Sevier Stake).[35]

In 1928 the federal government by executive order created a small reservation for the Koosharem Indians in Grass Valley. The creation of the Koosharem Reservation occurred at a time when the federal government was dismantling Indian reservations in the West and allotting reservation land to individual Indian families. This nearly fifty-year-long federal policy of Indian allotments ended with the New Deal. Under the Wheeler-Howard Indian Reorganization Act passed in 1934, Indians were given the opportunity to reestablish their collective tribal identities and to organize tribal governments. Public land was set aside for new reservations. As a result, an additional 320 acres of land was added to the Koosharem Reservation in 1937; this acreage included land that became a cemetery as well as a much-needed spring. Even with the changes in the federal Indian program, the Koosharem Indians continued to rely heavily on the county and the Mormon church for assistance.

In the years following World War II federal Indian policy underwent a drastic change known as "termination." Essentially, termination revoked the trust relationship between the federal government and the various tribes. With roots stemming as far back as the Dawes Allotment Act (1887), which began to allocate reservation lands to individuals (thus effectively reducing the amount of tribal protected reservation land), the termination policy sought to treat Indians just like any other citizen—without any special protection or help.[36] The plan called for dismantling the Bureau of Indian Affairs (BIA), relocating Indians to urban areas, and transferring BIA functions to local governments.

The Indians of Sevier County were in no position in 1947 to be cut loose from their federal support system. Also, the poverty of the Indians along with the history of dependence and white paternalism or outright hostility made the county's native peoples poor candidates for assimilation. The Paiutes were the nation's first tribe to be considered for termination. Utah's Republican Senator Arthur V. Watkins was among the federal leaders who vigorously pushed termination regardless of Native American desires.[37]

The termination of four small bands of Southern Paiutes in his home state fulfilled Watkins's "driving" need to answer the call of religious paternalism. His zeal for termination can be linked to his sincere beliefs as a Latter-day Saint. He was acting upon a Book of Mormon passage (2 Nephi 30:7) to the effect that one day the Lamanites were destined to become a "delightsome people." "These Indians," wrote Watkins in 1954, "have a God given right to manage their own affairs as soon as they are able to do so."[38]

The Southern Paiutes, however, were opposed to termination. On 21 May 1954, Jimmy Timikin, Speaker of the Paiute Tribe at Richfield, Utah, sent the following telegram to the Association of American Indian Affairs protesting termination on behalf of his people: "We do not wish termination. Hoping to better ourselves."[39] The Native Americans obviously felt that they could improve themselves more effectively with governmental assistance than without it.

The BIA gave Sevier County's Native Americans until 21 February 1957 to prepare for termination. After that date they were to lose their special status as Indians.[40] The Indians of the county, once exempted from paying various state and local taxes, were now required to pay those taxes.[41] The Indians lost their limited special sovereignty. This change of federal policy once again disrupted the economic and social well-being of the twenty-seven Indians living in Koosharem and the Koosharem Paiutes/Utes living at a private camp at the north end of Richfield. Their income was severely limited. Workers earned half as much as non-Indian workers of the county. For the Southern Paiutes, as with many other Indian tribes, the next twenty years were devastating. As termination became a reality, most tribes faced increased taxation and a loss of the limited sovereignty they had formerly enjoyed.[42] Fortunately for the Southern Paiute and other tribes, Congress's fascination with termination soon cooled.[43] Liberals began to speak in favor of assisting Indian economic development instead of continuing termination. By the 1970s the policy of unilateral termination had ended with the establishment of a new federal program of tribal self-determination.

At roughly the same time that the Southern Paiutes saw termination collapse, the Mormon church began to step up its efforts with the Indians. This effort was very evident in Sevier County. LDS Apostle Spencer W. Kimball, who was destined to head the church three decades later, began to pay special attention to the plight of the Indians during the 1940s. In 1947 the LDS church informally began its Indian Placement Program when Helen John, the sixteen-year-old daughter of a seasonal Navajo agricultural worker, requested permission to remain in Richfield after the harvest to attend school. Golden Buchanan, president of the Sevier LDS Stake, took in the girl to live with his family. He was assisted locally in his efforts to house Indian students by Miles Jensen. Official institutional sponsorship of the program followed within seven years.[44]

James Levie, who served as bishop of the LDS Sevier Ward between 1933 and 1942, remembered being present at a meeting in Monroe during the fall of 1948 at which President Buchanan was the speaker. By that time, Buchanan had been called by the LDS church First Presidency to work with the "Lamanite, or Indian people." He explained to those in attendance "the adverse conditions the Indians were living in and told the help the Indians would get if this people [of the Sevier Stake] would respond to a call to take an Indian girl into their home and give her a chance to go to school and learn to live with white people and live as they were living."[45]

Levie waited after the meeting to "see how many would accept such a call." To his surprise "every man walked out of the church without going to Brother Buchanan and saying the program was good." The old stereotypes regarding Indians were apparently still alive in Sevier County. James Levie finally told Buchanan, "Golden, I will take a girl for the next year's schooling."[46]

Six years later (1954), the program was formalized under the direction of the LDS church's Social Services Department. At this time, the program was eagerly accepted by Anglo Mormons and by Native American church members as well. Growing rapidly, by 1972 the Indian Placement Program peaked at 4,997 students churchwide. Initially the program accepted children who were at least eight years of age, had been baptized into the LDS church, and whose parents requested participation.[47]

Some Indian Placement Program participants in Richfield recounted the impact the program had on them. In August 1955, for example, brothers George and Roger Lee arrived at the Richfield Indian Placement Center by bus from the Navajo Reservation in Arizona. George Lee later remembered Richfield as a beehive of activity. Scores of local men began unloading luggage, trunks, and boxes from the bus. "They reminded me of ants," George wrote.[48] Lee amplified on his experiences in his later published memoirs which dealt with this and other life experiences.

During the mid-1970s, however, at the urging of tribal leaders and the federal government, which was now offering dramatically improved educational programs on the reservations, the LDS church began to limit participation in the placement program to high school students. In 1990 the LDS Indian Placement Program served about 500 students, generally providing for the needs of students living with Mormon families while they pursued educational opportunities.

In 1972 a Paiute Tribal Corporation was incorporated in Utah to assist the tribe's members. With the assistance of the Department of Housing and Urban Development, over one hundred HUD housing units were built in southern Utah, including at Richfield and Joseph in Sevier County. Federal recognition of the Paiute Tribe was accomplished on 3 April 1980 with the signing of documents by President Jimmy Carter. On 17 February 1984 the Paiutes received what has been called "4,470 acres of poor BLM land scattered throughout southwestern Utah" as well as a $2.5 million trust fund from which members can draw interest to facilitate tribal projects and services. Some of this money has been used to build new homes and businesses as well as to improve health care and educational opportunities, giving area Paiutes and other Native Americans more reason to have hope for their future well-being in the county as well as the region as a whole.[49]

## ENDNOTES

1. Ronald L. Holt, *Beneath These Red Cliffs: An Ethnohistory of the Utah Paiutes* (Albuquerque: University of New Mexico Press, 1992), 3.

2. George W. Tripp, "A Clovis Point from Central Utah," *American Antiquity* 31 (January 1966): 435–36.

3. David B. Madsen, "The Fremont and the Sevier: Defining Prehistoric Agriculturalists North of the Anasazi," *American Antiquity* 44 (October 1979): 711–39.

4. David B. Madsen, *Exploring the Fremont* (Salt Lake City: Utah Museum of Natural History, 1989), 2.

5. Jesse D. Jennings, "Prehistoric and Historic Peoples of Utah," in Jesse D. Jennings, Elmer R. Smith, and Charles E. Dibble, "Indians of Utah: Past and Present," University of Utah, Department of Anthropology (1959), 1, unpublished manuscript, copy at Utah State Historical Society.

6. Michael S. Berry, *Time, Space and Transition in Anasazi Prehistory* (Salt Lake City: University of Utah Press, 1982), 15; Michael S. Berry, "Fremont Origins: A Critique," in "Fremont Perspectives," edited by David B. Madsen, *Antiquities Section Selected Papers* 16 (1980), 17, Utah State Historical Society.

7. Duncan Metcalfe, "Gooseberry Archaeological Project," University of Utah Anthropological Papers (Salt Lake City, 1993), 41, 123.

8. Jesse D. Jennings, Preliminary Report 1978 Archaeological Excavation: Nawthis Village, 1978, manuscript, Archaeology Office, Utah State Historical Society.

9. See Jesse D. Jennings et al., "Sudden Shelter," University of Utah Anthropological Papers 103, (1980), 168–69.

10. For an extensive technical study of Backhoe Village see David B.

Madsen and La Mar W. Lindsay, "Backhoe Village," *Antiquities Section Selected Papers* 12 (1977), Utah State Historical Society.

11. La Mar W. Lindsay, "The Workshop Knoll Site, Sevier County, Utah," (1979), Antiquities Section, Utah State Historical Society, 1, 7.

12. Joel C. Janetski et al., "The Clear Creek Canyon Archaeological Project: A Preliminary Report," Brigham Young University Museum of Peoples and Cultures Technical Series 85–99, (September 1985), 51.

13. Holt, *Beneath These Red Cliffs*, 5; Pamela A. Bunte and Robert J. Franklin, *From the Sands of the Mountains: Change and Persistence in a Southern Paiute Community* (Lincoln: University of Nebraska Press, 1987), 23, 29.

14. Madsen, *Exploring the Fremont*, 9–11.

15. Ibid., 13–14.

16. See Bunte and Franklin, *From the Sands to the Mountains*, 8–9.

17. Frank D. Gardner and Charles A. Jensen, *Soil Survey in the Sevier Valley, Utah*, reprint (Washington, D.C.: U.S. Department of Agriculture, 1900), 280–82.

18. Milt Daily, oral interview conducted at Cedar City, Utah, 2 August 1968, American Indian Oral History Project, Doris Duke Collection, Ms. 333, Special Collections, Marriott Library, University of Utah.

19. Mabel Dry, oral interview conducted at Kaibab, Arizona, 18 July 1967, American Indian Oral History Project, Doris Duke Collection, Ms. 106, Special Collections, Marriott Library, University of Utah.

20. Robert C. Euler, "Southern Paiute Ethnohistory," *Anthropological Papers* 78 (University of Utah, 1966), 1–3.

21. Robert A. Manners, *Southern Paiute and Chemehuevi: An Ethnohistorical Report* (New York: Garland Publishing Inc., 1974), 21.

22. Holt, *Beneath These Red Cliffs*, 3.

23. See Tyler, "The Earliest Peoples," 27; Holt, *Beneath These Red Cliffs*, 20–22; William J. Snow, "Utah Indians and Spanish Slave Trade," *Utah Historical Quarterly* 2 (July 1929): 70–73; and Toney Tillohash, oral interview conducted at St, George, Utah, 16 June 1967, American Indian Oral History Project, Doris Duke Collection, Ms. 119, Special Collections, Marriott Library, University of Utah.

24. Holt, *Beneath These Red Cliffs*, xiii.

25. Ibid., xv; Isabel T. Kelly and Catherine S. Fowler, "Southern Paiute," in *Handbook of North American Indians*, vol. 11, edited by Warren L. D'Azevedo (Washington, D.C.: Smithsonian Institution, 1986), 387.

26. Kelly and Fowler, "Southern Paiute," 368; Bruce R. McConkie, *Mormon Doctrine* (Salt Lake City: Bookcraft, 1979), 528–29.

27. Holt, *Beneath These Red Cliffs,* 106.

28. Kelly and Fowler, "Southern Paiute," 392.

29. *Utah Labor Market Information* (Salt Lake City: Utah Department of Employment Security, 1972), 41.

30. Ibid.

31. *Statistical Abstract of Utah, 1990* (Salt Lake City: Bureau of Economic and Business Research, Graduate School of Business, University of Utah, 1990), 26; *Statistical Abstract of Utah, 1993,* 23.

32. Holt, *Beneath These Red Cliffs,* 152.

33. *Annual Report of the Secretary of the Interior, 1933* (Washington, D.C.: United States Government Printing Office, 1933), 138.

34. Holt, *Beneath These Red Cliffs,* 36.

35. Ibid., 43.

36. Ibid., 63–65.

37. Carolyn Grattan-Aiello, "Senator Arthur V. Watkins and the Termination of Utah's Southern Paiute Indians," *Utah Historical Quarterly* 63 (Summer 1995): 268–81. See also Kenneth R. Philip, "Termination: A Legacy of the Indian New Deal, *Western Historical Quarterly* 14 (1983): 165–80.

38. Quoted in Grattan-Aiello, "Senator Arthur V. Watkins and Termination," 282.

39. Quoted in Holt, *Beneath These Red Cliffs,* 80.

40. Holt, *Beneath These Red Cliffs,* 82.

41. "Conference Report on Termination of Federal Supervision over Certain Tribes and Bands in Utah," 83rd Cong., 2nd sess., House Report 1904, serial set 11740.

42. See Charles Wilkinson and Eric Briggs, ""The Evolution of the Termination Policy," *American Indian Law Review* 5 (1977): 152–54.

43. Francis Prucha, *The Great Father* (Lincoln: University of Nebraska Press, 1986), 351.

44. David J. Whittaker, "Mormons and Native Americans: A Historical Introduction and Bibliography," *Dialogue: A Journal of Mormon Thought* 18 (1985): 3; *Encyclopedia of Mormonism,* ed. by Daniel H. Ludlow (New York: Macmillan Publishing Company, 1992), 679.

45. James Lionel Levie, interview, Monroe, Utah, February 1978, Ms 2735 347, LDS Church Historical Department, Salt Lake City, 23.

46. Ibid.

47. *Encyclopedia of Mormonism,* 679.

48. George P. Lee, *Silent Courage: An Indian Story* (Salt Lake City: Deseret Book, 1987), 111.

49. See Ronald L. Holt, "Paiute Indians of Utah," in *Utah History Encyclopedia,* ed. by Allan Kent Powell (Salt Lake City: University of Utah Press, 1994), 409–11.

3

# Exploration and Early Settlement of the Sevier River Valley to 1875

In 1776 the Spanish Catholic fathers Francisco Domínguez and Silvestre Vélez de Escalante recorded the first known glimpse of the Sevier River Valley by non-Native Americans. Their view was fleeting and was not well publicized. Scouting the terrain and settling what is now Sevier County was not within the scope of the padres' assignment. Nevertheless, they passed near a portion of the Sevier River Valley as part of their assigned mission to locate a route from Santa Fe, New Mexico, to the Pacific Coast of California for the religious, military, and commercial purposes of Spain. While they never traveled far enough east to enter the Sevier Valley, one of their campsites was but ten or fifteen miles west of the present site of the Sevier Bridge Reservoir.

The priests were unable to complete their mission due to bad weather and other factors and returned from Utah to New Mexico. Spanish government authorities did not send other explorers or Catholic priests to Utah; however, the report of Domínguez and Escalante and the map Don Bernardo Miera y Pacheco made of the expedition's travels helped entice other explorers and traders to the area who gradually established the eastern segment of what today is called the Old Spanish Trail.

The Old Spanish Trail was more than a single trail; rather, it consisted of a series of trails or variant routes taken by overland commerce and traders between Santa Fe, New Mexico, and the Spanish and (after 1821) Mexican villages and towns in southern California. At least two branches of the Old Spanish Trail passed through Sevier County. Before forking in eastern Sevier County, one of the main branches of the trail heading west entered Emery County at the important (and traditional Indian) crossing of the Green River just north of the present community of Green River. The trail looped in a northwesterly direction north of Buckhorn Wash to Cottonwood Creek southeast of Castle Dale. There the road turned southwest where it entered Sevier County at Ivie Creek near Fremont Junction. At Red Creek, this stem of the Old Spanish Trail forked into two branches. The northern branch followed Salina Canyon to Salina, where it turned south following the Sevier River to Bear Valley Junction, where the trail turned west crossing over the Hurricane Cliffs to Parowan Valley.

The southern fork, or Fish Lake Route, began at Red Creek in the northeastern corner of the county and headed south, passing through what is now Johnson Valley Reservoir. The trail passed the west side of Fish Lake and from there dropped into Grass Valley in Piute County. The trail followed Otter Creek down to its junction with the East Fork of the Sevier River and followed the East Fork to its junction with the Sevier River and the main trail near Junction.[1]

Historians have as yet found no written record of the trail's use between the expedition of Domínguez and Escalante and the first decade or so of the nineteenth century. There are Spanish records that indicate Spanish slavers and traders visited the Utah Lake region and probably central Utah in 1805 and again in 1813, and it is likely that other trading expeditions made their way to parts of Utah. In 1805 Manuel Mestas reportedly traveled to the Sevier Valley to recover stolen horses. A now discredited story was current for years that an American general, one John Sevier, was supposedly sent in 1820 to the area by the U.S. government with an exploring party of Kentuckians, giving his name to the valley, river, and county. Sevier,

Jedediah Strong Smith (1799–1830), Mountain Man, Trailblazer, Explorer of the Sevier River Valley in 1826. (Utah State Historical Society)

however, was never in the region, and the name is a corruption of the Spanish *Rio Severo* (severe), named for the river's sometimes turbulent character.

By the 1820s, however, the lure of fur, trade, and commerce had brought Mexicans, Americans, and others who were quite familiar with the eastern portion of the Old Spanish Trail and its various branches to central Utah and Sevier County. In 1826 the intrepid American fur trapper and explorer Jedediah Strong Smith, accompanied by fifteen other trappers, traveled south through Sevier County from Bear Lake, eventually reaching southern California.[2] Smith and his men traveled through Sevier Valley. When Smith came to the junction of the Sevier River and Clear Creek, he veered west following Clear Creek to present Cove Fort. The group reversed this route on their return.

Following Smith's travels on the western half of the Old Spanish Trail and those of Mexican trader Antonio Armijo, one of the earliest to traverse the entire trail from New Mexico through Utah and Sevier County to California, during the 1830s, 1840s, and early 1850s the trail was heavily traveled and used by Mexican and American traders and fur trappers, explorers, guides, Ute Indian horse traders (including Chief Walkara), and emigrants seeking their fortunes in California.

In the fall of 1830 Americans Ewing Young and William Wolfskill left Taos, New Mexico, with a company of trappers bound for the central valleys of California. This company used a variant of the Old Spanish Trail. They crossed the Colorado River near present-day Moab and then proceeded northwest, crossing the Green River at the ford north of the present-day town of Green River in Emery County. The expedition traveled west to Salina Canyon and the Sevier River Valley.[3] Wolfskill's and Young's entrance into the Sevier Valley disrupted momentarily a large Ute Indian funeral ceremony being held for an important chief. The Wolfskill-Young company was welcomed to the valley by the Ute Indians and was invited to hunt and trap in the territory.[4]

During the thirty years of extensive use of the Old Spanish Trail, the Sevier River Valley was an important stop where caravans of men and animals rested. In 1841 the William Workman-John Rowland company—made up of at least twenty-six emigrants, including several families, two physicians, and several scientists—made its way along the Old Spanish Trail from New Mexico to California to settle. The pack company was well stocked with provisions and 150 head of sheep to provide fresh meat for the company on the overland journey. B.W. Wilson, a member of the Workman-Rowland company, later wrote of the valley's splendor and their fishing experience:

> On the River Sevier, in Utah Territory, Dr. Lyman and myself had stopped behind the train to fish; it was in the evening, the Doctor being with his hook and line in the water, the fish biting very well. He spoke to me that a very large fish had bit at his hook and got off. Just as he was talking a ball from an Indian gun struck the ground near him.

Like any good fisherman, nothing stopped the good doctor from continuing to fish when they were biting. Wilson continued with his fish story, " . . . he remarked very coolly, 'That fellow can't hit me, so therefore I will stay and get this fish before I leave,' and he did so."[5]

The Old Spanish Trail through Sevier County also was used as a livestock trail. Horses and mules were trailed east from California to New Mexico and beyond. James P. Beckwourth, a mulatto frontiersman employed in the late 1820s by William Henry Ashley as a trapper, in the 1840s worked for commercial traders Andrew Sublette (brother of William Sublette) and Louis Vasquez. He herded 1,800 head of horses from California to New Mexico on the trail in 1844. Others in succeeding years followed Beckwourth's lead, driving horses and mules eastward from California to New Mexico to trade.[6]

Kit Carson made several trips through Utah in which he traveled on segments of the Old Spanish Trail, acting as guide and courier for the federal government. In 1848, Carson accompanied Lt. George D. Brewerton on a branch of the Old Spanish Trail, identified as the East, or Fish Lake, Trail. The Fish Lake branch separated from the main trail near the confluence of Salina and Niotche creeks; it then followed the latter upstream and continued along the present-day Gooseberry Fremont Road south to Fish Lake. From Fish Lake the trail followed Otter Creek down to the East Fork of the Sevier River and on to Kingston, where it rejoined the main trail.

The Old Spanish Trail in central Utah and Sevier Valley was busy with government travelers in 1853 and 1854. Congress had appropriated funds to conduct a series of surveys in the West for a possible transcontinental railroad to the Pacific Coast. In 1853 Lt. Edward Fitzgerald Beale, who was serving in California as Superintendent of

Indian Affairs and was in the east on government business, was asked to unofficially survey a central route on his return to California. Accompanied by Gwinn Harris Heap, who kept an excellent journal of the expedition's trip to California, Beale had reached the head of Salina Canyon and the headwaters of Salina Creek by the end of July 1853. Heap called Salina Creek Rio Salad ("salt"). Near the mouth of Salina Canyon, Heap recorded seeing a new wagon road which was being used by Mormon freighters and miners to haul salt rock from the salt mines near Salina to the newly established settlements in Sanpete County.

The expedition turned south at Salina and followed the Sevier River upstream. While traveling through the future county, Heap complained of the heat and the dryness of the valley floor. "The weather was exceedingly hot, without a breath of air; and the dust raised by the animals, in traveling over the loose and dry soil, hung over us in clouds."[7] Although the weather was hot and dry, Heap remained impressed with the Sevier Valley, writing that it "surpassed in beauty and fertility anything we had yet seen." The company left the county following the Sevier River to present-day Marysvale and Kingston, where "we struck a trail which we supposed to be the old trail [Spanish Trail] from Abiquiu to California."[8] Heap and the others continued on the trail, eventually reaching California.

The next summer, Lt. John W. Gunnison, accompanied by seven surveyors and scientific men, teamsters, minor government officials, and a military escort of thirty-two soldiers, was ordered to conduct the official survey of the central route of the proposed transcontinental railroad through central Utah, including future Sevier County. The Gunnison Expedition was one of four government expeditions sent to map and survey various possible routes in the West to the Pacific Coast. By mid-October the survey party had reached the summit of Wasatch Pass; ahead of them to the west was the Sevier River Valley. Gunnison and some of his surveyors, after arriving in the valley, followed the Sevier River downstream. A few days later, southwest of present-day Delta, most of this advance party of surveyors, including Gunnison, were killed by Indians.

For most of three decades from the 1830s to the 1850s the Old Spanish Trail through central Utah and Sevier County was an important commerce trail linking New Mexico and the commercial towns in Missouri and the Southwest to the Pacific Coast. Parts of the Old Spanish Trail, developed by Ute and Paiute Indians earlier, was the precursor to sections of Interstate 70 used presently by motorists, truckers, and tourists. Now as then, the county continues to be an important transportation link for transcontinental travelers and commerce.

Nearly one hundred years after Domínguez and Escalante, U.S. Army Captain Clarence E. Dutton surveyed the geological features of the region. As we have already seen, he was extremely interested in the terrain of today's Sevier County. But it was the passing of the Catholic priests which started Utah's "process of becoming."[9] Following the long natural history of an area or region, the human experience unfolds to fill the canvas only partially sketched out by nature. If Domínguez and Escalante can be said to have launched the process of becoming, then to Dutton could go the credit for elucidating the sketch of central Utah. Before Dutton, however, following the Spanish and the mountain men came the Mormon pioneers.

The Mormons first came to the Great Salt Lake Valley in July 1847, refugees from religious persecution in the midwestern United States. Their prophet, Joseph Smith, Jr., had been murdered in 1844 at the hands of an anti-Mormon mob at Carthage, Illinois. Under the leadership of Smith's successor, Vermont-born Brigham Young, the majority of the Mormons fled to what they hoped would be a safe haven in the Rocky Mountains. Here their national image might be transformed. They would, it was hoped, no longer be hated religious outcasts but instead be considered hearty pioneers settling the wilderness.

Colonizing ventures and the expansion of the Mormon "Zion" were activities and goals dear to the heart of Brigham Young. In Utah the Mormons developed some of their most distinctive institutions and practices in the process of colonizing. Colonization helped create harmony among Mormons; it helped to foster group cohesiveness. The climax of the Mormon withdrawal from the larger society could be considered to have occurred not with their arrival in Salt Lake City but in the colonizing process—"the call, the move, group control over land and water, and the farm village life,"[10] as one historian expressed it. All of these Mormon experiences were present in the colonizing of the Sevier Valley and helped to make the harsh land habitable.

During Brigham Young's thirty-year tenure as church president, Mormon colonies were established at such far-flung places as San Bernardino, California, Carson Valley, Nevada, Fort Lemhi, Idaho, and across the reaches of Utah from St. George in the south to the Bear Lake Valley and Cache Valley in the north.[11] Richfield in the Sevier River Valley was settled in 1864.

In 1848, following the defeat of Mexico in the Mexican-American War which produced sizable American territorial gains in the Southwest, Mormon Utah became part of the United States. In 1849, just two years after the Mormons arrived in the Great Salt Lake Valley, they proposed to Congress what they called the State of Deseret. Deseret included not only most of present-day Utah, Nevada, and Arizona but also parts of Wyoming, Idaho, Oregon, and California. Congress rejected the idea and instead created the much smaller, but still extensive, Territory of Utah in 1850.

Neither the Mormons nor the federal government knew much about the territory very far south of present-day Manti in Sanpete County. In 1849 Brigham Young commissioned a fifty-man exploring company led by Parley P. Pratt, a Mormon apostle, to "explore Southern Utah for possible settlement locations." Pratt and his men were to go to the "outside of the Rim of the [Great] Basin."[12] Their journey would lead them through the Sevier River Valley.

The Pratt party included fifty men, twelve wagons, one carriage, twenty-four yoke of oxen, seven beef, thirty-eight horses and mules, and assorted supplies and items to trade with the Indians. The oldest man on the trip was Samuel Gould at seventy-one years of age; the youngest was Alexander Abraham Lemon, age eighteen years. The average age was about thirty-five. Eight members of this exploring party had crossed the plains with Brigham Young in 1847.[13]

Pratt's party carefully recorded soil conditions, topography, vegetation, water sources, the availability of timber, promising pasture lands, and other natural resources which might benefit future Mormon settlers of Utah Territory. Proceeding down the Sanpete Valley, the explorers reached the Sevier River by early December 1849. A few weeks later, on Christmas Day, Robert L. Campbell, a

Parley P. Pratt (Utah State Historical Society).

member of the company, penned a report to church leaders Brigham Young, Heber C. Kimball, and Franklin D. Richards from a site in southern Utah recounting the difficulties of the trek:

> We have about used up our oxen in getting our wagons thus far . . . over the mountains of snow, in places 2–4 feet deep, which has taken us a week [to proceed 45 miles], with water only in two camping places. Nearly perpendicular pitches where men had to draw up the oxen, then the oxen draw up the wagons. . . . [14]

This exploring venture, rather credulously undertaken during the winter, proved a harsh test for the participants.

Of the Sevier country Campbell wrote, "The thermometer has been at 21 degrees below zero on the Sevier bottom."[15] Campbell described the Sanpitch country between Salina and Manti in neighboring Sanpete County as "a barren, rugged, mountainous country." The trail was strewn with rocks and snow for most of the trek down the Sevier River Valley. The harshness of the environment was starkly clear to this expedition. Few other human beings were seen. The region which includes Sevier County was, to say the least, inhospitable.

Although Campbell's view left the region wanting in regard to colonization, the same area when seen through Parley P. Pratt's eyes was a land of great potential. Pratt gave the following assessment regarding the Sevier Valley:

> The land is rich, is beautiful and undutating [*sic*] westward, and the best calculated watering of any place we have seen of late. Two small streams rather less than [Salt Lake City's] city creek come out high and run nearly on a level with the top of the ground . . . and throw out their surplus floods in times of high water dispersing fertility in every direction. The grass, willows, weeds, and other grasses grow exceedingly dense over thousands of acres. Pasture lands extend for miles north and south of the farming land. . . . Good building timber . . . shows itself in abundance among the mountains.[16]

It would appear that a more promising country to settle would be hard to find for these Mormon colonists. Pratt reported the presence of coal near the present site of Salina and had praise for the rich bottomlands of the Sevier River Valley where Richfield would eventually stand.[17]

On 15 July 1863, the year before settlement of the area actually began, another exploring party of six men, led by George W. Bean, explored the Sevier Valley once again with an eye toward future settlement.[18] They were sent by church leader George A. Smith. A later report, recorded in the history of the Sevier LDS Stake, expounded upon the natural resources of the region:

> Plenty of deer and other game, besides good farm and grass lands and water . . . examined Salt Creek and not liking the uneven,

> poor land, they [the exploring party] went across the river to the large springs near the present settlement of Redmond. Keeping on the west side to the big spring, now Richfield, it was decided that here would be the large settlement of the valley because of the quantity and quality of the soil.[19]

This seeming abundance of game, water, and pasture lands certainly negated the "uneven, poor land" first found near Salt Creek. At least some hardy souls from neighboring Sanpete County must have thought so.

The increasingly limited availability of land and water in Sanpete County to the north, not only for new arrivals but also for the younger generation, accounted for the increased regard for the Sevier River Valley, particularly from the 1860s to the late 1870s.[20] A good portion of the population growth in Sanpete County was a result of successful Mormon missionary work in the Scandinavian countries, and many Danish Mormon immigrants settled in Sanpete County. This situation may well have provided much of the stimulus for the settlement of Richfield in 1864 and much of Sevier County in the immediate years thereafter.

Upon their return, members of Bean's party reported both to George A. Smith and to Apostle Orson Hyde. There seemed to be a brief controversy over which church leader would be responsible for settlement of the area, but in the end Hyde was given the responsibility.

Robert W. Glenn, Isaac Sampson, and several other men, all of whom had been part of the 1863 exploring expedition led by George W. Bean, were attracted by two cool springs on the east side of the Sevier River Valley about five miles from Richfield. They envisioned wonderful possibilities for irrigation and water in the area. Probably based upon their favorable report, Brigham Young called Glenn, Sampson, and several other men to return to the site to initiate a settlement.[21] The first families of Glenwood included those of Glenn, Sampson, Joseph Wall, George Pectol, Thomas Bell, George Powell, A.T. Oldroyd, Peter M. Oldroyd, Seth Wareham, Artimas Miller, Henry Hendrickson, James Killian, and several others. These settlers arrived during the summer of 1864.

Robert Glenn, after whom the community was named, presided over the new community that first summer. James Wareham was appointed by Apostle Orson Hyde to take over the direction of Glenwood in November 1864. Hyde changed the name of the community from Glen's Cove (also known as Glencoe) to Glenwood.[22] This name stuck, possibly because it was selected by an LDS apostle, and the place has been known as Glenwood ever since.

The settlement of Richfield occurred earlier that same year. Contrary to many of the ecclesiastically organized pioneering efforts launched by Brigham Young in mid-nineteenth-century Utah, nine men from Sanpete communities led by Albert Lewis of Manti came to the Sevier Valley on their own initiative from neighboring Sanpete County. "Nobody sent these pioneers here," wrote Pearl F. Jacobson, a local historian.[23] These men, however, "knew it was the wish of their leader, Brigham Young, that all of the valleys of Deseret [Utah] should be settled." The apparent natural richness of the Sevier River Valley drew these men to settle the area. Good, rich soil, a reliable, close source of spring water, and the nearby forest with its available growth of timber all attracted these pioneers who arrived at the present site of Richfield on 6 January 1864. By February, Albert Lewis had built the first house.

The settlers included New York native Nelson Higgins, who at fifty-eight years was the oldest of the pioneers.[24] Higgins, a veteran of the Mormon Battalion of the Mexican War, was known as "Father" Higgins by his younger compatriots. He held a solid military reputation among his fellow Latter-day Saints, having served first as a colonel of the Nauvoo Legion (the Mormon militia) and later as a captain in the Mormon Battalion. In March 1855 Brigham Young had commissioned Higgins a major in the Sanpete County militia. By age and reputation, Nelson Higgins was a leading figure in early Sevier County. He was later unofficially considered the first LDS bishop of Richfield, replacing Albert Lewis as leader of the first settlers in the spring of 1864.

In the winter of 1864 Orson Hyde called for thirty families from Sanpete County to join those already at Richfield. Initially the settlement seems to have been briefly referred to as Warmsprings and as Omni (from the Book of Mormon); very soon, however, it was named Richfield, undoubtedly for the richness of the farmland, and it was that name that was printed in a report by Orson Hyde in the *Deseret News* of 15 June 1864.

Sevier County was officially created in early 1865, at which time there were a number of small settlements, including Richfield Glenwood, and Monroe (known at the time as Alma). In 1865 at least another 100 families came to settle the county, many from neighboring Sanpete County, which became closely linked with Sevier. A schoolhouse was built in February 1865, with Hans P. Miller as the first teacher.[25]

Armed conflict soon threatened to destroy the first settlements in the county. During the middle of the 1860s, the Black Hawk War swept across south-central Utah like a prairie fire, temporarily suspending Mormon settlement efforts. The background of this confrontation with the Ute Indians can be traced to conditions in the Sanpete region and the Sevier River Valley, which bore the brunt of the conflict and suffering. As Mormons increasingly colonized the territory, the Native Americans of the region became increasingly restricted in their movements and hunting territory, causing increasing suffering and anger. With the recent settlements of Fillmore, Parowan, and Cedar City, along with those in Sanpete County, many Indians were forced to rely more upon the Sevier River Valley. Its settlement came to be viewed by some as a challenge and threat.

The winter of 1864–65 was a difficult one for the Ute Indians living near Gunnison. The weather was harsh and food was scarce in the area. A smallpox epidemic swept the Indian camps causing much sickness and some deaths. Some of the leaders of the Utes placed the blame for the troubles on the Mormons.[26] The Indians were accustomed to providing for themselves from the bounty of the land, and the choicest land was increasingly being taken by Mormons who, despite their protestations of friendship, then denied Indians use of the land and of the crops and herds they placed upon the land, restricting the Native Americans to more marginal lands and making them more dependent upon Mormon and U.S. government handouts and aid. Soon the hunger and suffering led some of the more militant Indians to profess that they would "kill Mormons and eat Mormon beef."

Several bands of Utes under the leadership of Black Hawk (Autenquer) became restless because of their need for food, clothing, and shelter. Theft of cattle by Black Hawk and others increased local Mormon anger toward the Indians, who they felt should be confined to the Uintah Indian Reservation in the Uinta Basin. One particularly irate Manti resident, John Lowry, tried to take matters into his own hands. At that Sanpete County community during a meeting of whites and Indians on 9 April 1865, Lowry disrupted the gathering by claiming that a horse held by Yenewood, a Ute Indian, was his property. He knocked Yenewood down and proceeded to beat him. In a shrewd observation, George W. Bean, an early settler of the area, later asserted "our Indian troubles have generally been brought about by some foolish act of the white men."[27]

It was this "foolish act" of John Lowry that precipitated Utah's Black Hawk War, which thoroughly disrupted the nascent settlement of the Sevier Valley and central Utah for several years. Though it is labeled a "war" by many, it was actually a series of raids, chases, and skirmishes between the settlers with their territorial militia and various bands of Utes (and, towards the end, Navajos) in central and southern Utah. The United States Army was not involved. The Civil War was just ending in the east and the orders of Colonel Patrick Conner and the California Volunteers stationed at Camp Douglas near Salt Lake City were to protect the overland mail route from Indians and keep a watchful eye on the Mormons. The territorial government's response to Black Hawk was the mustering of the territorial militia of about 2,500 men over the course of the three or four years of hostilities. Some of the men for the militia came from recent settlers in Sevier County.

Barney Ward and James Anderson, both of Salina, were killed in Salina Canyon in April 1865 at the hands of Black Hawk and his discontented followers. Following the raid, Black Hawk's warriors retreated up Salina Canyon to Castle Valley. During the course of the war, Salina Canyon was used frequently by the Utes as a route of retreat to the open, rough, and as yet unsettled Castle Valley to the east.

Most of the confrontations between settlers and Utes occurred during the spring, summer, and fall months, which were critical months for the settlers of the county to plow, plant, irrigate, and harvest their crops. During winter months, Black Hawk and his band of Utes laid low in Castle Valley, between Fish Lake and the Green and Colorado rivers. During 1865 the Indians drove off many head of cattle in Sanpete and Sevier counties—one source claimed that 2,000 head were driven off[28]—occasionally killing settlers and travelers. The pioneers of the county also battled a grasshopper infestation in 1865 that destroyed much of their crops.

In April 1866, Indians attacked several wagons near Glenwood. Some families from Glenwood and Monroe briefly moved to Richfield for greater security. Later in the month, a small group of settlers in Marysvale were set upon by Black Hawk's warriors. That same month it became quite clear to the settlers of the Sevier River Valley and church and government leaders in Salt Lake City that central Utah was engaged in a general Indian uprising. Albert Lewis was among those killed that year; he died in an ambush in April while pursuing hostile Indians. On 25 July 1866 General Daniel H. Wells, commander of the Nauvoo Legion, arrived in the county with fifty men and camped for some time between Glenwood and Richfield. By summer's end, the territorial militia patrolled the area around Salina and Salina Canyon. By the end of fall, raids and confrontations in central Utah subsided as Black Hawk returned to safety in the deserts of eastern Utah.

The following year, Indian raids became more widespread. On 21 March, three settlers—Jens Peter Peterson, his wife Amalia, and fourteen-year-old Mary Smith—were killed between Richfield and Glenwood. Their bodies were said to have been somewhat mutilated, and county residents reacted with shock and horror. As the hostilities mounted, counsel was received from Mormon church leaders in April 1867 to evacuate the valley and "move to some other Settlements" where the settlers would feel more secure.[29] Some 200 teams and wagons reportedly were sent from Sanpete County to help the evacuation of Sevier County, and most of the evacuees settled temporarily in Sanpete County. At least nine central Utah communities were evacuated during the Black Hawk War, including several in Sevier County.[30] Hence, the Mormon occupancy of the Sevier River Valley took a forced hiatus until the cessation of hostilities in 1871.

A fort was begun in Richfield in 1865. During the "forting-up" process of the Black Hawk War, many settlers from outlying areas initially relocated to the relative safety of Richfield and Alma. The approximately thirty families in Alma (Monroe) were themselves in a precarious position, according to a visitor to their community, Mormon church apostle George A. Smith. Among the ninety-six town lots laid out, Smith reported that the thirty or so families were

> scattered all over the town plt. Most of them are living in holes in the ground with dirt roofs, as the Indian war has prevented them from getting timber in the mountains. The brethren reported themselves in possession of 23 guns and several revolvers and said they had facilities for 50 families and more. We held a meeting and my suggestion that they would be safer in a fort than living in such a scattered condition.[31]

Apparently the settlers in Alma took the advice of Smith and built themselves a fort. According to a typescript found in the Works Progress Adminstration papers at the Utah State Historical Society, by July 1866, only a few months after the visit and inspection of Alma by Smith, the settlers at Alma were protected by a wooden fort: "The southwest quarter of the block was occupied by the fort proper, while a livestock corral was constructed on the northwest quarter of the block."[32]

Some of the settlements in the Sevier River Valley were without adequate leadership during the Blackhawk War. In a letter to General Daniel H. Wells, head of the Utah territorial militia, Orson Hyde vented some of his frustrations with this problem of the lack of leadership. He wrote:

> Just over from Glenwood, Alma [Monroe], and Richfield where I have been laboring for the past few days. I think with much profit. In the military capacity the people there are like sheep without a sheperd. It is said that Colonel Smith has command of the forces in that county but he is a nonresident, and for all advice and efficient aid to that people he might almost as well reside in St. Louis, Liverpool or London. . . . [33]

Hyde's complaint may have been overstated. For the most part, settlers in the county were not called by church leaders to settle the various settlements, nor were there always clear leaders appointed from Salt Lake City to direct the colonizing and settlement of the area. Also, the settlements in the county were very young and had not developed a cadre of local leaders.

By late summer 1868 a formal peace treaty was reached with Black Hawk and most of his warriors in Ephraim. A year earlier, Black Hawk had been wounded by members of the militia and probably felt that his cause to rid the settlers from his homeland was futile. However, there were still a few of the younger Ute men who resisted peace. From 1868 to July 1875 sporadic raids continued, primarily south of Sevier County. In April 1868 one attempt to resettle Richfield was repelled by Indians, who killed one of the men attempting to return. The skirmish, near Sigurd, was known as the Battle of Cedar Ridge.

Finally, in the summer of 1870, Brigham Young gave permission for the settlers to return to the county. Most were anxious to return to their homes, and a small group including probate judge William Morrison arrived in Richfield in November. They found that the Indians had not done much damage to the structures. By 1871 many more began returning to their homes. That year, the settlers again faced a plague of grasshoppers.[34] By July 1872 some 150 families had returned to the county; by March 1874 there were 145 families, with 753 people, in Richfield. There were some occasional worries and troubles with the Indians, but safety was increasingly provided by the increasing number of white settlers.

By July 1873 a peace treaty was negotiated with the Indians in Grass Valley near Koosharem.[35] Brigham Young had ordered a party from Utah County to explore the country east of the Sevier Plateau and to make peace with the Indians of the area. The expedition was headed by Bishop A.K. Thurber of Spanish Fork, George W. Bean, General W.B. Pace, and an influential Ute leader from the Uintah Reservation, Tabby. Bishop W.H. Seegmiller of Richfield and several others from the county joined the expedition when it passed through the county. According to George W. Bean, the Indians were advised, and agreed, to congregate in Grass Valley which was in effect in great part set aside as a reservation where they would "cultivate the arts of peace and industry."[36] Brigham Young subsequently directed

A 1910 photograph of one of the first meat shops in Richfield owned by Nicholi Johnson and Jeremia Hawn. (Utah State Historical Society)

Bean and Thurber to settle in Grass Valley and assist the Indians there. Orrin Porter Rockwell, among others, was also sent to the area for a time to work with the Indians. Peaceful relations were established, and the Native Americans kept their pledges to keep the peace.[37]

In the early 1870s, Sevier County was resettled. Contrary to the first settlement of the valley, Brigham Young this time exercised full control over the resettlement movement.

An internal conflict which initially disrupted the resettlement of Sevier County directly involved Nelson Higgins and another early settler, Probate Judge William Morrison. The LDS Sevier Stake was unofficially founded at Richfield on 18 December 1870 with Morrison assuming the mantle of leadership.[38] This first "stake," which functioned through May 1874, was never officially recognized by the LDS church, since it had been effected without institutional approval. Self-appointed stake president Morrison and unofficial bishop Nelson Higgins apparently were both strong-willed men. Each believed he was rightfully the ecclesiastical "power" within the locale. Local history recounts that the "petty rivalry" between Morrison and Higgins eventually escalated to strong "bitterness." Neither man respected the self-proclaimed authority of the other. Finally, Higgins, under the guise of his role as the ecclesiastical leader of Richfield, summoned Morrison before a bishop's council.[39]

The animosity between Higgins and Morrison seems to have centered upon a land dispute. In his opening remarks to the bishop's council which commenced 7 August 1871, Higgins laid out the charge against Morrison. Higgins maintained that "Reports had come to him that Bros. Wm. Morrison and L.M. Farnsworth had struck [claimed] some Quarter Sections and laid out one or two town sites."[40] Then Higgins called upon Morrison to answer this charge. As an original settler of Richfield, Higgins clearly felt some proprietary voice in land-settlement matters.

Morrison bluntly responded that he "did not acknowledge the bishop nor any of the men he had appointed to assist him to be his supervisors." He professed to have no knowledge of why he had been called before the council. In Morrison's words, nobody had "any business" calling him in front of an ecclesiastical court. Furthermore, he countered that he would not be under "the control of the Bishop and . . . would not be under such bogus rule and Authority." Having said that, William Morrison walked out of the meeting.[41]

Morrison's supporters seem to have perceived the entire difficulty in quite a different light than did Higgins and his people. At the bishop's inquiry, L.M. Farnsworth, presumably a co-conspirator in Higgins's eyes, spoke in defense of Morrison's actions. He said that he did not believe that William Morrison had claimed the disputed land for his own gain but had acted merely "to secure the land from being jumped by outsiders."[42] This was a legitimate fear in light of earlier Mormon experiences in the Midwest and the ever-increasing number of gentiles (non-Mormons) in the territory and the immediate region. From Farnsworth's perspective, Morrison had acted in good faith for the benefit of the community.

Higgins, however, was not easily turned in his thinking. He told the council that "he neither could nor would fellowship such a man" who would jump land his brethren had worked so hard for. Furthermore, Higgins was appalled that, when called upon to discuss the problem, Morrison would "insult" the local priesthood by calling them a "bogus organization."[43] The historical record gives no indication of a resolution of the problem at that time.

Presumed property rights (both land and water) often proved troubling for the early settlers of the American West. In days before the establishment of a federal land office, such disputes often festered, as each party believed he had the right to use the resource or property to his own best advantage.[44] In the instance of the Higgins-Morrison feud, the former felt that the latter had unscrupulously preempted land that rightfully belonged to others.

Seven months later, another bishop's council was convened "to transact business in relation to Br. Morrison." Morrison did not even appear at this meeting, so Higgins dispatched men to bring him to the gathering. At this second tribunal several formal charges were filed against Morrison. He was accused of "claiming the presidency of Sevier County without proper license,"[45] a charge which technically was true. But, though Morrison had acted inappropriately in assuming leadership of the unsanctioned stake, Higgins's calling as bishop was equally in question.

A second charge, that of "defying and insulting the priesthood . . . by saying that the Bishop and those who gathered around were bogus," was also levied against Morrison. But, in all likelihood, the very idea that Higgins would even presume the right to call the nominal stake president before a bishop's council must have seemed highly unusual to Morrison and his backers. In the end, William Morrison refused to plead guilty to any of the charges against him, surmising that "Bp. Higgins had no authority to cut him off."[46]

Sevier River Valley pioneers gather for a celebration in the last quarter of the nineteenth century. (Utah State Historical Society)

This very uncomfortable situation tore at the unity of the local Latter-day Saints until later in 1872 when Apostle Orson Hyde, the ecclesiastical overseer of the colonies in central Utah, chastised Higgins, Morrison, and others for the lack of harmony they were exhibiting. "There was," Hyde concluded, "no good cause for the troubles that exist here [in Richfield]."[47] Before departing, Apostle Hyde called Joseph A. Young, one of Brigham's sons, as the president of the now-legitimate Sevier Stake.

Both Morrison and Higgins were able to weather what must have been an intense trial of each man's faith. Later records show both men still active in local church activities. In May 1873 Nelson Higgins was the first man called by Joseph A. Young to serve on the High Council of the Sevier Stake. The following year, William Morrison was serving as an assistant secretary for the Richfield United Order.[48]

Along with Nelson Higgins and William Morrison, other early Mormon settlers of Sevier County included George Ogilvie, a native of Nova Scotia, who for a number of years acted as Richfield's doctor. Robert Wilson Glenn and Albert Lewis each did some early surveying in the county. Danish (and fellow Scandinavian) converts to the Mormon church constituted many of the earliest settlers of the county. Jorgen Smith had the first store in Richfield, at 408 South First West; Hans Olsen Hansen and his younger brother Christian Olsen Hansen were among the first settlers; August Nielson supervised the construction of the first road through Clear Creek Canyon and later served as a Sevier County commissioner (1893–95); Andrew Poulson was a veteran of Utah's Black Hawk War, a director of the Richfield United Order, a constable in Richfield for many years, and built and operated the first flouring mill in the Sevier River Valley (later to become the Richfield Roller Mills); and Eskild Christian Peterson, who was described as "a most capable and useful man." Peterson served on the Richfield city council for three terms and was president of the Otter Creek Reservoir Company for many years.[49] The reservoir, a product of the unrelenting efforts of Robert D. Young, Andrew Ross, and James H. Wells, was started in 1897 and completed in 1901.[50]

The many Danes among the pioneers of the county in 1864 were just a vanguard of more Scandinavians to come after resettlement following peace with Black Hawk and his warriors. Sevier County's allure for Danish immigrants remained strong through at least the early twentieth century. In the year 1910, Sevier County Danes numbered 699.[51] Naturalization records to 1910 indicate that immigrants from Denmark made up 48 percent of the naturalized citizens of the county. Other nationalities represented in the county included Great Britain, 24 percent; Norway and Sweden, just over 8 percent; Scotland, 2 percent; Australia, France, and Germany, about 1.3 percent each; and New Zealand, Hungary and Romania under 1 percent apiece. Somewhat surprisingly, residents from Greece constituted 5 percent of the populace and those from Syria 2.5 percent of the county's residents.[52]

Earlier, in May 1864, Apostle Orson Hyde, who presided over the Mormon settlements in Sanpete County, visited the small community of Jericho (now Joseph), not far from Clear Creek Canyon southwest of Richfield. Only a few, scattered residents were trying to eke out a living there. He observed that the people of Jericho were "kind" and treated him well.[53] The original settlers were forced to leave in 1865 because of the Black Hawk War, however, and no one returned until six years later.

Monroe was also settled in 1864. Following a call from Brigham Young, Walter Barney left Lehi in Utah Valley and moved south to the Sevier Valley. His family was soon joined by thirty-two others.

Originally naming their new community in honor of the Book of Mormon prophet Alma, Barney and others, including the Allred, Davis, David Jones, and twenty-two other families, located their homes near hot springs about fifteen miles south of Richfield.

Wiley Allred was chosen as the first LDS bishop of Alma (Monroe) and served until the post-Black Hawk War resettlement of the town in March 1871.[54] Bishop Allred was forced to hold the first religious meetings at Alma in dugouts. In 1871, after the Indian hostilities had abated, several of the original settlers returned. Having learned in the interim that another settlement near Salt Lake City also bore the name Alma, these returning colonists renamed their village after early United States president James Monroe.[55]

In November 1871 four related families, those of Beason Lewis, Tarlton Lewis, Jr., William M. Carter, and Christian Johnson, settled at Cove (now Sevier) about two miles southwest of present Joseph. During the following winter and spring, five other families also settled in Cove. They built houses, constructed a canal from the Sevier River to irrigate their fields, and planted crops. James Hale, a resident of neighboring Monroe, was appointed by Moses Gifford, Mormon branch president at Monroe, to preside over the newly created Joseph Branch of the church in 1877. The community was named after stake president Joseph A. Young, and a log meeting- and schoolhouse was built in 1876.[56]

The environment of early Joseph was not very inviting. There were no trees, with only rabbitbrush and willows to break up the landscape. The first few homes in the area consisted of wagon boxes set upon the ground in a manner similar to the earliest days of settlement of the earliest pioneers in the Great Salt Lake Valley twenty-five years earlier.

The harshness of the land was made evident to the hopeful agriculturalists of Joseph when they began planting crops. Local historian Revo Morrey Young has noted that "In order to farm a man had to first grub the land, dig a ditch, and then put in his crops with such crude implements as he had."[57] In many ways, Joseph was a stereotypical Sevier County pioneer village. Its farmland was rendered productive only through much hard work and the liberal application of irrigation water. Joseph was located near the Indian travel route

The Joseph H. Thurber blacksmith shop in Richfield. (Utah State Historical Society)

between Fish Lake and the Cedar City area. After the conflicts with the local Indians ceased, as many as 500 Indians camped near Joseph in their periodic travels across the territory.

Another early Mormon village in the county was Salina, twenty miles northeast of Richfield, which also was founded in 1864. Its name is derived from the Spanish word *salada*, which means "salty."[58] This town name reflects the area. The high mineral content of much of the county's soil makes it very alkaline or salty. In the case of Salina, there were actual salt outcroppings that were mined from settlement times.

The first families who settled Salina came from the nearby Sanpete County settlements of Moroni and Gunnison. In October 1863 Peter Rasmussen, Neils C. Rasmussen, and William Haywood of Moroni, along with Morten Mortensen of Gunnison, came south to scout out a site for a settlement.[59] These pioneers of Salina were likely facing the same pressures from the increasing shortage of available land and water in Sanpete County that had motivated others to settle Richfield, Glenwood, and the other earliest towns of Sevier County. A small early settlement between Glenwood and Richfield was called Prattville, but after resettlement was no longer considered a town.

With the end of the Black Hawk War, by 1874 the population of Sevier County was steadily increasing. Villages founded after the Black Hawk War included Annabella (1871), six miles southeast of Richfield; Sevier Ward (1872), the county's southernmost community; Sigurd (1873), located on the west side of the Sevier River; Central (1873), situated almost in the center of the county; the Grass Valley (1873) area in the southeast corner of the county, which includes the hamlets of Koosharem, Burrville, Greenwich, and Box Creek; Elsinore (1874), eight miles southeast of Richfield; Aurora (1875), about three miles southwest of Salina; Venice (1875), a small village on the east side of the Sevier River; and Redmond (1875), Sevier County's northernmost town, situated twenty-two miles north of Richfield.[60]

The families of Henry Dalton and the Joseph Powell were the first to settle Annabella in the spring of 1871. The settlers originally called their village Omni Point, from its proximity to Richfield (known early as Omni). The first homes were dugouts. The log cabins with dirt floors and dirt roofs that followed must have seemed a great improvement for the pioneers. In the 1880s a sawmill was set up in the nearby mountains, making it possible for the settlers to have wooden floors, doors, and window frames. The community's name was later changed to Annabella, probably in honor of the first two white women to live there—Anna Roberts and Isabella Dalton.[61]

As was the case with other towns of Sevier County, the digging of canals to bring water to the local farms was vital to the growth of Annabella. The Annabella Canal, finished in 1872, was constructed under the supervision of Niels M. Peterson. However, this canal ran only to the center of town. Residents later dug the Roberts Canal, which was used to irrigate the higher lands. This ditch was abandoned before long in favor of the more recent South Bend Extension Canal. However, debris from seasonal floods from the foothills often made this extension costly to maintain.

The boundaries of Sevier Ward, a small community in the southwest corner of the county, extend from the mouth of Sevier Canyon to the rolling hills south of Joseph. In July 1872 the heads of nine

This house, one of the oldest remaining in the county, was constructed 1873–74 in Richfield by Ralph Ramsay a skilled wood carver who immigrated to Utah from England in 1856. (Allan Kent Powell)

families living near Clear Creek Canyon began settling southwest of Joseph and eventually established Sevier Ward. James Evans Powell was the first to move his family to what became the town. With his wife, Elizabeth Jane Carter, and their eleven children, Powell built a house in the vicinity and made preparations to stay. His daughter Minnie was born on 6 July 1874—the first child born in the new community.[62]

Between 1872 and 1879 the Powells were joined at Sevier Ward by the families of Robert Bridges, Worthy Bridges, Samuel Mackey, James Riley, John Lott, Charlie Robinson, Joseph Hyrum Levie, Thomas Gilbert, and Orval Hardy. Like elsewhere in the county, the most pressing issue facing these men was that of water. After studying the problem for a time, the pioneers of Sevier Ward concluded that they would have to take water from Clear Creek.[63] They set to work and dug 2.5 miles of irrigation ditch by hand. Water was first used from the canal in 1872. This canal was later incorporated as property of the Clear Creek Canal and Irrigation Company.

James Riley, Charlie Robinson, and John Lott, who made their homes up Clear Creek Canyon, dug other private ditches to water their fields. As soon as water became available, the people of Sevier Ward began planting. Local farmers grew such diverse crops as apples, apricots, peaches, pears, grapes, and black walnuts. Most found Sevier County a "very good location for fruits."[64]

With crops planted, the settlers of this small community began to think of schools. A school board was chosen which included Bob Bridges, Caroline Mills, and Joseph Hyrum Levie. Bridges leased land to the village for ninety-nine years for a schoolhouse. Sevier Ward's first school, a long log structure with one large room, was built on the site. A second log school was later built in Clear Creek Canyon to serve the needs of the people there.[65] In 1910 local demands had increased so much that a new, two-story rock school building was built to serve Sevier Ward.

Located near the heart of Sevier County is Sigurd, first known as Vermillion. Actually the community is really two villages—Sigurd Ward on the south and Vermillion on the north; yet the two are so closely connected by history, schools, and incorporation that they are one for all practical purposes. Local historians say that a "lively rivalry" exists between the two towns. In 1871 Henry Nebeker settled land in the Black Knolls region south of today's Sigurd.[66] Soon thereafter Peter Gottfredson and Isaac Smith came from Glenwood to claim land about two miles north of the Nebeker claim on the west side of the Sevier River. They must have liked what they saw, for they decided to make their homes there. After clearing eight acres of land and planting a wheat crop, Gottfredson and Smith engaged Henry Nebeker to care for their wheat while they went to Mt. Pleasant to harvest their crops in Sanpete County.[67]

By 1875 there were at least thirteen men, including Lew Gerber, Ransford Colby, Elisha Hoopes, and Ott Cuddleback, farming near what is today Sigurd. Others came and settled in Sigurd during the next three years. Near Sigurd are two battlesites of fights between the Indians and Mormon pioneers in 1868. The locally famous fights of Cedar Ridge and Rocky Ford were stamped indelibly in the minds of Sevier County residents by an Indian ambush which killed two men—Alexander Justensen and Charles Wilson.[68] The Vermillion LDS Ward was created on 15 July 1877. Peter Gottfredson was the first bishop of the Vermillion Ward and was later the author of an important book about the Black Hawk War, *Indian Depredations in Utah.* The local Mormons were later divided into two wards, the second taking the name of Sigurd after its creation in 1895.[69]

In the fall of 1873 Joseph Evans and William A. Stewart decided to make the present location of Central their permanent homes. The two were enthralled with the "lovely" spot, known briefly as Inverury. Local historians have assumed that it "must have been the Sevier River flowing nearby which seemed attractive and inviting to them." The Stewart and Evans families wintered at the spot in 1873 and were joined by twelve others from Beaver and Kanosh, Utah, the following spring. In 1875 William Morrison, probate judge of Sevier County, was called upon to lay out the townsite and also to name the community.[70] It seems possible, given the circumstances surrounding the naming of Central, to speculate that this was at least one of the parcels of land which had provoked the earlier feud between Morrison and Nelson Higgins.

The village of Elsinore was founded by James C. Jensen, Jens Iver Jensen, Christian Julius Jensen, Niels Peter Jensen, Lars Hansen, Niels Erickson, Vigo Smith, and William Smith—all from Richfield. In 1874 they homesteaded land adjacent to the Richfield Irrigation Canal.[71] In 1874, acting upon the request of Jens I. Jensen, James C. Jensen, and Charles H. Nielson, Sevier LDS Stake President Joseph A. Young selected the town's name. "I have passed by there several times," said Young, "and every time I think of my visit to Denmark and the little site of Elsinore situated on the right hand of Oressund." So it was decided to name the town Elsinore.[72] Due to its name and the large number of Danish residents, the town came to be known regionally as "Little Denmark."

Beginning in 1875, the three Jensen brothers directed their labors toward digging a new Elsinore canal. By the following year, the canal was partially finished and the small community had access to irrigation water. In 1876, following this mammoth human effort, nature intervened to nearly bring their work to naught. Difficulty was experienced through the sinking of the land when water was turned upon it, causing the canal to break in several places. Still, the harvest that fall was considered "bountiful"—1,800 bushels of wheat having been grown.[73]

In August 1873 Brigham Young called George W. Bean and Albert K. Thurber to settle in Grass Valley to teach the Indians the arts of cultivating crops, industry, and peace. Soon after their arrival at Grass Valley these Mormons not only were teaching the natives the skills intended to further their success in white society but also were teaching the LDS religion.[74] The valley townsite became known by its Indian name, "Koosharem," meaning "clover blossom."

Among the first Grass Valley area settlers was Charles C. Burr (for whom Burrville was named) and his four sons. Another small community in Grass Valley, Box Creek, was named after Thomas Box and his family.[75] Ranching has always been the main source of wealth for Grass Valley. Herds of cattle and sheep have foraged on the foothills of Grass Valley since at least the early 1870s.

Nestled between the mountains and the river in the northern part of the Sevier Valley is the farming village of Aurora, or Willow Bend, as it was originally known. Later described as "one of the most prosperous agricultural communities in Utah," the Aurora area was first investigated by George T. Holdaway, J. Alma Holdaway, and Elliot Newell of Provo during the early 1870s. The men returned to Utah County with glowing reports of their find, encouraging others to return with them. Consequently, in March 1875, the two Holdaways and Newell, in company with Franklin Hill and Ezra Curtis and his wife and sons, brought a small herd of cattle and some farming implements and returned to stay.[76]

They immediately began clearing land and digging an irrigation ditch to get water from the Sevier River. However, their first efforts proved futile. Their crops were lost because of the lack of water, which only exacerbated the hardships of pioneering a new land. Sevier County, after all, was more arid generally and the soil drier than that of their former home country in Utah Valley. The Sevier River was considered to be "barely able" to provide the needed water for irrigation.[77] In 1879, however, the settlers of Aurora purchased an additional canal from John W. Coons and his sons. Coons had wed Eliza Oglivie, the daughter of one of Richfield's founders, George

Gottleib Ence, one of the area's early settlers, and family. (Utah State Historical Society)

Oglivie.[78] After enlarging this canal, the people of Aurora were able to provide the necessary water for their fields.

Eventually, more canals were dug and additional water was made available to the once-unyielding soil. Three canals, the Rocky Ford, the Vermillion Extension, and the State Canal, eventually ran out of the hills west of Aurora. The farming district at last had a good water supply. Within a few years more settlers came to Aurora. Among these new arrivals were Jabez Durfee, James Kennedy, John W. Curtis, Amos Sly, Andrew Anderson, and Harry M. Payne, to name just a few. Aurora, like much of the rest of Sevier County, experienced notable growth during the 1870s and 1880s.

On the far northern fringe of the county is the village of Redmond, named for three red knolls to the west of town. As a local history has noted, "The people [of Redmond] are not recognized for their great wealth or costly mansions, but like most people who live close to the soil they . . . are free and independent."[79] In 1875 John Johnson of Salina in company with A. D. Ferron, a surveyor for the government, surveyed the land around Red Butte Springs (now

This early commercial store in Richfield was known as the "Old Green Store." (Utah State Historical Society)

Redmond Lake), located some twenty-two miles north of Richfield, for a possible townsite. Soon thereafter, two brothers, Charles and James S. Jensen, laid claim to a quarter-section of land bordering on the springs. By the spring of 1876 they had been joined by several other settlers. Grain was planted and a canal, incorporated as the Spring Ditch Irrigation Company, was dug.[80]

Happily for the settlers, their grain came up beautifully. Then the unpredictable forces of nature interrupted progress at Redmond. In 1876, rabbits devoured the entire crop. Most of the settlers were so disheartened they wanted to leave Redmond. But John Johnson convinced them to stay. They replanted their grain, watered it faithfully, and tried to persevere. Then, the following June, a heavy frost came and blackened their entire crop. Discouragement took hold again; but once more the very persuasive Johnson pleaded with them to turn the water on their fields. They did so, perhaps rather doubtingly, and the grain actually came up. The settlers of Redmond were able that year to harvest a good crop of grain.[81]

The small farming village of Venice was initially settled by Francis G. Wall in 1875. On his first glimpse of the area, Wall thought it "must be very rich as the brush and weeds grew so high." A visionary, he foresaw fields filled with rich, green alfalfa, golden grains, and many comfortable homes. After building a cabin on the east side of the Sevier River, Wall sent to Manti for his family and for his father, William Wall. In a short time, there were eleven families living at Venice.[82]

Even at the earliest stages of development, the pioneers of Sevier County projected irrigation canals from the Sevier River. Taking their lead from the now well-known Mormon irrigation activities in the Great Salt Lake Valley, Sevier County pioneers embarked upon the manipulation of local water sources with knowledge based upon earlier Utah experiences. The river flowing through the valley came to serve as the life-giving artery nourishing the many small agricultural communities which in time came to dominate the local economy.

In March 1864, less than three months after the first settlers from Sanpete County arrived, the *Deseret News* reported efforts by the settlers "to get a canal from the Sevier River, but nothing was accomplished that season."[83] However, the planned canal became a reality the following month when a "canal from 6 to 10 feet wide[,] 2 or more feet deep and 11 miles long" was pushed to completion. Following what must have been the backbreaking efforts of 123 men for nearly forty days, the canal was finally completed on 26 April 1864 and the water was "turned in."[84] The first settlers were able to raise what they later described as "large crops" by also drawing water from the local spring.

This canal-digging effort was only the beginning of such activities in Sevier County. The pioneers of the county dug many miles of canals in order to bring lifegiving water to their crops. This human effort was so successful that nature's harshness was largely offset. Before long, the Sevier River Valley was being described locally as "one of the most desirable locations in the Territory."[85]

Irrigation projects were probably the most visible communal economic enterprises in the county in the nineteenth century. In 1873 LDS church president Brigham Young intimated that land owners in Sevier County might secure patents on their land and then claim additional property by "excavating 20 cubic yards on the canal for an acre of land." Employing what might today be seen as sound ecological advice, Young further counseled the local Mormons, "One big ditch should be made instead of cutting up the country into a number of small ditches." To the occupants of the east side of the Sevier River Valley, he recommended that "every acre of land at Annabella Springs could be cultivated between Monroe and Glenwood from a ditch as high up on the bench as practicable."[86] Sensible planning combined with hard work was Brigham Young's formula for success.

Along with digging canals, other efforts at community building made the county a beehive of activity in the 1870s. A survey of Sevier County's water resources was "prosecuted vigorously" in 1872 as the Annabella, Glenwood, and Rocky Ford irrigation districts laid what now seem credulous plans to draw "unlimited supplies of water by ditches or canals from [the] Sevier River."[87] Further exploration of the county was also undertaken in 1872. According to a report in Salt Lake City's *Deseret News* on 29 July 1872, "The object of the explorations was the discovery of resources for the development and building up of that part of the territory."

By the turn of the twentieth century, at least nine rather extensive canals had been dug, crisscrossing the northern Sevier River Valley. Bearing geographically descriptive names like the Old Gunnison Canal, the New Gunnison Canal, the Highland Canal, the West View Canal, and the Vermillion Canal, these many waterways served regional communities from Gunnison (Sanpete County) on the north to Redmond and Salina farther southward. In the 1870s and 1880s most of the important canals serving the southern portion of the county—including Richfield, Elsinore, Joseph, and Monroe— had been constructed.[88] Each canal was the joint property of the local land owners; watermasters were elected and water allocations were determined according to shares and water availability. Watermasters were some of the most trusted and respected men in the county. Individual irrigators chose their watermasters because of their integrity and fairness of character.

County irrigators quickly moved from the informal cooperative irrigation organization centered on the commonweal and the Mormon church to a more formal organization based on law. The mutual irrigation company, a non-profit association established for the purpose of distributing water at cost, became the rule among the cooperative-minded Mormons of Utah.[89] In 1865 the territorial legislature passed legislation providing for the creation of mutual irrigation companies by farmers in the counties of the territory. These mutual irrigation companies were first called irrigation districts, and were formed through mutual agreement and consent of the farmers involved in the proposed district. During the resettlement of the county following the Black Hawk War and in the decade of the 1880s, large numbers of mutual irrigation companies were incorporated in Utah and in Sevier County.[90]

While it certainly was of extreme importance, irrigation was not the only cooperative activity in which the residents of Sevier County were engaged during the second half of the nineteenth century. Cattle grazing and range use was another issue of concern to the early settlers of the county. Some believed they had found an "excellent range" on the mountains west of Richfield (the Pahvant Range). Brigham Young encouraged the organization of local stock into cooperative herds.

The local joint stock herd suggested by Young initially consisted of 393 head of cattle worth $6,457. On 22 March 1873 articles of association were adopted incorporating the Sevier Cooperative Stock Herd Company. County residents also owned 650 sheep in Richfield, 650 more in Monroe, and more than 1,200 at Glenwood. Cooperative economic action came more easily to some in Sevier County than it did to others. According to the contemporary records of the Sevier LDS Stake, "The brethren at Monroe did not fully understand the subject of cooperation in stock, but the brethren at Glenwood had subscribed liberally for stock in the cooperative stock herd."[91]

This attitude among the Mormons of Monroe may have been due to a lack of commitment to cooperative action on the part of local church leaders. In 1875, as the Mormon church's cooperative plan, the United Order, was being embraced in parts of the county, Bishop Moses Gifford of Monroe reportedly "failed to get the . . . spirit & resigned his office."[92] In a largely Mormon community such as Monroe in the 1870s, the personal commitment of local leaders would weigh heavily upon community actions.

Brigham Young also suggested the construction of a road up

Clear Creek Canyon linking Sevier County with Coal Creek in Millard County.[93] This road construction project was directed by August Nielson.

Water, land, cattle, and communal action all helped to shape the character of nineteenth-century Sevier County. On 19 April 1874 a branch of the LDS United Order was organized in Richfield.[94] The plan usually entailed that participants would deed all their property and labor to the church, receiving in return what they needed to live on from the local order's officials, generally the bishop and stake president. By November, Bishop William H. Seegmiller of Richfield reported that "most of the brethren had taken hold of the United Order and were working well." Surprisingly, the order was also prospering at Monroe. At Salina it was reported that "the people there were divided on the United Order though those who had joined it were doing well."[95] Within one year of its founding, the United Order was reportedly "prospering" in the Sevier County communities of Richfield, Monroe, Glenwood, and Elsinore and was succeeding to a lesser degree at Salina and Joseph.[96]

According to local church accounts, most of those communities entering into the United Order in Sevier County received positive results. According to Bishop Seegmiller's report, the order was strong at Richfield and elsewhere; but community participation in the United Order was not complete. At Annabella it was reported that only half the people and joined the order but that "the brethren who had joined the United Order were doing well." At Salina, however, "only 16 families had joined the United Order while 21 families had not entered." At Joseph City "difficulty existed among some of the brethren based upon experiences in the United Order."[97]

With some sense of satisfaction, the official stake record observed in March 1875: "The people of Richfield, and in fact almost all the people in the county, are working in the United Order, and as far as we can see, were all working harmoniously."[98] Still, some noteworthy problems did face the Untited Order principle in Sevier County. Many of the wealthy and prominent men of the county proved unable or unwilling to "see the principle" and fell away from the church. Gottlieb Ence, a Swiss emigrant living in Richfield, observed of the United Order in 1874,

The Richfield rock school, constructed during the winter of 1864–65, serves as the backdrop for this photograph of Sevier County students. (Utah State Historical Society)

> Two thirds of the People in Richfield were favorable toward this move and entered into obligation an Covenant, about nearly two third of the People were poor and still more poor People Emigrants were coming an joint us. This made it verey hard for does [those] that had means, because it was devidet [divided] to all does that had Nothing.[99]

Ence's words make the economic implications of the United Order in Sevier County quite clear.

Following Stake President Joseph A. Young's sudden death at age forty-three in August 1875, the Sevier County United Order began to crumble.[100] Extremely capable, energetic, and well respected, he had been the glue which held the experiment together. Comparing it with the Latter-day Saints' oft-criticized practice of plural marriage, Young had knowingly cautioned the brethren of the Sevier Stake in December 1874, "The United Order will try men as plurality has tried women."[101]

At the quarterly conference of the Sevier Stake in November 1877, just over three years after it began, the United Order in Sevier

County was dissolved. In summarizing what went wrong with the order in Richfield, Gottlieb Ence concluded, "We had some verey good men in the U. Order but some very poor not good for much [men] made it disagreeable for the good ones, so it would create bad feellings."[102] In terminating the United Order, Apostle Orson Hyde counselled the local Saints, "[B]e not discouraged . . . you have tried to do the will of the Lord, and it will be a record in your favor."[103]

The words "you have tried to do the will of the Lord" could provide a fitting legacy for the trailblazers of Sevier County. They battled a harsh environment and eventually greatly subdued it. These men and women brought human life to the land. They built homes and reared families. They certainly proved worthy of the accolade cited earlier, they were "no longer outcasts but 'pioneers.'"

Endnotes

1. See C. Gregory Crampton and Steven K. Madsen, *In Search of the Spanish Trail: Santa Fe to Los Angeles, 1829–1848* (Salt Lake City: Gibbs Smith, 1994), and LeRoy R. Hafen and Ann W. Hafen, *The Old Spanish Trail, Santa Fe to Los Angeles* (Glendale, CA: Arthur H. Clark Company, 1954), 84–89.

2. Dale L. Morgan, *Jedediah Smith and the Opening of the West* (Indianapolis: Bobbs-Merrill Company, 1953), 196–97; and Hafen and Hafen, *Old Spanish Trail,* 114–15.

3. Dale L. Morgan, *The Great Salt Lake* (Indianapolis: Bobbs-Merrill Company, 1947), 98.

4. Hafen and Hafen, *Old Spanish Trail,* 148–49.

5. Quoted in Hafen and Hafen, *Old Spanish Trail,* 211.

6. Ibid., 190; Thomas D. Bonner, *The Life and Adventures of James P. Beckwourth* (Lincoln: University of Nebraska Press, 1972), 474–75.

7. Gwinn Harris Heap, *Central Route to the Pacific,* ed. Leroy R. Hafen (Glendale, CA: Arthur H. Clark Company, 1957), 218.

8. Ibid., 220.

9. Charles S. Peterson, *Utah, A History* (New York: W. W. Norton & Company and American Association for State and Local History, 1977), 3.

10. Ibid., 36.

11. Ibid., 38; also see Leonard J. Arrington, *Great Basin Kingdom: Economic History of the Latter-Day Saints, 1830–1900* (Cambridge: Harvard University Press, 1958), 215.

12. Donna T. Smart, "Over the Rim to Red Rock Country: The Parley P. Pratt Exploring Company of 1849," *Utah Historical Quarterly* 62 (Spring 1994): 172. Also helpful is Rick J. Fish, "The Southern Utah Expedition of Parley P. Pratt, 1849–1850," (Master's thesis, Brigham Young University, 1992).

13. Smart, "Over the Rim to Red Rock Country," 172–73.

14. Brigham Young Collection, Incoming Correspondence, 25 December 1853, LDS Archives, quoted in Fish, "The Southern Utah Expedition," 130.

15. Fish, "The Southern Utah Expedition," 130.

16. Quoted in Fish, "The Southern Utah Expedition," 131–32.

17. Smart, "Over the Rim to Red Rock Country," 187.

18. Irvin L. Warnock, comp. and ed., *Thru the Years: Sevier County Centennial History* (Springville, Utah: Art City Publishing Co., 1947), 16–17.

19. See the Sevier Stake Manuscript History (1874–1949), LDS Archives.

20. Edward A. Geary, *The Proper Edge of the Sky: The High Plateau Country of Utah* (Salt Lake City: University of Utah Press, 1992), 13.

21. Warnock, *Thru the Years*, 167.

22. Ibid., 167–68.

23. See *Golden Sheaves from a Rich Field: A Centennial History of Richfield, Utah,* compiled and edited by Pearl F. Jacobson, et al. (Richfield, Utah: Richfield Reaper Publishing Company, 1964), 43. See also Hubert Howe Bancroft, *History of Utah* (San Francisco: History Company Publishers, 1890), 706. On the usual practice of obtaining a "call" before undertaking a colonizing venture in Mormon Utah see Leonard J. Arrington, "Taming the Turbulent Sevier: A Story of Mormon Desert Conquest," *Western Humanities Review* 5 (Autumn 1951): 393–94.

24. Jacobson, *Golden Sheaves*, 51–52.

25. Ibid., 19.

26. See Deloy J. Spencer, "The Utah Black Hawk War 1865–71," (Master's thesis, Utah State University, 1969), 8. See also Revo Morrey Young, *Ten Penny Nails: Pioneering Sevier Valley* (n.p., n.d.), 29–39.

27. Quotation in Spenser, "The Utah Black Hawk War," 10; George Washington Bean, Dictation, H. H. Bancroft Papers, Bancroft Library, University of California at Berkeley, microfilm copy, Utah State Historical Society.

28. Warnock, *Thru the Years*, 22.

29. Nelson Higgins, Papers, incoming letter dated 5 April 1867, Utah State Historical Society.

30. Spencer, "Utah's Black Hawk War," 57. While Spencer failed to number Joseph among the abandoned communities, Revo Morrey Young notes in her entry on Joseph in *Thru the Years* (191) that "the place was abandoned in 1865, because of the Indian troubles" and no more attempts were made to settle it until November 1871.

31. Quoted from LDS Journal History, 25 March 1866, in Works Progress Adminstration papers, Utah State Historical Society, Salt Lake City.

32. Typescript history of Monroe quoting Andrew Jensen, History of Sevier Stake, in WPA papers.

33. Quoted in Spencer, "The Utah Black Hawk War," 62.

34. Jacobson, *Golden Sheaves*, 21.

35. Works Project Administration papers, Utah State Historical Society, Box 81; "Forts" and "The First Settlements in the Sevier Valley," *Utah Geneaological and Historical Magazine* 6 (April 1915): 83ff.

36. "The First Settlements in the Sevier Valley," 144–45.

37. Warnock, *Thru the Years*, 38.

38. See Young, *Ten Penny Nails*, iv, 12.

39. Warnock, *Thru the Years*, 15.

40. See Sevier Stake Historical Record & Minutes, 7 August 1871, LR 8243, Ser. II, LDS Archives.

41. Ibid.

42. Ibid.

43. Ibid.

44. Patricia Nelson Limerick, *The Legacy of Conquest: The Unbroken Past of the American West* (New York: W.W. Norton and Company, 1987), 73.

45. Sevier Stake Historical Record & Minutes, 21 March 1872, 10.

46. Ibid., 11.

47. Ibid., 33.

48. See President and Mrs. Irvin L. Warnock, *Memories of the Sevier Stake Church of Jesus Christ of Latter-day Saints: Diamond Jubilee Memorial Volume, 1874–1949* (Springville, Utah: Art City Publishing Co., 1969), 15, 18.

49. Jacobson, *Golden Sheaves*, 45–49.

50. Warnock, *Thru the Years*, 203–204.

51. See Cynthia Jane Sturgis, "The Mormon Village in Transition: Richfield, Utah, as a Case Study," (Master's thesis, University of Utah, 1978), 25.

52. Naturalization Records, Sevier County, 1896–1910, Utah State Archives, Salt Lake City.

53. See the *Deseret News,* 15 June 1864.

54. Warnock, *Thru the Years,* 226.

55. Ibid., 227.

56. Ibid., 191–92.

57. Ibid., 193.

58. Ibid., 371.

59. Ibid., 372.

60. See Ibid., 87, 107, 127, 143, 269, 425, 435, 459.

61. Ibid., 87, 89.

62. Ibid., 425–26.

63. Ibid., 426.

64. Ibid., 426–27.

65. Ibid., 427.

66. Ibid., 435; *Richfield Reaper,* 29 April 1971.

67. Warnock, *Thru the Years,* 435.

68. Ibid., 435.

69. Jeanne Dastrup, "The Sigurd Story," paper, 1971, copy at Utah State Historical Society Library, 28.

70. Quotation from *Richfield Reaper,* 29 April 1971; Warnock, *Thru the Years,* 127.

71. Warnock, *Thru the Years,* 144–46.

72. Ibid., 144–45.

73. Ibid., 146; Elsinore Ward Manuscript History, c. 1876, LDS Archives.

74. Warnock, *Thru the Years,* 38.

75. Ibid., 215–16.

76. Ibid., 107, 108.

77. Young, *Ten Penny Nails,* 47.

78. Ibid., 12.

79. Warnock, *Thru the Years,* 269.

80. Ibid., 269–70.

81. Ibid., 270.

82. Ibid., 459, 462.

83. *Deseret News,* 30 March 1864.

84. *Deseret News,* 30 April 1864.

85. Sevier Stake Historical Record & Minutes, Microfilm LR 8241, Reel 2. See also Harold H. Hiskey, "Optimal Allocation of Irrigation Water: The Sevier River Basin," (Ph.D. diss., Utah State University, 1971), 2.

86. Sevier Stake Manuscript History, 1879.

87. Sevier Stake Manuscript History, 1872.

88. See Frank D. Gardner and Charles A. Jensen, "Soil Survey in the Sevier Valley, Utah," U.S. Department of Agriculture, c. 1900, 249–50, copy at Utah State Historical Society Library, Salt Lake City.

89. See Orson W. Israelson, J. Howard Maughan, and George P. South, *Irrigation Companies in Utah: Their Activities and Needs* (Logan: Agricultural Experiment Station Utah State Agricultural College, 1946), 11–12. Copy available at Utah State Historical Society Library.

90. Israelson, Maughan, and South, *Irrigation Companies in Utah,* 13. In 1946 there were twenty-four irrigation companies operating in the county and 509 mutual irrigation companies in the state, page 15.

91. Sevier Stake Manuscript History, 1872.

92. Sevier Stake Historical Record & Minutes, 1875, 42.

93. Sevier Stake Manuscript History, 1872.

94. Sevier Stake Manuscript History, 1874. Also helpful on the United Order is Leonard J. Arrington, Feramorz Y. Fox, and Dean L. May, *Building the City of God: Community and Cooperation Among the Mormons* (Urbana: University of Illinois Press, 1992).

95. Sevier Stake Manuscript History, 7 November 1874.

96. Sevier Stake Historical Record & Minutes, 1875, 42–43.

97. Sevier Stake Manuscript History, 1875.

98. Sevier Stake Manuscript History, 19 March 1875.

99. Gottlieb Ence, Autobiography, typescript, 37, Utah State Historical Society Library. The authors of *Building the City of God* contend that the actual figure in Richfield was four-fifths who favored the Order (see page 179).

100. Arrington, Fox, and May, *Building the City of God,* 195.

101. Sevier Stake Historical Record & Minutes, December 1874, 84.

102. Ence, Autobiography, 41.

103. Ibid., 140.

4

# Social, Political, and Economic Development of Sevier County, 1865–1896

In 1850 the Utah Territorial Legislature created six counties: Great Salt Lake, Weber, Tuilla, Utah, San Pete (later Sanpete), and Little Salt Lake.[1] Each of these entities was formed around pockets of white settlement. County borders and names changed over time until 1917 when the creation of Daggett County gave Utah its present twenty-nine counties.

On 16 January 1865 the territorial legislature created Sevier County out of the southern portion of Sanpete County. The boundaries of the county were outlined as follows:

> That all that portion of Sanpete county lying south of an east and west line passing through the ford of Willow Creek between Gunnison and Salina, and east of the main range of mountains dividing Round and Pauvan valleys from the valley of the Sevier is hereby created and named Sevier county, with county seat at Richfield.[2]

The county's northern, western, and southern boundaries were essentially the same as they are today. However, the county's eastern border extended to the present Utah-Colorado state line, making Sevier County a long and narrow rectangular county. In 1880 the citizens of Castle Valley petitioned the territorial legislature to separate themselves from Sevier County. Their petition was granted and Emery County was formed out of the eastern ends of Sevier and Sanpete counties.[3] A small change in the county's boundaries was made in 1890 by the territorial legislature. That year, a section of Sevier County located between Axtell and the Sevier River was removed from the county and added to Sanpete County.[4]

Probate courts executed the basic law to Utah's settlements from 1852 until statehood in 1896. Each county probate court was composed of a probate judge elected by the territorial legislature for a term of four years. The probate judge held unusual judicial powers: in addition to deciding matters regarding probates, he held original jurisdiction of civil and most criminal cases.[5]

The territorial legislature gave additional powers to the probate courts, frequently called county courts. The county court, which also included three county selectmen (or county commissioners), elected for terms of three years, served as the executive and legislative branches of county government—in short, to take care of the management of all county business.[6] The county court was to create school and road districts in the county and ensure the proper management of them. Additional authority was given to the county courts and selectmen a year after the creation of Sevier County. The Sevier County Court was given the responsiblity for the proper distribution and management of the county's natural resources. The county courts, the laws of the territory stated, shall

> have the control of all timber, water privileges on any watercourse or creek; to grant mill sites and excercise such powers as in their judgement shall best preserve the timber and subserve the interests of the settlements in the distribution of water for irrigation or other purposes.[7]

The Sevier County selectmen were also responsible for care and maintenace of "insane persons" and others incapable of conducting their own affairs.

The county probate judges, selected by the territorial legislature,

Looking north along main street in Richfield about 1875. (Utah State Historical Society)

were generally bishops or men of high standing in the Mormon church, as were also the county selectmen.[8] The county courts held unusual political and economic power in the county until 1896.

William Morrison was selected by the Utah Territorial Legislature in 1865 to serve as the first probate judge in Sevier County. James Crawford, Peter Rasmussen, and James Mecham were elected the county's first selectmen. Morrison was involved in local promotional activities and land speculation in the Richfield area and he built the county's first gristmill in 1865.

In 1856 the Sevier Valley was reportedly surveyed by U.S. government surveyor Charles Mogo. The territorial legislature in 1866 designated Richfield the county seat of the newly created Sevier County. Richfield was first surveyed in 1872 by Edmund Fox. In 1873 the townsite of Richfield was officially established in the federal land office in Salt Lake City, and in 1874 settlers began to receive official title to their claimed property. In 1878 the territorial legislature incorporated Richfield, after an earlier charter had been vetoed in 1876 by Governor George Emery. Elections were held in August 1878 and Franklin Spencer became the town's first mayor.[9]

By the early 1870s the Sevier River Valley, with its hub at Richfield, was on its way to becoming a major regional commercial center.[10] During the 1870s and 1880s Elsinore with a population of 400, Joseph with about 300 people, Glenwood with 500, and Monroe with 600 inhabitants challenged Richfield as the county's leading population center.[11] By 1890, however, the population of Richfield reached 1,531, surpassing all other communities in the county, Monroe being the closest with a population of 850.[12] In 1885 the first city hall had been erected in Richfield at a cost of $750.

Roads were gradually improved and created during the early years, and bridges also were constructed across the Sevier River, further improving communication between the county's settlements. A bridge was built across the Sevier River between Richfield and the Glenwood area in 1875; another was built in 1876 between Elsinore and Monroe. In July 1872 it was decided by LDS church and county leaders to extend the telegraph line south from Gunnison through Sevier County. Joseph A. Young led the local telegraph movement. Each community in the county was given an allotment of telegraph poles to provide so the desired construction could begin. Richfield was called upon to provide 450 poles; Monroe, 240; Glenwood, 225; and Salina, 90. By December 1872 the telegraph line was completed as far south as Monroe.[13] It is recorded that Monroe had a post office in 1872, and although information about other early post offices has not been found, it is to be assumed that Richfield and other towns of the area had official U.S. postal service at an early date. In the 1870s Peter Miller was the postmaster at Richfield.[14]

Other economic endeavors embraced by county residents during the second half of the nineteenth century included a tannery, a dairy, some mining, a sawmill, a quartz mill, a gristmill, and a textile mill. Jens Jensen built lime kilns in the vicinity of Richfield at an early date, and later, in the 1870s, there was even an attempt to create a silk industry as mulberry trees were planted and silkworms brought in at the behest of LDS church leaders. Although this experiment failed, it did at least lead to the growth of the mulberry trees in the county. As the LDS ward clerk at Richfield noted, "The Saints were encouraged to sustain mechanic shops and manufactures."[15]

George Robinson is believed to have established a gristmill at

Richfield Creamery, located at 309 East 200 South, Richfield. Built in 1876 and operated by Archie M. Young. (Utah State Historical Society)

Monroe in the early days of settlement, and Andrew Bartleson established a gristmill shortly after resettlement.[16] Although they later became foes, Nelson Higgins and William Morrison were jointly operating a gristmill at Richfield by 1865. The whole community laid plans for a cooperative gristmill by 1871; it was completed two years later. Joseph Young established a sawmill on Cove Mountain in August 1872 which was moved three years later to Clear Creek Canyon.

At Koosharem, grazing was originally the sole economic pursuit; but by 1879 the residents could proudly claim, "We have a co-operative tannery, also a dairy and a co-operative saw mill is under erection." At the Marysvale Ward, actually in Piute County, but then a part of the Sevier LDS Stake, a quartz mill was built in 1881 which brought in "quite an influx of miners and prospectors." Monroe had a gristmill by 1864, and "a new saw mill" commenced operation in 1871. A tannery was established for a brief period of time at

Glenwood by the local United Order in 1877. The cooperative store was built in 1878 as part of the United Order, and the building survives to the present, one of the few Mormon cooperative buildings still remaining from the time of the great communtarian experiment. Also at Glenwood, a committee was appointed in 1879 to secure the purchase of a carding machine from John W. Young, another son of recently deceased church president Brigham Young.

At Salina, steps toward light industrialization were taken in 1882 when the community built a flouring mill powered by the waters of Salina Creek. The following year, "a rude manufactory of salt" capable of an output of five hundred pounds of salt per day commenced business in the community.[17] According to another history, E.W. Crane built a salt refinery in 1880, and these two operations could well be the same. Salina residents were among the participants of the famous Hole-in-the-Rock expedition sent by Mormon church leaders to colonize the southeastern portion of the territory in 1880.[18]

Freighting was undertaken in the early decades of settlement, including west to the Nevada mining towns. This was often dangerous on account of the weather and road conditions as well as the outlaws that frequented the roads to the mining areas across the bleak and desolate stretches of western Utah. The enterprise, however, did provide a market for some county produce and brought cash to a cash-poor society. Saloons in the county served traveling freighters and miners as well as (no doubt) a few locals.

The *Deseret News* on 26 November 1875 in its "News From Sevier County" section noted "the excellent harvest" the county had experienced. Local farmers, apparently, felt strongly about the value of their agriculture products. "Parties there [in Sevier County] had been offering $1.10 a bushel for it [the local wheat]," the *Deseret News* reported, "but the people declined to sell at that price, preferring to hold it until they can get $1.25."[19]

Nature appeared to be on the side of the local agriculturalists in the summer of 1877. The Richfield Ward history of that time observed: "The crops are all a little backward, but are going finely, and it is the opinion of many that the prospects of a plentiful harvest were never seen to be as promising as they are now. Never before were so many rainfalls seen as in the last April and May."[20] This entry,

Inside the Richfield Bank. (Utah State Historical Society)

penned by an unidentified LDS ward clerk, is very telling about life in Sevier County about a decade after its founding. Obviously the people were confident in their ability to survive and even prosper. But the entry indicates that they were still dependent upon nature to advance their material condition. The rather tentative words seem to indicate that times had not always looked so bright.

The 1880s saw the residents of Sevier County busily engaged in various economic enterprises. At Glenwood, the year's harvest in 1882 was said to be "briskly in progress" with a "fair yield" of cereals being realized. Two years later, the people of Monroe were interested in building a reservoir and in planting trees. Tree planting was also carried on to "a considerable extent" at Salina in 1884. That same year, the Sevier Valley canal was "located and surveyed" from west of Richfield to the bench above Elsinore.[21] Sigurd (from Norse mythology) was officially assigned by the post office as the name for Vermillion on 11 June 1887 because of the same name being used for a Kane County settlement.

A report from Redmond in 1885 observed, "The crops as a rule throughout the valley look very well and give promise of an abundant harvest."[22] The following year, local opinion held that "the poorest land was taken first because it happened to be the most accessible to water, but now the people have grown strong enough to construct canals to irrigate the bench land . . . which is better adapted to tilling."[23] A stake history compiled in 1888 bemoaned the economic dependency and the somewhat underdeveloped character of the region:

> Markets for the produce of our county have been poor. The farmers hope for a good harvest, but to the stranger it looks very dirty. What is wanted here as elsewhere is manufactories. The country is overrun with sheep with no facilities to manufacture the wool into fabrics, though there are splendid water powers at some points in this valley.[24]

This was not really as much an outcry against sheep raising as it was a plea for economic expansion and integration; not really a manifestation of social discontent as much as a sign of economic discontent. Like others in a rapidly industrializing America, county boosters wanted textile mills, not simply more herds of sheep.

According to the *Pacific Coast Directory* for 1880–81 and its companion volume for 1883–84, Glenwood had nearly a dozen business owners and professional men including A. Shaw, groceries; O.H. Speed, physician; Joseph Wall, hotelier; A.T. Oldroyd, general merchandise; and T. Bell, carpenter and justice of the peace. In Monroe the businesses listed included N.J. Pates, musical instruments; F. Lundquist, bootmaker; R. Sorenson, tinsmith; as well as thirteen other businesses and professionals. The business directory listed more than twenty-two businesses and professions in Richfield. In the hamlet of Inverury (Central), located six miles south of Richfield, six business and professional men were listed, including James W. Stewart and William Greenwood as railroad contractors. J.L. Butler was listed as a sheepraiser and woolgrower, and six other businessmen were listed in Joseph. In Burrville, N. Linvik and H.J. Olson were listed as bootmakers along with seven other businessmen. In Koosharem, Linvik and Olson also were listed as bootmakers along with about a half-dozen other businesses. Monroe, according to the business directories, had two liquor stores, the Anderton Brothers store and J.H. McCarthy's establishment. The directories listed in Monroe nearly a dozen businesses and professional men including E. Crane, saltmaker, and Fred G. Willes, druggist. There were two hotels in Monroe and, at one time, eight grocery stores.[25] The first bank in the county was opened in Richfield in 1883 by James M. Peterson.

Another business in Sevier County with roots in the late nineteenth century was the *Richfield Reaper,* the local newspaper, which was founded in 1885 by Joe Thompson. Initially, Thompson bought a small printing press from H.P. Miller, who had ordered it from a Chicago mail-order house for the purpose of cataloguing his personal books. Editor and publisher Thompson kept his new press in a building in the southern end of early Richfield. Joe Thompson's publishing career must not have proved too lucrative, however, for soon he was trying to add to his income by selling "drugs," some of which were said to be nothing more than doctored liquor. This second enterprise landed Thompson in trouble with the law. He was indicted for fraud, and in order to pay his fine he had to sell his press.[26]

County residents enjoyed dancing from earliest settlement times. Academy (or Farnsworth) Hall in Richfield was built by brothers Austin, Alonzo, and Albert Farnsworth and finished in 1873. It was celebrated with a dance on Christmas night. A local dramatic company formed in 1876. Earlier there had been a ward chorus and theatricals were performed in the old rock meetinghouse/schoolhouse in Richfield. In 1881 Hans Peter Hansen and Ed Thurber built what became known as the Opera House, originally a 30-by-70-foot building that was enlarged over the years and hosted both local and touring productions and dances.[27] Hansen also organized a brass band in 1882, and other towns also featured dances and local musicians.

Outdoor activities included sleigh riding in the winter and parades in the summer, especially on Pioneer Day (24 July) and (later) the Fourth of July. Baseball was popular for both participants and observers. Mormon ward teams from the county played each

Looking east along main street in Salina, May 1917. (Utah State Historical Society)

other as early as the 1870s; later, organized teams were sponsored by the various communities.[28]

In earliest settlement times, medical service was rendered by those with the courage to attempt it. Midwives were important in all early communities and provided basic health care before the arrival of medical practitioners. George Ogilvie was Richfield's first doctor. Other early doctors—some with little or no formal training—included Elizabeth Burns Ramsay, Elias Blackburn, and Kennedy Neal. By the turn of the century, Richfield and other county towns were served by a number of qualified medical practitioners, nurses, and dentists. For example, Martin Hansen opened a dental office in Richfield in 1886.[29]

Light industries, although often largely oriented toward local consumption like Salina's flour mill and salt manufactory, were indicators along with the arrival of a regional railroad that Sevier County was moving beyond a simple grazing and farming economy.

Agricultural diversification and a growing industrial presence were beginning to sweep the nation, Utah, and Sevier County. By the late 1880s the county was knocking at the door of the modern world.[30]

The Sevier LDS Stake was officially organized with Joseph A. Young as stake president on 24 May 1874. During its years practicing the United Order, the Richfield Order owned a gristmill shingle mill, some 200 head of horses, 800 cattle, and 1,700 sheep. LDS wards were organized in most of the county's communities through the years, the larger towns eventually being served by more than one LDS ward. Meetinghouses, which often doubled as schoolhouses and civic social halls in the early years, were constructed in all LDS wards.

In 1888, the Mormons of Sevier County began construction of what became the county's most imposing structure, the Sevier LDS Stake Tabernacle, located on Main Street in Richfield. As the *Richfield Reaper* boasted following the edifice's completion, "There is no finer church building in central Utah than the Richfield tabernacle."[31]

The tabernacle was for Sevier County Mormons what the Salt Lake LDS Temple became for the entire LDS church in the 1890s.[32] The Sevier Stake Tabernacle became a visual sign of the dominant religion—an outward reflection of the people's inner devotion. While living in the United Order had represented the spiritual resolve and economic commitment of local Mormons, the tabernacle emerged as the manifest symbol of the importance of the church in the county. In what evolved into the traditional LDS way of accomplishing things, a building committee comprised of W.H. Clark, Simon Christensen, Paul Poulsen, I.K. Wright, and E.P. Bean was constituted in the spring of 1888. Its charge was to formulate plans to raise the building. The original design of the structure was the work of Niels Skowgaard.

Work on the tabernacle was intermittent at best. The *Richfield Reaper* somewhat disparagingly observed, "The work progressed fairly well at intervals until 1893 when it began to drag."[33] In 1896 W.H. Clark was succeeded as chairman of the building committee by Theodore Bradley. Bradley and the committee tried in vain to institute several "donation schedules"; however, the area residents were generally so impoverished that this brought little needed financial support. It was finally decided "to make the matter one of straight practice"[34] (possibly a direct monetary or labor assessment of each church member rather than a system dependent upon voluntary donations).

This new strategy was put into action in early 1898, ten years after construction began. The work was nearly pushed to completion by that fall. Then, as so often was the case for the Latter-day Saints of Sevier County, tragedy struck. On the evening of 14 October 1898 the nearly completed structure caught fire. Much damage resulted. But the resiliency developed by life in an austere environment and the deep religious commitment of the county's people prevailed. "Without waiting any length of time," according to a church account, these faithful people "resumed [work] and the building was again completed eight months after the fire." The Sevier Stake Tabernacle was "appropriately dedicated" on 16 July 1899.[35] Unfortunately, it was condemned as unsafe in 1914, necessitating the building of yet another tabernacle, which was completed in 1930.[36]

Contemporary with the tabernacle was the second Sevier County Courthouse. The first county courthouse had been erected in Richfield during 1876–77, just six years after the resettlement of the county. Then, in 1890, county officials, led by commissioners A.W. Buchanan, James L. Jensen, and A.D. Thurber, decided to construct a new courthouse. The Sevier County voters of the time were not all convinced that such a building was needed, however.

Perhaps the fact that the tabernacle construction was still in progress deterred some residents. The ensuing bond election to secure financing for the new public structure brought enough votes to carry the measure, 321 (59 percent) voters favoring the proposed courthouse to 223 (41 percent) opposed. It was approval, yes, but not an overwhelming mandate. The second county courthouse, a two-story building constructed primarily of brick, featured a tall central tower bounded by smaller corner towers. Combining an eclectic blend of classical motifs with the familiar American courthouse architectural style, this Sevier County Courthouse was quite typical of civic buildings of the 1890s. It was begun in 1892 and completed in July 1893 and featured a separate jail.[37]

The courts of Sevier County before statehood had limited power. That is to say, the penalties that the county's courts were empowered to impose for crimes were fixed or established by other authorities. When Utah was admitted as a state in 1896, the county's trial court functioned at only one level. The county's population was not yet great enough to warrant other court levels and jurisdictions. Only courts in the more metropolitan areas, such as Salt Lake City, Ogden, or Provo, were initially granted powers to try criminal cases.[38]

Nearly eighty years later, in the 1970s, the state legislature created the circuit court system in Utah. Circuit courts replaced the earlier city courts in less populated areas of the state. The three areas covered by the newly created circuit courts were headquartered in Spanish Fork, Vernal, and Richfield. Under Utah law, the circuit court does not adjudicate marital disputes (divorces), child custody cases, or property matters. Such rulings fall under the purview of probate courts.[39]

Before the creation of Utah's circuit courts, the most powerful judges serving Sevier County were those in probate courts. The county's probate judges between 1865 and 1896 were William Morrison (appointed in 1865), George W. Bean (1874), W.G. Baker (1878), Andrew Hepler (1883), J.B. Kenney (1888) and W.W. Wallace (1894).[40] A probate judgeship was a desirable appointment. It might have been used as a political reward or for proven service to the community. In 1874 Congress passed the Poland Act, which severely restricted the power and authority in civil and criminal matters of county probate judges. The Utah state constitution abolished the office in 1896. That same year county commissions replaced county selectmen as the executive and legislative heads of county government. The county commission functions were also changed. No longer directly involved with the management and distribution of natural resources in the county or to serve as a court, the commissions' responsibilities were expanded in the areas of road maintenance, education, health care, and the care of the poor.

Education is a primary function of government and was a concern of county residents from earliest settlement times. Schools were generally established and schoolhouses built in area towns at an early date, generally within a year of the town's founding; however, the quality of education was often less than could have been hoped for, especially considering the lack of facilities and funds. County resi-

Richfield Schoolhouse. (Utah State Historical Society)

dents did endeavor to provide schooling as they were best able to do so.The first school in Richfield was held in the home of Betsy Gardiner in 1864; forty pupils were enrolled. A rock schoolhouse was built the next year; Hans Peter Miller was the first teacher at this school. Sevier County officers selected school trustees on 6 March 1865, and after resettlement educational activities resumed in all the towns of the county. In 1876 Richfield residents applied to the Sevier County Court for the establishment of a school district. Their petition was granted.[41]

Until statehood, free universal public education was unknown, and in rural counties like Sevier much of the organized education was provided by local LDS church organizations. For example, the Sevier Stake established an academy for older students in 1887 that operated for a few years in the county. Other Christian denominations increasingly saw education as a means to establish a foothold in Mormon-dominated Utah. Quality schools were opened throughout the state by Protestant denominations beginning in the 1870s in an attempt to attract students and their parents by means of the improved educational opportunities they offered.

In Sevier County, along with growth came perceived threats to

Richfield Presbyterian Church. (Utah State Historical Society)

area Mormons from the non-Mormon world, and the late nineteenth century also witnessed the coming of Protestant missionaries and churches into the county. Seeking to save Mormon souls, Presbyterians and Methodists launched missions and schools in Utah. In Sevier County, unfortunately, early records are somewhat incomplete or at variance in their dates regarding the establishment of other religious denominations. The basic facts remain, however.

Monroe Presbyterian Church. (Utah State Historical Society)

Under the direction of Dr. D.J. McMillan, Presbyterians founded mission schools, including a grade school at Richfield in 1880 (some sources say 1877), with Miss J.A. Olmstead as the teacher, which also served as a mission station.[42] Primary schools were also established in Monroe (1877), with Phoebe Wheeler as instructor, and in Salina (1884). A Presbyterian church was built and dedicated in Richfield in 1889–90 with Reverend P.D. Stoops as the first minister. It was preceded by a church in Monroe in 1884. The Richfield Presbyterian school closed in 1908, the Salina school in 1918, and the school in Monroe in 1929.[43] The establishment of a school in Salina was followed by the construction of a small chapel built with funds from a Mrs. Crosby of New York City in memory of her daughter.[44]

In rural Utah the missionary ministers often were circuit riders

Richfield Methodist-Episcopal Church, 1886 (Utah State Historical Society).

(itinerant preachers). Locally, the Reverend D.J. McMillan oversaw large geographic districts during the 1880s. Reverend McMillan, whose home station was Richfield, usually preached in that town on Sunday, then traveled his circuit, which took him to Gunnison on Monday, back to Richfield on Wednesday, and then to Monroe and to Marysvale later in the week. In Monroe, McMillan held Sunday services in the school built in 1877. For all of this effort, however, there is no evidence of any conversions of Sevier County Mormons to the Presbyterian church.[45]

The Methodists were also active in the county. One source reported a Methodist Episcopal church organized in Richfield in 1884 by Rev. Martin Anderson, preceded by a Methodist mission established in Salina in 1864. A Methodist church congregation was established in Richfield in 1886 among area Scandinavians and included many area miners. Reverend Emil Mork was the first pastor.[46] Grade schools were established at Richfield (1886) and at Monroe (1890), hoping to persuade young Mormons to embrace Methodism. A church was built at Monroe. A primary Methodist focus was upon the Scandinavian Latter-day Saints. A Scandinavian mission was established in Utah which operated fourteen churches and at least thirteen grade schools. The ministry had a Norwegian conference and a Danish conference. Sunday services were conducted in both English and appropriate Scandinavian tongues, and a Scandinavian-oriented periodical, *Utah Tidende,* was published, starting in 1890. Along with a proselyting focus upon Scandinavians, the Methodists also vigorously attacked Mormon polygamy.[47] After the establishment of free public schools with Utah statehood in 1896, mission schools declined. Methodists in Sevier County discontinued organizational worship after the turn of the century, area Methodists joining with local Presbyterians for worship at that time.

Evangelical Protestants were not all that Sevier County's Mormon residents had to be concerned with during the 1880s and 1890s—their religion during these very decades was locked in an intense struggle with the federal government over the practice of plural marriage, better known as polygamy. While the available evidence is too incomplete to determine the extent of polygamy within the county, there is enough information to give some idea of the practice of plural marriage within Sevier County during the late nineteenth century.

The story of polygamy in Sevier County has never been as completely told as it has been for some other Utah counties—Davis and Washington, for example.[48] Given the secrecy surrounding the practice during the 1870s, 1880s, and 1890s due to the fear of prosecution under several federal anti-polygamy laws, the full story may never be known. While the extent of plural marriage in Sevier County is difficult to determine, there are some limited extant records.

At a Sevier Stake general priesthood meeting held in February 1879 there was "considerable discussion of plural marriage." The second counselor in the stake presidency, later to become stake president, William H. Seegmiller, commented on "the nature and design of the institution of plural marriage." He characterized the recent decision of the U.S. Supreme Court in the George Reynolds case as being tantamount to a "Declaration of War against the Kingdom of God." Seegmiller further charged that the "elders would come under the censure of the Almighty God for not sufficiently honoring the Ordinance."[49]

The trials endured by the Latter-day Saint practitioners of plural marriage were great. Let us look at four practitioners of the principle from Sevier County to help understand the impact plural marriage had upon life there. Gottlieb Ence, a Swiss immigrant living at Richfield whose views were noted in regard to the United Order, wrote of his wife's struggle with plural marriage:

> My dear Wife Elisabeth being a good Latter Day Saint wished to obey all the Principles the Lord has revealed unto man in order to obtain a place in his Celestial Kingdom, she was willing to sacrifice her own feellings in order to be able to inherit a place in his Celestial Kingdom. She then consented an let me have her sister Caroline for my second wife, this she don[e] in full faith that it was a commandment of God, and she would be rewarded for doing so.[50]

Some years later, Ence happily noted, "My two wifes, Elizabeth and Caroline have lived together with their families for mainy years in peace & love as one united Familie."

Unfortunately, life was not always so serene for Gottlieb Ence. He, like other polygamists, lived with the fear of arrest for unlawful cohabitation. As Ence noted in his autobiography,

> By the interpretation of the law by the Courts or judges, . . . it was not alowd for two Women as Wifes could live to gether in one haus [house]. If so a Man would surly be convicted for Cohabitation or adultery, so they [his two wives] supperated an each lived in thier [sic] own home since 1885, in order to comply that much with the law.[51]

Even after Elizabeth and Caroline were living in separate residences, Gottlieb Ence feared the coming of the marshals to spy on suspected polygamists. "During the Winter [of] 1886 & 87," noted a worried Ence, "the Deputies would call around pretty often." Probably in order to avoid arrest, Gottlieb Ence decided to go "on the underground," a Mormon phrase signifying hiding to evade apprehension.

In late January 1887 Ence in company with his son Alma and a few other men made a trading trip to Silver Reef, a mining town located in Washington County. While the stated purpose of the journey was to sell grain and flour to the miners, it appears likely that at least Ence, if not some of the others, was seeking to disappear for a

Elsinore Livery Stable owned by Henry C. Larsen. (Utah State Historical Society)

time. "After selling out," he wrote, "the others return[ed] home." But Ence chose to go on to visit his brother at Santa Clara, "whom I had not seen for mainy years." That he was really on the underground in southern Utah becomes clear when Ence writes, "I stayed with them about one month as things look a littel more favorable [than] around home in regards to deputies." Gottlieb Ence finally returned to "my dear home" sometime later when he felt it safe to do so.[52]

The memoirs of Hans Christensen of Richfield, written in 1890 while he was incarcerated at the Utah Territorial Penitentiary at Sugar House near Salt Lake City on charges of illegal cohabitation, provide an additional record of plural marriage in Sevier County: "I had maried another wife [Johanne Catherine Jensen] two years before [in 1877], and rented a place for her to live, untill the year after [1879] when I bought a House and Lot in the outskirt of town, for her to occupy." Christensen knew he was facing the "prospects of being sent to this place [prison]" for polygamy.[53]

Albert King Thurber, a native of Rhode Island, converted to Mormonism while on his way to the California gold fields in 1849. Following his return to Utah, Thurber married Thirsa Malvina Berry, daughter of John W. Berry, with whom he had traveled on his return trip. They wed in February 1851.[54] About thirteen years later, around 1873 or 1874, after moving to Sevier County, Thurber took Agnes Brockbank as a plural wife. Between his two wives, Thurber fathered fourteen children, at least four of whom were born at Richfield.[55]

Another area resident, Joseph Smith Horne, married Lydia Ann Weiler in Salt Lake City's Endowment House on 7 November 1868. Just weeks before this wedding, Horne, described by Brigham Young as "a good, faithful, energetic man," had been called to serve as the bishop of the Gunnison Ward. Lydia, although friends and relatives viewed it as "somewhat of a trial for her," was willing to go with him to Gunnison.[56] Ten years later, just days after Lydia had died, Horne was called as bishop of the Richfield Second Ward. He arrived in Richfield in December 1878, a widower with three small children. Caroline Ence, one of Gottfried's wives, was Horne's housekeeper that winter.

In the end of February 1879, Caroline Ence returned to her home and Maria Snow, the estranged wife of Warren Snow of Manti, along with her children came to live with the motherless family. Joseph Horne described her as "a woman of experience [who] can do well for the children." According to Horne, Maria and Warren Snow "had not associated as husband and wife for several years." In the summer of 1879 Maria Snow, who had been a plural wife for over twenty years, obtained a divorce and assumed her maiden name of Baum. In October 1879 Joseph Horne asked Maria Baum to marry him. "She hesitated a little," Horne wrote, "wondering what her children and friends would think, but finally consented." They were married in the St. George LDS Temple on 5 December 1879.[57]

Horne's story concerns aspects of plural marriage in nineteenth-century Utah (note that Mrs. Snow had already been a plural wife before getting a divorce). It also addresses the issue of rearing small children without a mate. Horne remarried fairly quickly after his wife's death (about one year). By comparison, one of Horne's contemporaries, Henry W. Bigler, another widower with children who served as an ordinance worker at the St. George LDS Temple, lost his wife of many years in the mid-1870s and then waited three years before remarrying.[58]

At almost the same time as his marriage to Maria, Joseph Horne was already looking for a plural wife:

> I had paid some attention to Martha Maria Morrison, daughter of William Morrison, and Anne Maria Hansen; and while I was in S.L. City, in the legislature, she came to the city and we were married in the Endowment House Feb. 14, 1880 by Jos. F. Smith.[59]

The bridegroom made no mention about his wife's thoughts on this union. While he and his three children returned home after the legislative session (Maria was not mentioned), Martha Morrison "went to Mt. Pleasant to visit friends and relatives." Perhaps tellingly, it was not until two months later that Martha actually joined the Horne household.

Joseph S. Horne's plural marriages once again illustrate the legal risks faced by polygamists. In 1880 a federal judge, believing "we must break this thing up," sentenced Horne to one and a half years in prison. "What consistency! How noble!" Joseph S. Horne sarcastically wrote in his autobiography. "In one breath [the judge] acknowledge[s] a woman as my wife, asks when I married her, and in the same breath sentences me for committing adultery with her, she not being my wife!" It would seem safe to say that Sevier County's other polygamists must have felt trepidation about their own situations.

In Utah Territory, particularly Salt Lake and Weber counties, the coming of the railroad and the influx of non-Mormons it brought had a marked impact upon local politics. Following their mid-nineteenth-century move west, the Latter-day Saints attempted to shape, in one historian's view, "a community which conjoined church and state, politics, the economy, and society into one whole."[60] In Sevier County, isolation allowed the luxury of continuing local Mormon control. Social and economic change was most evident in the attempts at diversification of the county's economy from almost solely agricultural pursuits to manufacturing, such as Monroe's gristmill or Salina'a salt manufactory.

The value—in fact, the necessity—of such diversification became clear to many in Sevier County when, in the summer of 1887, the county faced a brutal drought. During a July meeting of leaders of

A funeral procession for James M. Peterson makes its way along Richfield's main street 11 April 1899. (Utah State Historical Society)

the LDS Sevier Stake, George W. Bean, first counselor in the stake presidency, spoke of the "scarcity of water that exists at the present time." At the same gathering, G.A. Murdock told those in attendance that "we received water through the blessings of the Lord . . . and the Lord may dry the water away from us."[61]

In the midst of this crisis, some long-term residents of the county were apparently contemplating legal action against newcomers to ensure that they continued to receive their share of the available water. Simon Christensen denounced the very idea of "going to the law with the people of this valley on the water question." Instead, William H. Clark, a stake leader, suggested that the different irrigating companies be organized into one company so that "water may be distributed satisfactorily."[62] While this hardship did not break the will of the pioneers of the Sevier Valley, two decades later the problem of access to available water proved very divisive.

The water controversy continued unresolved into the next year. In the spring of 1890 Stake President William H. Seegmiller twice addressed the problem which the water issue was causing for the people of the Sevier Valley. At an April stake priesthood meeting

> Bro. Seegmiller spoke with considerable force in relation to the pending water suits; [he] said that we had departed from the original object in settling ourwater difficulties. [Seegmiller] said it is all wrong for us to spend our money foolishly and that we ought to settle our water troubles peaceably and amicably in place of feeding shyster lawyers.[63]

The following month, at the Sevier Stake's quarterly conference, the stake president, whose counsel in April must have been ignored by at least some parties, charged that there were "influences at work in the stake tending to cause disunion and distrust." Apostle John Henry Smith, visiting the conference, remarked, "in reference to our disputes," that "we should as far as practicable settle these matters among ourselves by church courts or arbitration and keep out of civil courts." Then Smith offered the Mormons of Sevier County some very practical suggestions: build more reservoir sites; store the water which goes to waste at certain times of the year; use the water wisely; and plant fruit trees to assist in conservation.[64]

Do not "let the opportunities of storing water pass us," cautioned Apostle Anthon Lund to the conference attendees, "but secure them while we have an opportunity lest we have to pay tribute to others and to a certain extent come under the yoke of bondage." The words of the LDS general authorities must have been heard, for three months later William H. Clark reported that the "reservoirs movement" had proven "very favorable." By November he reported that "the adjudication of our water rights up and down the Sevier River and its tributaries [had] a fair prospect of having this matter settled without much trouble or expense and with good feelings."[65]

All across Sevier County, as in Utah Territory, modernization and economic diversification was occurring by 1890. As the county's people struggled to adapt to and succeed in a rapidly modernizing world, they sought to avoid the caprices of the ever-expanding marketplace. A major sign of impending modernity was still to come.

Inexpensive and reliable routes of transportation serving rural western areas were critical to their economic expansion. When the Denver and Rio Grande Western (D&RGW) railroad steamed into Salt Lake City in the early 1880s it signaled the end of the Union Pacific's monopoly over Utah's rail traffic. This competitor from

Colorado was able to accomplish what Mormon entrepreneurs had tried in vain to do for over two decades.[66] Freight rates to and from Utah dropped. Not only did the capital city of Utah benefit from the entrance of the D&RGW, so too did Sevier County.

In 1888 the Salt Lake City Chamber of Commerce praised the new road for its shipping policies, which the chamber described as "conducive to the development of Utah Territory."[67] Without a doubt, the people of Sevier County welcomed the Denver & Rio Grande Western with open arms. By the late 1880s it was almost essential for a community's future for it to have a rail link to the outside world.

In 1891 the Denver & Rio Grande Western Railroad began serving the northern Sevier Valley. That year a great step forward in the progress of the county was made when the railroad reached Salina.[68] Five years later, the line extended to Richfield, and in early June 1896 the first passenger train arrived at the county seat. Eliza Shelton Keeler, a local woman, excitedly recorded that event:

> Now we have a railroad in Richfield, the depot is one block south of our house. It is making times pretty lively around here; this is something new but we are glad to have it. June 2nd was a great day in Richfield, the first passenger cars came in at fifteen minutes of four p. m. with 1,500 passengers aboard, from Salt Lake City and all the way along. A great many from the surrounding settlements were here to witness the great event.[69]

This event created a holiday mood in Richfield and throughout Sevier County. The railway seemed to offer something to please everyone. Sevier LDS Stake records, reflecting a more restrained view than that of Mrs. Keeler, proudly noted in 1897 at least one accomplishment of the new line: "The railroad has furnished . . . one of the finest stockyards and chutes for loading sheep and cattle on the cars, that is to be found in the state."[70]

The railroad undoubtedly spurred economic growth in the county, especially in the livestock industry. According to the report of the Utah State Board of Equalization for 1896, more than 110,000 head of sheep were assessed (taxed) in the county, ranking Sevier County fourth behind Sanpete County (332,728 sheep), Tooele County (202,890 sheep), and Millard County (152,378 sheep). In that same year, Sevier County ranked ninth in the number of cattle assessed, with 8,776 head. San Juan County ranked first in the state, with 14,078 head.

This economic diversification and reaching out to embrace the outside world was not achieved without a social cost for the people of Sevier County, however. Just as LDS church members had been warned by church president Brigham Young during the California gold rush of the late 1840s and 1850s about the potential evils of worldly riches, members of the Sevier LDS Stake were counselled by their leaders four decades later to put aside thoughts of worldly riches and concentrate on building up the kingdom of God. The Sevier LDS Stake presidency warned church members in 1883, "We should not go to the mines and work for our enemies and build them"; rather, the Saints were advised to "stay at home and help to build temples."[71]

The concerns of LDS church leaders and parents regarding the evil influences of the gentile (non-Mormon) world upon their youth was very similar in the 1890s to those voiced years earlier.[72] Apparently, local youth wishing to escape what they likely saw as the confining nature of rural America wanted to leave home and find work in larger cities. In 1891 Sevier Stake President William H. Seegmiller cautioned the parents of the stake "against letting [out] their girls to Provo, Salt Lake and Ogden cities to work at hotels, etc."[73] Three months later, the youth of the stake were exhorted "to stay at home with their fathers and mothers instead of going abroad to the world, railroad camps, etc. to get work as their [*sic*] was danger in boys and girls going to ruin if associated with evil society."[74] For Sevier County's Mormons, whether young or old, being *in* the modern world but not *of* it was becoming more and more of a challenge.

During the closing years of the nineteenth century and the dawning of the twentieth, in order to reach accord with the federal government and achieve statehood for Utah, Mormon church presidents Wilford Woodruff and Lorenzo Snow promoted the development of two-party politics in Utah. Importantly, the two aging presidents appear to have "supported the establishment of a strong Republican Party."[75] This was somewhat surprising in light of the fact that Mormons had long considered the Republicans to be the party of their oppressors, for they were the national party holding power dur-

The cast for a locally produced play in Richfield. (Utah State Historical Society)

ing much of the later nineteenth century. However, the politics of Utah's drive for statehood dictated support of a two-party political system by Mormon voters. By the late 1890s some Mormon church leaders were consistently voicing support for national Republican politicians, and in state races some Mormon leaders backed the candidacy of Republican, and Catholic, Thomas Kearns in his successful bid for the U.S. Senate.[76] This political reorientation also affected Sevier County.

The off-year elections of 1894 show that many Utahns were ready to back Republican candidates. The Republican congressional candidate, George Q. Cannon, defeated his Democratic opponent by almost 2,000 votes statewide (in Sevier County, 672 votes to 516 votes).[77] The following year, 1895, when delegates were chosen for the state constitutional convention, there were fifty-eight Republicans (including three from Sevier County: Theodore Bradley of Richfield, George F. Miller of Monroe, and Joel Ricks of Salina) and only forty-nine Democrats selected.[78] It would seem that Utahns were getting more comfortable with Republicans. Utah's desire for admission to the Union was answered at last in 1895. The reasons for suc-

An early Independence Day Celebration in Richfield. (Utah State Historical Society)

cess included the growing national belief in the sincerity of the Woodruff Manifesto issued in 1890 encouraging Mormons to obey the national laws regarding plural marriage. Utah's increasing integration into the national mainstream helped make statehood possible at last.

On 4 January 1896 President Grover Cleveland issued the proclamation admitting Utah as the forty-fifth state. Locally, the Sevier LDS Stake president delivered the long-awaited news announcing that he had received a telegram informing him of President Cleveland's actions.[79] Two days later, Utah's first state officials were inaugurated in the Salt Lake LDS Tabernacle. Throughout the new state it was a day of celebration.

Despite the joy felt as a result of statehood, Utahns were experiencing some troubles. The financial depression which had struck the nation with the Panic of 1893 continued and economic dissatisfaction was mounting. Many Utahns, including those of Sevier County, bolted from their new friends, the Republicans, opting instead to support Democrat/Populist presidential candidate William Jennings Bryan. In this instance, local concerns were paramount. In the 1896 presidential race, the majority of voters in Utah and in Sevier County cast their ballots in favor of Bryan, whose policies, including support of silver as a treasury base (popular in the silver-mining West), were looked upon with favor by most Utahns. The Democrat/Populist more closely represented local concerns than did the Republican candidate, William McKinley. Bryan carried the state of Utah, including agrarian Sevier County, which voted for him overwhelmingly. The nation, however, chose Bryan's opponent, McKinley, as the new president to lead them into the new century.

Sevier County was growing rapidly as the new century approached. In 1890, the county recorded 6,199 inhabitants, and by the turn of the century there were 8,451 residents of Sevier County—almost double the 4,457 count of the 1880 census just twenty years before. Ground was broken for a major area reservoir in 1897, and, with a bustling county seat, a railroad connection with the world, statehood status, and a number of thriving smaller communities, Sevier County residents looked forward to the twentieth century.

## ENDNOTES

1. Miriam B. Murphy, "Utah's Counties," *Beehive History* 14 (1988): 2.

2. *Acts, Resolutions and Memorials of the Utah Territorial Legislature,* 1865, 16, Utah State Historical Society.

3. James B. Allen, "The Evolution of County Boundaries in Utah," *Utah Historical Quarterly* 23 (1955): 261–78.

4. *Laws, Memorials, and Resolutions of the Utah Territorial Legislature,* 1890, 13–14, Utah State Historical Society.

5. For further information on probate courts see James B. Allen, "The Unusual Jurisidiction of County Probate Courts in the Territory of Utah," *Utah Historical Quarterly* 36 (Spring 1966): 132–42.

6. *Acts, Resolutions and Memorials . . . of the Legislative Assembly of the Territory of Utah,* 1855, 126, Utah State Historical Society.

7. *Acts, Resolutions and Memorials . . . of the Legislative Assembly of the Territory of Utah, from 1851 to 1870 Inclusive,* 1870, 206.

8. Allen, "The Unusual Jurisdiction of County Probate Courts," 134.

9. Pearl F. Jacobson, compiler and editor, et al., *Golden Sheaves from a Rich Field: A Centennial History of Richfield, Utah* (Richfield, Utah: Richfield Reaper Publishing Company, 1964), 123–27.

10. Murphy, "Utah's Counties," 24.

11. Glenwood, Monroe, and Salina surpassed Richfield in the number of commercial establishments listed in the 1883–84 *Utah Directory* published by J.C. Graham.

12. *Twelfth Census of the United States, 1900* (Washington, D.C.: U.S. Census Office), 477.

13. Irvin L. Warnock, compiler and editor, *Thru the Years: Sevier County Centennial History* (Springville, Utah: Art City Publishing Co., 1947), 40.

14. Jacobson, *Golden Sheaves,* 225.

15. Richfield Ward Manuscript History, 23 May 1880. See also Richfield Ward Manuscript History, 1865–1873, 1879; Koosharem Ward Manuscript History, 1876; Marysvale Ward Manuscript History, 1879, 1881; Monroe Ward, 1871, 1878; all LDS Archives.

16. Wilford Murdock and Mildred Murdock, *Monroe, Utah: Its First One Hundred Years* (Monroe: Monroe Centennial Committee, 1964), 26.

17. Richfield Ward Manuscript History, ca. 1865, 1871, 1873; Koosharem Ward Manuscript History, ca. 1879; Glenwood Manuscript History, 22 February and 3 May 1879; Salina Ward Manuscript History, ca. 1882 and 1883.

18. Warnock, *Thru the Years,* 385, 392.

19. *Deseret News,* 26 November 1875.

20. Sevier Stake, Richfield Ward Manuscript History, 10 June 1875, LDS Archives.

21. *Deseret News,* 21 August 1882.

22. Redmond Ward Manuscript History, 17 June 1885, LDS Archives.

23. Ibid., 1886.

24. Ibid., 28 May 1888.

25. *Pacific Coast Directory for 1880–1881* (San Francisco: L.M. McKenney & Co., 1881); *Pacific Coast Directory for 1883–1884* (San Francisco: L.M. McKenney & Co., 1884); Murdock and Murdock, *Monroe,* 53.

26. Coquette Ross, "*The Richfield Reaper,*" Richfield High School Honors English paper, 17 January 1988, Utah State Historical Society.

27. Jacobson, *Golden Sheaves,* 76–87.

28. Ibid., 75, 81.

29. Ibid., 40, 116.

30. On this transition in Utah see Leonard J. Arrington, *Great Basin Kingdom: Economic History of the Latter-day Saints, 1830–1900* (Cambridge: Harvard University Press, 1958), 223–25.

31. *Richfield Reaper,* 6 March 1902, 1.

32. Regarding the contemporary significance of the Salt Lake LDS Temple, both within and outside of Utah see M. Guy Bishop and Richard Neitzel Holzapfel, "The 'St. Peter's of the New World': The Salt Lake Temple, Tourism, and a New Image for Utah," *Utah Historical Quarterly* 64 (Spring 1993): 136–49.

33. Quoted in "The Sevier Stake Tabernacle," 1.

34. Ibid.

35. Ibid. In 1914 the tabernacle was condemned because of earthquake damage and in 1918 was razed.

36. Jacobson, *Golden Sheaves,* 64.

37. Sevier County Historic Sites File, Utah State Historical Society, Salt Lake City.

38. Aimee Mower, "The Court System in Sevier County," 2, Richfield High School Honors English paper, 25 April 1988, copy at Richfield City Library, Richfield, Utah.

39. Ibid., 3.

40. Ibid., 5.

41. Warnock, *Thru the Years,* 45; Jacobson, *Golden Sheaves,* 148.

42. Thomas Edgar Lyon, "Evangelical Protestant Missionary Activities in Mormon Dominated Areas: 1865–1900," (Ph.D. diss., University of Utah, 1962), 91. See also Jacobson, 69–70.

43. Carl Wankier, "History of Presbyterian Schools in Utah" (M.S. thesis, University of Utah, 1968), 40. See also Warnock, *Thru the Years,* 55.

44. Wankier, "History of Presbyterian Schools in Utah," 30.

45. Lyon, "Evangelical Protestant Missionary Activities," 99.

46. Warnock, *Thru the Years,* 56, 321; Jacobson, *Golden Sheaves,* 72.

47. Lyon, "Evangelical Protestant Missionary Activities," 156.

48. See Lowell Bennion, "The Incidence of Polygamy in 1880: 'Dixie' versus Davis Stake," *Journal of Mormon History* 11 (1984): 27–42.

49. Sevier Stake Historical Record & Minutes, 1 February 1879, Reel 1, LDS Archives. For background on the Reynolds case see Dean L. May, *Utah: A People's History* (Salt Lake City: University of Utah Press, 1987), 126.

50. Gottlieb Ence, Autobiography, typescript, 39, Utah State Historical Society.

51. Ibid., 64.

52. Ibid., 64. On the Mormon underground see Richard S. Van Wagoner, *Mormon Polygamy: A History,* 2nd ed. (Salt Lake City: Signature Books, 1989), 108–17.

53. Hans Christensen, Memoirs, Utah State Historical Society.

54. Albert King Thurber, "A Brief Biographical Sketch of Albert King Thurber," 1, Utah State Historical Society.

55. Albert King Thurber, Genealogical Record, Utah State Historical Society.

56. Joseph Smith Horne, Autobiography, 28, Utah State Historical Society.

57. Ibid., 53.

58. Erwin G. Gudde, *Bigler's Chronicle of the West* (Berkeley: University of California Press, 1962), 134.

59. Horne, Autobiography, 53.

60. Thomas G. Alexander, *Mormonism in Transition: A History of the Latter-day Saints, 1890–1930* (Urbana: University of Illinois Press, 1986), 3–4.

61. Water Records Index, Part III, 6 July 1889, LDS Archives.

62. Water Records Index, 5 August 1889.

63. Sevier Stake Minute Books, 10 April 1890.

64. Ibid., 22 May 1890.

65. Ibid., 22 May 1890, 4 November 1890.

66. See Arrington, *Great Basin Kingdom,* 348; and M. Guy Bishop, "More Than One Coal Road to Zion: The Utah Territory's Efforts to Ease Dependency on Wyoming Coal," *Annals of Wyoming* 60 (Spring 1988): 8–16.

67. [Chamber of Commerce], *Salt Lake City* (Chicago: Rand McNally & Company, 1888), 68–69. For a contrary, pro-Union Pacific opinion see H.W.B. Kantner, *A Handbook on Mines, Miners, and Minerals of Utah* (Salt Lake City: R. W. Sloan, 1896), which argued, "There has been no greater factor in the development of the manifold mineral resources [of Utah] than the Union Pacific Railroad" (1).

68. Warnock, *Thru the Years,* 50.

69. Kate B. Carter, comp., *Our Pioneer Heritage* (Salt Lake City: Daughters of Utah Pioneers, 1962) 5: 303.

70. Sevier Stake Manuscript History, 12 November 1897, LDS Archives.

71. Sevier Stake Minute Books, 7 January 1883, Reel 2, LDS Archives.

72. See M. Guy Bishop, "Preparing to 'Take the Kingdom': Child-

rearing Directives in Early Mormonism," *Journal of the Early Republic* 7 (Fall 1987): 288.

73. Sevier Stake Minute Books, 26 May 1891, Reel 2.

74. Ibid., 23 August 1891.

75. Charles S. Peterson, *Utah, A History* (New York: W. W. Norton and Company and American Association for State and Local History, 1977), 162.

76. Ibid., 163.

77. Wayne D. Stout, *History of Utah*, 2 vols. (Salt Lake City: Wayne D. Stout, 1970), 1: 482–83.

78. Ibid., 1: 491–94.

79. *Memories of Sevier Stake Church of Jesus Christ of Latter Day Saints: Diamond Jubilee Memorial Volume 1874–1949*, compiled and edited by President and Mrs. Irvin L. Warnock (Springville, UT: Art City Publishing Co., 1949), 29.

5

# THE COUNTY MATURES, 1896–1929

In the years between Utah statehood (1896) and the beginning of the Great Depression (1929) the county's residents experienced, among other things, battles over water rights, population and civic growth, wars, agricultural prosperity and depression, and political conflict. The county would also experience further economic growth, the introduction of new industries, the development of mineral resources, and the growth of the dominant religion, the Mormon church. As the Great Depression approached, public exposure to poverty and unemployment mounted.

Ground was broken on Otter Creek, a tributary of the Sevier River in nearby Piute County, on 19 October 1897 for a major dam that would serve Sevier County water needs. By 1901 the dam was completed, with a height of forty-eight feet. This was a major development for the entire region, helping to harness the lifegiving water of the region. In 1907 another reservoir—the Piute Reservoir—was also begun in Piute County that would further help control the Sevier River and serve downstream users. Other small reservoirs such as the Rocky Ford Reservoir near Sigurd were built over the years on small tributaries of the Sevier River to serve county farmers and other residents.

As they struggled to help control nature, the turn-of-the-century inhabitants of Sevier County demonstrated their determination to achieve a more modern way of life. This was perhaps most easily seen in the transportation revolution which swept the county during the decades of the late nineteenth and early twentieth centuries. Even before the automobile came to Sevier County, local entrepreneurs formulated plans for a wagon toll road to run in a northwesterly direction from north of Richfield to the foothills. It was hoped that the road would be used primarily by those bringing lumber from the mountains. The concept of privately owned toll roads had a history both in the eastern United States and in Utah Territory.

In December 1901 R.R. Farnsworth, L.R. Bean, Frank Isabell, and William Isabell of the county commission along with five other men won the right "to construct, maintain and keep in repair a certain road [and] the right to collect tolls for travel upon said road." The tolls could not, by law, "exceed fifty cents per trip for one team and heavy wagon; twenty-five cents per trip for one team and light wagon; [or] ten cents per head . . . for horses, cattle, and sheep."[1] While it is not known how much the men may have made from the toll road, its very presence in a rural area such as Richfield was a sure sign of economic growth.

Sevier County was a beneficiary, of sorts, of the economic wrangling of western railroad builders. By 1879 the so-called "Rio Grande War," pitting the mighty Union Pacific and its subsidiary the Kansas Pacific against the Atchison, Topeka and Santa Fe line, had ended. With this railroad war over, the way was opened for the Denver and Rio Grande Western Railroad (D&RGW) to build westward. And build they did—westward from Colorado toward Salt Lake City.[2]

General William Jackson Palmer, president of the Denver and Rio Grande Western Railroad, convinced stockholders that the route between Salt Lake City and Denver should head south from Salt Lake City to Nephi, then through Salt Creek Canyon, and then south to Salina. At Salina the proposed railroad was to split, with one branch headed south to the Arizona border, the other east from Salina over

One of the tunnels blasted by the Denver and Rio Grande Railroad through Salina Canyon in the 1880s, in use as part of a wagon road when this photograph was taken in July 1917. (Utah State Historical Society)

Salina Pass into Castle Valley and then east along the foot of the Book Cliffs to Colorado.

The Union Pacific Railroad, fearing the loss of its markets in central and eastern Utah, organized the Utah Southern and Castle Valley Railroad Company. This company was to build a rail line generally along the same proposed route in the county as the D&RGW route. Critical to both railroads was which would build first through Salina Canyon. The railroad that accomplished this would control the critical right-of-way and thus would control rail traffic to eastern Utah from the Sevier River Valley. Further, Union Pacific Railroad officials believed that if they could control the Salina Canyon right-of-way, they could effectively block their new competitor from central and southern Utah from the east.

Circumstances elsewhere altered the plans of both railroads. The D&RGW built its Denver to Salt Lake City line through Carbon County and Spanish Fork Canyon to Provo and Salt Lake City. These developments delayed the coming of the railroad to the county until nearly the turn of the century.

In May 1891 the county's hope for a railroad was rekindled when the Sevier Railway Company was incorporated. The railroad's main line extended from Manti to Marysvale. Track was completed to Salina in June 1891 and the rails reached Richfield by June 1896. It took another four years until October 1900 to complete the line to Marysvale. The Sevier Railway Company was later purchased by the Denver & Rio Grande Western Railroad Company in August 1908.

Problems related to the construction of the D&RGW apparently caused some difficulties in Sevier County. The minutes of the Sevier LDS Stake quarterly conference, which convened in May 1898 and at which Francis M. Lyman was the visiting general authority, gave an indication of the local difficulties over unpaid wages from the D&RGW:

> Apostle F. M. Lyman . . . in refering [*sic*] to the troubles which have existed here in Richfield relative to the dealings with the railroad company, Brother Lyman said that President Seegmiller had been vindicated so far as the civil matters involved was concerned and so far as those parties are concerned who have worked on the railroad and not received their pay should be settled with and it belongs to the people of Richfield to see that this matter is settled.[3]

Such problems were not uncommon for western railroads. Capitalizing ventures such as railroad construction were always a risky business at best in nineteenth-century America. Securing financing for Western roads frequently was a problem. Brigham Young's son John W. Young was a member of the LDS church's First Presidency in the 1870s and also an accomplished railroad promoter. However, he struggled with problems that can, to a large degree, be laid at the feet of the eastern capitalists who financed many Utah railroad building endeavors.[4]

The *Richfield Reaper* was begun in 1898 by A.B. Williams, who purchased what was left of the fire-damaged printing equipment of the earlier town paper *The Advocate,* which was begun by George Hales in 1877.[5] The newspaper reported further difficulties with the railroad in 1902 when the people became "stirred up to a high pitch of wrath" over a new policy of the D&RGW railway. The cause of the tension was a report that the company was suspending Sunday rail service because "business on the road now does not justify [the] runs."[6] Apparently, the people of Sevier County viewed the decision as callous disregard of their needs. Since they had previously applauded the railroad's entry into Sevier County, even participating in its construction, they now must have wondered why the D&RGW was treating the people of Sevier County so cold-heartedly. This act, doubtless based by the company upon economic considerations, was, in the eyes of county residents, discriminatory.

"The company has the people of this section of the country at its mercy," charged the *Richfield Reaper*, "and just what can be done to get any relief is not now clear." Recapitulating what they saw as their contributions to the road and underscoring their current difficulties with the D&RGW, the paper charged:

> The people of this valley have purchased outright the costly right-of-way for this company. They have expended outright thousands of dollars in money and labor to encourage the advent of the railroad. They have extended to it a patronage that has made it one of the best paying lines in Utah. They have gone into an industry that put $7,000 to $10,000 into the coffers of the company this fall, and because they complained at the ill-treatment received in return, the company shuts off the Sunday trains.[7]

To the local people, canceling the Sunday train service was punishment plain and simple for their complaints about wages. The Denver & Rio Grande Western had by 1902 assumed for some residents the role of an adversary rather than that of the hoped-for ally in Sevier County.

A year later, in 1903, the Denver and Rio Grande Western Railroad added a spur on the Marysvale line from Salina through Salina Canyon to Nioche, a distance of about twenty miles. The purpose was to maintain control of the right-of-way through Salina Canyon.[8]

To accommodate the shipment of livestock from the county, several stockyards and loading facilities were built by the Denver & Rio Grande Western Railroad Company. The Elsinore stockyard and live-

The Hansen Harness Shop in Richfield, 1920. (Utah State Historical Society)

stock loading facilities could accommodate sixteen livestock cars at one time. The Richfield livestock handling facility was a little smaller, handling only twelve rail carloads of livestock at a time. The largest stockyard on the Marysvale line was in Salina, where a stockyard with a twenty carload capacity was built. In addition, the freight depot in Salina could handle fifteen railroad freight cars.

Railroad stops in the county included Salina, Aurora, Vermillion, Sigurd, Jumbo & Keene Mills, Venice, Richfield, Central, Nibley, Elsinore, Joseph, Vaca, and Sevier; and on the Salina Canyon spur the stops included Gooseberry, Saw Tooth, and Crystal.

From the creation of the county until 1909 it was the responsibility of the Sevier County Court and later county commission to direct road designations, road construction, and road improvements within the county. Funds for roads were raised within the county; the most common means was through the annual poll tax of two days of labor per year or three dollars per year paid in cash. Special appropriations were made to the counties by the legislature to help build

The Richfield Branch of the Utah Implement Company. (Utah State Historical Society

specific roads or bridges. In 1882, for example, the territorial legislature appropriated one thousand dollars to help build a road from Clear Creek south to Marysvale.

Beginning in 1907 the county received revenue derived from the national forests in the county to help with funding of roads and public schools in the county. In 1909 dramatic changes occurred affecting roads in the county. Hot on the heels of a national good-roads movement, the state legislature established the state highway system and state highway department. This removed from the county much of the responsibility for raising revenue and maintaining those roads that were designated state highways. In 1910 the soon-to-be U.S. Highway 89 was designated a state highway and extended from Salt Lake City south to Vermillion. The highway between Vermillion and Marysvale remained a county highway for several more years; however, the segment of road between Richfield and Glenwood was declared a state highway in 1910.

In 1909 funding for roads in each of the counties became more uniform. Statewide vehicle taxes, and later gasoline taxes, collected by the county were applied to roads in the county. Federal funds were made available for road improvements in the county; however, the county was required to raise an equal amount to qualify for these federal funds. Further, the engineering, design, maintenance, and construction of roads in the county were subject to state standards.

Efforts to bring electric power to Sevier County in the early 1900s put local residents in a possibly risky financial situation when Richfield entrepreneur Thomas Brown "and other public spirited citizens" sought in 1904 to construct a steam power plant near the railroad depot on East Center Street.[9] The group built a generating station, bringing electric lights to Richfield's people for the first time. Brown's original Richfield scheme had appeared so promising that a group in Salina connected a small generator to a waterwheel and began distributing electrical power to that community the same year.

With his first attempt having proven so successful, two years later Brown built a small water-power plant and distributing lines at nearby Glenwood. In 1908 he incorporated his holdings as the Richfield Electric Light and Power Company.[10] That same year, the similar undertaking at Salina, which also powered the operation of their flouring mill, was incorporated as the Sevier Light, Power and Milling Company. Sevier County's nascent power companies were soon faced with outside competition. Lucien L. Nunn, the builder of the first alternating current power station in the world at Telluride, Colorado, in 1890, purchased both the Richfield and the Salina companies in 1911. Then in 1912 and 1913 he connected these properties with a 44,000-volt line running from Beaver Canyon to Gunnison. Nunn then built distribution systems at Aurora, Sigurd, Venice, Vermillion, Central, Annabella, Elsinore, and Joseph—none of which had enjoyed electrical service before.[11] By 1913 most of Sevier County had electric power. Since 1918 the county's power system has expanded and the area is now linked with generating stations stretching from Nephi on the north to Panguitch on the south. In 1929 it was connected with the Utah Power and Light Company system.

Physical improvements were apparent throughout Sevier County during the early 1900s as the county continued on its path toward modernization. As local LDS stake president William H. Seegmiller enthusiastically observed at a meeting in the fall of 1899, "The people of this valley have been and are still busy constructing reservoirs and storing water, which in the near future will materially aid us in developing the resources of this valley; . . . we can begin to look for better times."[12]

In 1902, the residents of Richfield took steps to improve their city's public water service. "The city council meeting last Thursday started at a lively pace and kept it up until adjournment," reported the *Richfield Reaper*. "The water works question was as usual the principal feature of the deliberations."[13] Whether large projects for the public good such as reservoirs, or smaller, local improvement projects, all helped develop the county, and many of these developments, such as the coming of the telephone in 1901, served to enhance life in Sevier County. In July 1901 Rocky Mountain Bell Telephone Company was "empowered to sit in poles and string its wires" to bring telephone service to Sevier County residents. Many of the projects brought the residents of the county more into the mainstream of American life. But, as often is the case, modernization and growth were accompanied by social problems. Such was the case for Sevier County as some more urban dilemmas descended upon this still rural, largely agrarian area during the early decades of the twentieth century. In May 1902 the newspaper reported that Councilman H. N. Hayes pointed out the fact that "a number of people in various parts of the city have tapped the [water] mains with one-inch pipe," resulting in an "unproportionate [*sic*] supply of water to the people of this city."[14] Hayes suggested that an ordinance be adopted to further regulate culinary water use.

Two ordinances intended to promote crops were passed in Sevier County in 1903. Neither ordinance was unusual to the rural American West. The first established a bounty on jackrabbits; the second placed a bounty on grasshoppers. The amount to be paid was not stipulated in either ordinance. An ordinance passed eight years later placed a bounty of "one half cent" on all ground squirrels destroyed in Sevier County.[15]

Despite the county's general rural character, the residents enjoyed a number of developments related to civic and business growth. The Richfield Commercial & Savings Bank was incorporated in 1899 with a net capital of $25,000. The bank's organizers included Hans Tuft, president; Andrew Ross, vice-president; and Guy Lewis, cashier.

The Elite Barber Shop in Richfield. (Utah State Historical Society)

During the first fourteen years of its operation, the bank's assets grew to $500,000.[16] A decade after the organization of the Richfield Commercial & Savings Bank, other financial institutions were established in the county; they included the First State Bank of Salina, the State Bank of Sevier in Richfield, and the Monroe State Bank in Monroe, organized in 1910.

At the turn of the century, Richfield boasted banks, cafes, hotels, barber shops, a saloon, a billiard hall, a freight and bus line, and theaters. The Star Pavilion was completed in 1898 and was used as a community social and recreational hall, including hosting basketball games of the local high school boys and girls teams. The Johnson Hotel was built in the 1880s and was described by the *Richfield Reaper* as "one of the best hotels south of Salt Lake City." The Arlington Hotel was built by H.B. Jennings in 1903; it became the Southern Hotel in 1916 and continued until it was razed in 1946. The Anona Dance Hall was built in 1906. The Lyric Theatre was established on Main Street in 1907 to show the new motion pictures; other theaters followed as that entertainment medium grew in popularity.[17] By August 1909 Richfield had its first paved sidewalks, and the Richfield Commercial Club was formed in the early 1900s to boost the city throughout the region, state, and nation. A national chain came to Richfield in 1911 in the form of a J.C. Penney store, known at the time as a Golden Rule store.

The Richfield Roller Mill, before it was destroyed by fire in 1923, was established in the 1870s as a United Order mill as part of the Richfield United Order. When the Richfield United Order was dissolved in 1877, Andrew Poulsen purchased the mill and rebuilt it elsewhere in town. Over time, Poulsen modified the mill, installing a boiler and engine and changing the name to the Richfield Roller Mill.[18]

The Christensen Hardware store had its commercial roots as a blacksmith shop in the 1880s. John Christensen, a blacksmith by trade, expanded his blacksmith business and sold buggies, wagons, wagon-wheel spokes, and other hardware. After John Christensen's death in 1930 the store's name was changed to Christensen Hardware Company by his sons.[19]

Serving the entire county, the Richfield Monument Company was established by Arthur Henrie in 1895. Henrie was originally from Manti, where he learned stonecutting skills laboring on the Manti LDS Temple. A hundred years later, the Richfield Monument Company continues to provide gravestones and markers in the county.[20]

An indicator of Richfield's and the county's economic growth at the turn of the century was the establishment of a retail jewelry business by Peter C. Peterson in 1900. Ten years later, James Peters Christensen purchased the business and took the business name of J.P.C. Norman. The jewelry company struggled and was nearly ruined because of the slow mail and freight delivery service to the area. In 1918, Christensen sold the jewelry business and moved to California.[21]

During the first two decades of the twentieth century, Aloia Strobel and Clarence Littlewood started the Richfield Shoe Shop (so named in 1918). Later, a harness shop managed by David Hansen and Alma Nielson was added to this business. Then, in 1925, Strobel's son, Elmer, started a shoe-repairing business at the site.[22]

Besides dancing and motion pictures, county residents enjoyed baseball and even horse racing—a track was established about 1903 between Richfield and Glenwood. It was the scene of a tragedy in September 1905 when a spectator was killed by lightning.[23] Various dramatic companies were formed around the turn of the century, and they provided county residents with dramatic performances. Lyceum and chautauquas were popular nationally at the turn of the century, and the county was included on a number of tours, particularly in the second decade of the new century. Lectures and entertainments provided edification for local citizens, who also formed their own civic clubs and societies, including a chapter of the Daughters of Utah Pioneers and a literary study club.

Agriculture remained a mainstay economically. Sugar beets became one of the crops grown after the turn of the century, and the Utah-Idaho Sugar Company built a sugar processing plant in Monroe in 1911; but livestock remained the primary factor economically. The first county fair was held in 1907 to celebrate and boost the county's agricultural products. Livestock auctions became important events in the county and the region, growing in importance over the years through the century. In 1910 the Monroe Creamery Company was established in Monroe, the participating diary farmers building a small processing plant.[24] A cheese factory was started in 1916 in Richfield by Sevier Dairy and Produce Company. The plant was sold in 1926 to Sego Milk Company but was closed in 1929. In 1918 an ice company was started in Richfield by H.A. Andelin.

Some area prosperity came from the gold mining operations in nearby Piute and Millard counties, but much of it was through providing markets for county agricultural products and business for area merchants. The railroad also provided export opportunities for area produce and mineral products.

Manufacturing was limited, although salt was still produced in the northern part of the county. Gypsum began to be mined around the Sigurd area in 1908 by the Jumbo Plaster and Cement Company. Its plaster mill provided welcome employment opportunities for area residents until the plant was destroyed by fire in January 1932, with a loss estimated at $500,000. The company also built lodging for its non-resident laborers. In 1909 the American Keene Cement Mill was also built, the two companies beginning what has become perhaps

Sevier County's most important industry. The Utah Potash Company planned a mill in Monroe in 1919 that was never developed.[25]

Between statehood in 1896 and 1930 the county's educational system changed and developed significantly. Territorial law had authorized individual communities within counties to establish, fund, and maintain their own educational districts through a school-district board of trustees. All of the school districts in the county were directed by the county's superintendent of education. During the late territorial period, the average school year in the county was twenty-five weeks. In September 1897 Richfield High School was formed.

In 1898 there were sixteen school districts in the county: Annabella, Burrville, Central, Elsinore, Glenwood, Joseph, Monroe, Richfield, Redmond, Salina, Vermillion, Aurora, Wallsville, Cove, Plateau, and Sigurd. The Plateau School District had nineteen students enrolled, while the Richfield district had 588 students. Plateau received $1.14 in state funds and Richfield received $35.28. Additional funding was raised within the individual school districts. The total enrollment in the county in 1898 was 2,873 students, and the total state appropriation for the county was $172.38.[26] Of those students enrolled, 2,471 could read and write.[27] Superintendent Jacob Magleby reported that a countywide two-mill tax levy on property raised $3,577 for educational purposes.

Male and female teachers received different salaries in the county and in the state early in the twentieth century. In 1901, male school teachers in the county earned $49.68 a month while female teachers earned $33.32 a month. The state average was $57.64 a month for male teachers and $40.20 for female teachers.[28]

By 1902 a Koosharem school district was added, making seventeen school districts in the county. For the school year 1901–02, county commission maintained a two-mill levy on all property to support the schools, while the citizens of the Burrville School District levied a special two-mill tax on themselves to provide additional support for their school; this was the lowest special mill-levy rate in the county. The citizens of the Aurora School District levied a hefty twelve mills on themselves to help support their school. The county received $11,476 from the state school fund and the county school fund, excluding the special mill levies each of the seventeen school districts taxed themselves, which raised another $4,000 for the schools in the county.[29]

By the end of the 1906 school year, all of the school districts but two owned their school buildings. All of the school districts had been bonded to pay off the debts incurred in building and buying schoolhouses. Three new schools were built between 1905 and 1906: a twelve-room school in Richfield costing $25,000, a four-room school in Sigurd, and a four-room school in Koosharem, these latter two each costing about $3,500 to build. The Monroe School District added four rooms to its school and updated the heating system with a "modern steam" system for the entire school costing about $10,000.[30] In 1908 the Richfield School District completed construction of the Richfield High School building at a cost of $30,000. The new building included up-to-date conveniences such as "modern lavatories."[31] The high school building served a growing student enrollment. In the 1908 school year thirty-six male students were enrolled in the first two grades of high school (high school included ninth-grade students) and forty-six female students.[32] Salina High School was completed in 1910; four years later, Monroe also built a high school to serve its educational needs. The schools eventually became North Sevier and South Sevier high schools.

The construction of high schools in the county helped provide extended educational opportunities for many students. At the beginning of the 1910 school year, eleven former high school students from the county were awarded scholarships to attend the normal school in Salt Lake City.[33] By 1910, Richfield's population was 2,559.

The Sevier County Teachers Institute was organized in the first years of this century to provide teachers with additional education. On average, teachers in the county's various school districts had two years of education beyond the mandatory years of public schooling. Teacher institutes were held for several days annually and usually were well attended.

There seems to have been little public interest in the electing of school trustees in 1898. Superintendent Magleby complained in his report to the state that year that "people take but little interest in School Elections."[34] Ten years later, more women were taking an

The Richfield Militia parades on Memorial Day, 1910. (Utah State Historical Society)

active role in the various school districts in the county, being elected as school-district trustees.

In 1905 the state legislature authorized the consolidation of school districts. It became the responsibility of the county commission and county school superintendent to consolidate the seventeen school districts in the county. In 1912 the seventeen individual school districts in Sevier County were consolidated into the Sevier County School District, a major development in improving education throughout the county. Economics, efficiency, and quality of education were driving forces in Sevier County and elsewhere in the move to consolidate school districts in the state. This meant that many students in the county were required to travel greater distances to school. This in turn forced the county to make improvements to its roads and it required the county to purchase vehicles to transport students to school.

The United States had become increasingly involved in world affairs by the turn of the twentieth century. The United States was involved in foreign conflicts both in 1898 (the Spanish-American War) and in 1917–18 (World War I). Both impacted Sevier County residents in varying degrees, and men from the county were asked to do their part in each struggle. When President William McKinley called for volunteers to serve in 1898, several men from the county responded to the call. One man from Sevier County suffered from battle wounds and one from disease: James Thorsen was twice wounded in battle, and Jess Bean, like many volunteers, contracted malaria.[35]

With the coming of the First World War, Sevier County got even more involved with the bureaucracy and other facts of war. A county draft board, including Sheriff William S. Greenwood, County Clerk Samuel G. Clark, and Dr. J.J. Steiner, was established. Also, Sevier County, like counties across the United States, formed a council of defense. This council was chaired by Robert D. Young of Richfield; the secretary was Parley Magleby, also of Richfield; and members included J.L. Ewing, C.M. Heppler, J.R. Heppler, E.E. Hoffman, William Johnston, Guy Lewis, H.H. Peterson, Mrs. James M. Peterson, and Dr. J.J. Steiner, all of Richfield; Byron Hanchett, Aurora; and Peter Scorup of Salina. Sevier County furnished 520 men to the armed forces of the United States during World War I. Tragically, twenty-four of these men gave their lives in the conflict.[36] After the war an American Legion post was chartered on 1 October 1919. It was named the Jensen-Colby Post No. 45 in honor of Leo M. Jensen and Ira Colby, the first Richfield soldiers killed in World War I. A women's auxiliary was formed in 1926.[37]

Just as the war was ending, the nation was stricken by a fearful and deadly influenza epidemic. Medical services in the county had improved over the years, including the establishment of private hospitals by groups of doctors, such as one in Richfield in 1902, and another that operated between 1917 and 1920 in Richfield under the name of the Richfield General Hospital Corporation.[38] Despite the improved care and facilities, the villages of Sevier County were not spared from the illness. The epidemic caused great terror. The account of the sickness given by William Daniels, a teenager at the time, gives an indication of the community spirit shown by some of the local youth: "the flu was so bad in Annabella, [my sister] Madge and I helped when we could in the homes that were so bad one of them was Frank Gleaves home. Frank's wife was very bad and they sent Madge and I to Richfield to get some medicine."[39]

Golden Buchanan of Venice, also a teenager in 1918, remembered the human tragedy of the epidemic: "My [future] wife lost her sister Viola." Also "a girl by the name of Irma Cowley died of it," he recalled. In a rather dark claim to fame, his family was the "first in the community" to get sick. "I remember being delirious with it," Buchanan wrote of his own experience with the flu.[40]

Clifford L. Jones of Monroe was only seven years old in 1918. Still the epidemic seems to have been spoken of often in his home. When Jones was interviewed later in his life, he stated, almost certainly from hearsay, "It was evident from the first that this disease was a killer, . . . folks all around us began to die. The doctors were all baffled."[41]

As the disease continued to flourish into 1919, county medical professionals decided to impose a quarantine. Twenty years earlier, in April 1899, the county had wisely established health districts with local health officers across Sevier County. These officers were empowered in January 1919 to "quarantine all persons or families exposed to said diseases for such a period of time as may be necessary to determine whether or not such persons have contracted said disease."[42] Public-health service became an increasingly important function of county government as a result of the flu epidemic.

With the return to peace in 1918, the county resumed its civic, economic, and social pursuits. A federal building had been constructed in Richfield towards the end of the war in 1917–18, bringing new government offices and services to the county. Automobiles were becoming increasingly popular, being first offered for sale in Richfield in 1916. Public radio broadcasting grew rapidly after its beginning in 1920 and, being able to receive national broadcasts, county residents felt increasingly sophisticated, modern, and connected with the rest of the world. Advertising grew rapidly, as did consumption in general. The county's newspapers boosted the area and urged consumers to shop locally.

Sevier County has had a rich tradition of newspapers. *The Salina Sun* (1908–1917) was one of thirteen newspapers that served parts of Sevier County. The others were the *Monroe News* (1910–1913), *Monroe Record* (1916–1917), *Sevier Valley Banner* (1912) in Elsinore, *Sevier County Times* (1899) in Elsinore, *Sevier County Echo* (1884) in Richfield, *Richfield Advocate* (1887–1898), *Southern Censor*

Main Street in Richfield, June 1917. (Utah State Historical Society)

(1896–1898) in Richfield and later in Elsinore, *Richfield Reaper* (1898-present), *Sevier Sun* (1908–1917) in Sevier, *Central Utah Press* (1891–1898) in Salina, *Salina Sun* (1901-? and 1918–1923), *Salina Call* (1906–1916), and *Sevier Valley Call* (1916–1922) in Salina.[43]

The so-called "Roaring Twenties" was an interesting time for Sevier County, with an interesting mix of urban growth and general agricultural recession. The county had continued to rapidly grow in population during the first two decades of the new century, with 9,775 being listed in the 1910 census—an increase of more than 1,300 from ten years before. In 1920, growth had climbed to 11,281 people and Monroe was incorporated as a city, having more than 1,800 inhabitants. By 1930, however, the county showed a slight decrease in population to 11,199, showing that the economic prospects had dimmed even before the Great Depression.

The new growth brought some increased problems. A volunteer fire department was organized in the early 1920s to combat the increased fire danger and resultant property losses. In March 1920, for example, a headline from a front page of the *Richfield Reaper* pointedly stated, "RICHFIELD RANKS HIGH IN ROBBERIES." This increase in robberies was obviously shocking to the community. Three burglaries were said to have been reported during the past week alone. Two local businesses, the Essanay and the White Sewing Machine shop, had been broken into and the high school was visited by "evildoers" as well. Noting this rise in crime which seemed to have befallen the community, and linking this trend to urban areas, the newspaper asked, "Is Richfield getting to be a metropolis?" The article went on to note that "the crime wave is growing in almost a metropolitan way." Population growth and increased construction or other signs of progress would not be objectionable, but such an increase in villainy was clearly intolerable. No trace of the criminals had been found by press time, leading the now-crusading newspaper to call for "an increased police force" to impede crime in Richfield.[44]

Earlier, Richfield had become a "dry" town in 1913, enforcing a local prohibition of liquor option that had passed in 1911. Other nearby communities still provided alcoholic beverages, however, so the law did not do much to cease the drinking of those who wanted to. In 1917, Utah went dry as a state, slightly anticipating national Prohibition. Prohibition brought with it an increase in liquor and beer manufacturing, bootlegging, illegal drinking establishments, and other violations of the law throughout the nation, the state, and locally. Richfield Marshal Lee Isbell was fatally shot in a liquor-related incident. It was the first known murder in the county since statehood and shocked local citizens.[45] Crime was becoming increasingly evident in Sevier County.

With water being at such a premium to Sevier and adjoining counties, efforts to store and use water could always be expected to be major news items in the *Richfield Reaper*. Perhaps recalling the counsel of Mormon stake president William H. Seegmiller in 1899, reservoirs to store precious water remained a priority for county residents into the second decade of the twentieth century. In April 1920 shared rights to the use of Sevier River water were worked out between Millard and Sevier counties.

On 8 April 1920, the *Reaper* reported that negotiations had been taking place during the past several months between the Piute Irrigation Company of Sevier County and the state land board for

The Arlington Hotel Building, later known as the Southern Hotel. (Utah State Historical Society)

the purchase of the Piute Reservoir project. The irrigation company had recently agreed to the terms of the land board and a resolution was passed to this effect.[46]

As part of this settlement, both Sevier and Millard counties, along with portions of Sanpete and Piute counties, were to have access to Sevier River water. It was anticipated that the compromise "will do away with all further litigation." This decision laid to rest conflicts between the involved counties which, in the words of the *Reaper,* had been before the public and in the courts for the past twelve years. Several irrigation companies along the river were interested in the final outcome of the litigation. At the center of the controversy was the water use of the Sevier Bridge Reservoir & Irrigation Company of Millard County and the Sevier County–based Paiute Reservoir & Irrigation Company. In the words of the *Richfield Reaper* in November 1929, "The Sevier Bridge Co. claimed . . . an amount of water nearly equal to all the water that the Sevier river could furnish, a total of 280,000 acre feet."[47]

The Sevier Bridge Company had filed its claim prior to that of the Piute Irrigation Company, which believed that it had an equal

A car waits in front of the Southern Hotel Building to take passengers to Fish Lake. (Utah State Historical Society)

claim to Sevier River water. Interestingly, none of the reservoirs involved were located in either Sevier or Millard counties, although both the disputing irrigation companies were. The Sevier Bridge Reservoir is in eastern Juab County and the Piute Reservoir is in Piute County. Thus, businesses headquartered in Sevier and Millard counties were contesting water stored in neighboring counties.

Under a 1920 agreement governing the use of Sevier River water, the Sevier Bridge Reservoir & Irrigation Company was allocated 28,280 acre-feet of water, which was much less than it had been using; Piute and Otter Creek reservoirs respectively stored 48,000 and 40,000 acre-feet of water. Since these two reservoirs located in the upper Sevier Basin would receive run-off water first, the 1920 agreement required them to release any amount over 40,000 acre-feet to flow northward to the Sevier Bridge Reservoir for agricultural use in the lower basin. It was believed that in moist years the river and its tributaries would provide sufficient irrigation water for all concerned. In dry years, however, the Piute Irrigation Company might get less than the first 40,000 acre-feet.[48]

It would seem that Sevier and Millard counties prevailed in this early–twentieth-century contest over water rights to the Sevier River. Although it was on a much smaller scale, this 1920 water-rights agreement between four south-central Utah counties was similar to an accord reached two years later by several western states. The resulting Colorado River Compact served then, and still serves today, to allocate the water of the West's mightiest artery—the Colorado River.[49] This compact represented the first time that the several western states had actually negotiated a water-use pact. The 1920 Sevier River agreement may well have been the first time any Utah counties had discussed such an agreement. Some seventy years later, Utah officials would attempt to secure the cooperation of several counties to promote the Central Utah Water Project, and Sevier County would end up in the midst of a controversy at that time, too.

In 1920, Richfield experienced a disruptive political controversy involving its mayor and the county commission. Upon the death of commissioner A.K. Hansen, a Republican, in the fall of 1920, Richfield city councilman George H. Peterson, whom the local newspaper called "a well trained businessman with progressive ideas," was appointed by county commissioners A. D. Nebeker and Frank Herbert to fill the now-vacant seat.[50] According to the *Richfield Reaper*, "everybody, the Republican county committee included, considers the appointment of Mr. Peterson perfectly satisfactory."

Mayor N.C. Poulsen of Richfield, however, apparently believed that he, as chair of the Sevier County Republican committee, had been slighted in the selection process. "In a situation like this," Mayor Poulsen claimed to the newspaper, "it is customary that the commissioners consult the central committee of the party a member of which has to be appointed, as to their opinion regarding a proper choice." The mayor maintained that Hansen, when nearing death, had told his (Hansen's) brother-in-law, James M. Peterson, that he considered Morten Jensen "the best man for the place [of commissioner]." The sitting commissioners were informed of this while in the process of selecting a replacement but chose Peterson instead. The incensed mayor and Republican party chairman charged, "The central committee . . . should have been asked; this a long established custom."[51]

The following week, the county commissioners replied to Mayor Poulsen in the *Reaper:*

> In view of the fact that Mayor Poulson [*sic*], chairman of the Republican county committee . . . has seen fit, through the columns of The Reaper, . . . to criticize and express dissatisfaction over the action of the board of county commissioners . . . in the method pursued in making [the] appointment of Hon. George H. Peterson of Richfield as county commissioner to fill the unexpired term of Hon. A. K. Hansen, deceased, . . . we feel, as the members of the Board who made such appointment, that in justice to ourselves we should make a reply.[52]

Then, quoting county statutes, commissioners Nebeker and Herbert wrote, "Whenever a vacancy occurs in the board of county commissioners, the board must fill the vacancy by appointment." The commissioners went on to pointedly remind readers that "the appointment is to be made absolutely, without qualification, by the county commissioners, and not by and with the comment of the mayor of Richfield or any political county committee."[53]

Rising to the debate started by the mayor the preceding week, the commissioners bluntly stated that "we have no knowledge of such a custom [of consulting the central party committee] prevailing here, . . . and we challenge the mayor-chairman to point to any established precedent to show that any such a custom exists . . . with reference to appointing a county commissioner to fill [a] vacancy contemplated by the law referred to above." The commissioners claimed that A.D. Nebeker, the chairman of the board of commissioners, had called upon Hansen about two weeks before he died and asked him "point blank" concerning this matter. Hansen was reminded at this time that "his successor must be a Republican while the present chairman of the board is a Democrat." Commissioner Nebeker stated that "Mr. Hansen just dropped the subject and expressed no choice whatsoever."[54]

Therefore, both commissioners Nebeker and Herbert were inclined to believe that Hansen was willing to leave the choice of his successor to them. In his communication with the board of commissioners prior to their appointment of George Peterson, Hansen's

Richfield's Baseball Team about 1912. (Utah State Historical Society)

brother-in-law James M. Peterson passed on the information that "shortly after his [Hansen's] return from the east," which was about two months before his death, he "had in mind to suggest" Morten Jenson's appointment as his successor. But no mention of this inclination was made in his later conversation with Commissioner Nebeker. So, wrote Nebeker and Herbert, "We respectfully ask our readers to compare the language attributed to Mr. Hansen by Mr. Peterson with the version given by Mayor Poulson."[55]

Most knowledgeable people seemed to agree on George Peterson's competency. In 1921 the people of the county reelected Peterson to a second term. N.C. Poulsen continued to serve as Richfield's mayor through 1922.[56]

Local politics was not the only activity of interest in the county during the 1920s. The sport of baseball was sweeping the nation during these years and Sevier County was caught up in the game as well. From the conclusion of World War I to the outbreak of war in 1941, interest in the sport burgeoned across America. Baseball assumed a place alongside work as one of the major interests of life. Having a community ball team was a "source of major pride."[57] This was as true in rural Utah as it was in the larger communities of the state.

This down-home baseball not only stirred local interest and pride, but also fostered home-grown dreams of local youth of someday playing in the big leagues. By 1922 Richfield had an organized ball team that competed in the Southern Utah Baseball League, comprised of teams (Richfield, Elsinore, Monroe, Salina, Gunnison, and Manti) from Sevier and Sanpete counties.[58] The geographical extent of the league was a contested issue, as some wanted to include teams from northern Sanpete County (Mt. Pleasant, Ephraim, and Moroni), but the Sevier teams objected due to increased travel expenses.

Richfield newspaper advertisements demonstrated the interest with which local baseball was promoted, including full-page announcements of upcoming games.[59] Judging from reports of an early contest between Richfield and Monroe, local games were exciting affairs. "In a well played and interesting ball game," reported the *Richfield Reaper*, "our team was beaten by the Monroe boys with a score of 5 to 3." Of the effort of the hometown squad, the *Reaper* observed: "Our boys did well what they did, but they did not do enough. Their usual confidence was missing." The game featured three double plays by Richfield and some "heavy hitting."[60]

As part of the national conservation movement of the early twentieth century, national forests, monuments, and parks were created throughout the United States. Although no national parks or monuments were located in Sevier County, the Fishlake National Forest was created from an earlier forest reserve created by President William McKinley in 1899, perhaps responding in part to a petition sent that year by 114 Utah citizens, many of them residents of Sevier Valley, and supported by Utah Governor Heber Wells asking for protection and regulation of the forest areas. It was expanded by presidential proclamation in 1904. The national forest included more than 760,000 acres in the county (and many more beyond its borders, being the second-largest national forest in Utah, with more than 1.5 million acres). It provides increased recreation opportunities while helping protect the watershed by bringing increased regulation of grazing and timber harvesting uses of the land. Headquarters of the new national forest were in Salina in 1907; by 1959, the headquarters were located in Richfield.[61]

Although area ranchers and sheepmen did not like the new restrictions on the public land, overgrazing and timber cutting had greatly affected public lands in Sevier County as elsewhere in Utah. Permits were required for use of the national forests and other public lands. Further reform was effected in 1934 with the establishment of the Taylor Grazing Act, restricting some uses of public lands managed by the General Land Office that later came under the jurisdiction of the Bureau of Land Management following its creation after World War II.

Other outdoor recreational activities were provided to the residents of the county. Charles Skougaard built a splendid resort at Fish Lake known as the Skougaard Tavern. Development of the resort began in 1910–11. Skougard introduced Lake Trout (Mackinaw) to the lake, where they thrived, enticing fishermen from throughout the region. In 1928 Skougaard built a spruce-log building at the lake containing 23,000 square feet of floor space. In addition to the main building, Skougaard also built 100 cottages for sleeping.[62] By that time Fish Lake was looked upon as a recreational retreat for the entire region.

In a related vein, Glenwood was chosen as the site of a Utah Fish and Game Department fish hatchery. It was completed in November 1921 and was the state's third fish hatchery for trout. It has continued in operation to the present, being gradually improved and expanded from a capacity to produce 60,000 pounds of fish to 135,000 pounds by 1984. The state hatchery was perhaps inspired by a private fish hatchery in the area that had operated since 1912.[63]

Another resort of note was developed at the Monroe Hot Springs. This resort had its beginnings in the late nineteenth century, when Thomas Cooper first developed it. In 1908 there were some short-lived plans to use the waters for a chicken incubation facilities; however, by 1917, plans were established to fully develop the resort—a process that took place throughout the 1920s and 1930s.[64] Another public swimming facility—the Richfield Natatorium—was built in 1923. By 1933 a bandstand and pavilion were built nearby for dancing and other entertainments. In 1927, through the efforts of the Richfield Study Club, the Richfield City Park was established, and it has continued to be improved in the years since, providing area resi-

Richfield musicians and performers. (Utah State Historical Society)

dents with a fine place to meet and recreate. The era saw the growth of service organizations, and a Lions Club was chartered in Richfield in 1928; it was followed by a Rotary Club in 1948 and a Kiwanis Club in 1952.

The depletion of the number of young men in the county during the war years forced many farmers to look to new labor-saving devices. Steam power and the internal combustion engine began to replace horsepower on many farms in the county. Other improvements of farm machinery helped increase farm production at a time of labor shortage, although as late as 1930 only twenty farms in the county had a tractor; sixty-four had trucks. Other mechanical devices had become more widely used: the county's 653 farms reported 693 automobiles, 530 had radios, 436 used electric lighting, 189 had indoor plumbing, and 174 had telephones.[65]

In the 1920s, hard times came to agricultural areas across the United States, including Sevier County, as wartime markets dried up and increased production brought sharp declines in agricultural prices. All of this came after farmers had often gone into debt to buy more land or machinery in anticipation of continued prosperity brought on by the war-created demand. This recession hurt the nation's farmers long before the even more crippling effects of the Great Depression affected the nation's urban areas as well. Signs of the impending economic crisis began to raise their threatening heads in Sevier County. By the 1930s public aid would be a fairly common thing in Sevier County and across the United States. The precedent for such assistance grew out of the reforms of the progressive era of the first decades of the twentieth century.

In Sevier County, governmental assistance had been given to the needy at least as early as 1906. That year, according to county records, a "Mrs. Carlson of Richfield [requested] aid, stating that she is indigent and greatly in need of assistance." On 3 December 1906 the board of county commissioners allowed her five dollars. Also, a petition was received from E.A. Cawley "for aid to care for his demented wife . . . and allowed to the amount of $38.00."[66] Not all requests were granted, however. In April 1907, "A petition signed by persons from Sigurd precinct praying for an allowance to Jane Ann Shugart . . . to assist her in her indigent condition is denied it appearing that she is not a proper person to be placed as a charge upon the County."[67] Just what made Shugart ineligible for aid was never stated.

The economic growth and growing problems of the county during the 1920s can be traced through the pages of the *Richfield Reaper*. A sheet-metal works was established by A.W. Rowley in 1921. At first, the business consisted of a small shop; but it soon expanded and eventually incorporated. Ideal Cleaners (1924), started by Lewis J. and Vera B. Peterson, was originally located at 33 South Main Street; but in 1934 the Petersons moved their business to 68 North Main. In 1929 Christensen's Department Store was located at 149 North Main. In August that year Glen Beutler started the "Little Wonder Cafe" on the corner of 101 North Main. Of the many eating establishments in Richfield, it was one of the longest lived.[68] Richfield's Main Street was a hive of business activity in the 1920s. Businessmen were highly respected during this heyday of civic boosterism. In Richfield between 1910 and 1930 all eight mayors were either professionals or businessmen, none were farmers, though the county would still be considered rural.[69]

The growth of the dominant religion in Sevier County, the Church of Jesus Christ of Latter-day Saints, mushroomed during the

The Richfield LDS Church Tithing Office. (Utah State Historical Society)

first two decades of the twentieth century. A new tabernacle site was selected in 1917, and the building itself was begun in 1927 and completed in 1930. New chapels were being built throughout the county and the local Mormons were unable financially to complete the tabernacle in a rapid manner after the old tabernacle was declared unsafe in 1914. The new tabernacle was paid for and finally dedicated in 1936 by Mormon church president Heber J. Grant.

On 29 January 1921 the Sevier LDS Stake was divided into three stakes. The Richfield Stake now consisted of the Richfield First, Second, Third wards, Venice, Glenwood, and Koosharem wards, and the Burrville Branch. The new North Sevier Stake included the Salina First, Salina Second, Redmond, Aurora, Sigurd, and Vermillion wards. The new South Sevier Stake would be was made up of the Annabella, Inverury, Monroe North, Monroe South, Elsinore, Joseph, Sevier, and Marysvale (Beaver County) wards.[70]

The incumbent stake president, Robert D. Young, continued in that calling for the restructured Sevier Stake, with James M. Peterson as first counselor and John Christensen as second counselor. Moroni Lazenby was chosen president over the new North Sevier Stake, with James Arthur Christensen and Jesse Thornell as his counselors. In the fledgling South Sevier Stake, John Ephraim Magleby was named stake president; Joseph Levi Staples was called as his first counselor and Joseph William Parker was his second counselor.[71]

Although the county had experienced great growth during the new century, it was rather homogenous in its make-up. The Presbyterian church remained the only organized alternative for area Protestants, and it would not be until after World War II that area Catholics would dedicate a church in the county and that other Protestant denominations would be formally established. There were few Asians and Hispanics and no blacks in the county in 1930; one was reported in the 1920 census. There was cultural diversity to some extent, however, due to the more secular make-up of the county seat and its growing number of non-Mormons as well as in the diverse heritage represented by converts of the LDS church itself.[72]

School enrollments grew rapidly during the period, and school facilities were also improved. The county had hoped to get a junior college in the 1920s, but was unsuccessful in the endeavor. By 1925 the Sevier County School District owned seventeen buses, which transported an average of 508 students a day. There were more than 3,750 students enrolled in school in the county in 1925.[73] During the next few years smaller schools in the county were closed and consolidated with other elementary schools. By 1930 there were no one-room elementary schools and only one two-room, two-teacher school in the county.[74]

In 1910 a high school athletic association was formed in the state, and by 1925 all of the high schools in Sevier County were involved in the statewide athletic association. That year, the South Sevier High School football team shared the state championship. In addition to athletic competition in the high schools, the school district organized the annual Sevier Day for all junior high school students. All of the students were encouraged to participate in athletic and intellectual competitions.

The 1920s brought other changes to the county schools. By 1928 parent-teacher associations had been organized in each of the schools in the county. These associations aided in improving the education of the students. At Elsinore and Salina, for example, parents spent time and other resources improving the school grounds. In the summer of 1928 kindergarten classes were instituted in Richfield,

This building has served as Richfield's public library since its construction in 1913 with a $10,000 grant from philanthropist Andrew Carnigie. (Utah State Historical Society)

Monroe, and Aurora. Sevier County was one of about ten rural Utah counties that adopted some kind of kindergarten program for children.[75] In 1929 North Sevier High School dedicated a new building in Salina. Four junior high schools were also established that year in the Sevier School District at Salina, Richfield, Monroe, and Elsinore.

Education prompted improved health care in the county. The concern for the health of students in the county resulted in the establishment of a school health program and the hiring of a school nurse. In 1928, the second year of its operation, county school superintendent A.J. Ashman reported that the school nurse examined 2,438 students; of these, 1,143 students were reported as having "defective teeth." There were 349 cases of "bad tonsils," 612 students were "underweight," and there were a number of cases of hearing, vision, and speech problems.[76]

Sevier County residents joined with others in the state to develop public and school libraries. In 1911 the citizens of Richfield applied to the Carnegie Foundation for assistance in building a library. In 1913 the endowment was granted, and the library building was dedicated on 14 May 1913. The Richfield citizens agreed to support the

The Bonny Theater in Richfield. (Utah State Historical Society)

library at a yearly rate of $1,000. By 1925 Salina citizens were taxing themselves to maintain a free public library. The Monroe Ladies Literose Club spearheaded the drive to establish a free public library for their community in 1930. The Monroe Public Library was first located in the basement of the Monroe State Bank. Desks, chairs, and other furnishings were provided by the local Lions Club. Nearly 1,500 books were obtained for the library when a house-to-house canvass was undertaken by the women of the Literose Club.[77]

On 24 October 1929, just five days before the stock market crash which dates the beginning of the Great Depression, the newspaper informed Sevier County residents of a new industry that was soon to begin in Richfield. The county's poultry industry was going to have a new brooder, or heated shelter, for young fowl. This was to be a "strictly modern," state-of-the-art plant. The new plant's organizers included J.J. Spendlove and J.I. Curtis.[78]

In November 1929 the *Richfield Reaper* announced a commercial concern setting its sights on the county. At a meeting of Richfield's Commercial Club, St. Louis glass engineer W.H. Cochran reportedly spoke very enthusiastically about the resources Sevier County had to offer for the manufacture of glass. It was further claimed, "Eastern capitalists have agreed to furnish $3,250,000 of the $5,000,000 required for the establishing of a factory."[79] The *Reaper* was informed that "several prominent Sevier county people" were already "making plans" to assist with the financial negotiations for the plant.

The proposed glass factory was mentioned in the local newspaper again in mid-December. "The alleged intention of eastern capital and manufacturers of plate glass to establish a plate glass manufacturing plant somewhere in Sevier County again came up for discussion at the Commercial club luncheon Monday," the *Richfield Reaper* noted.[80] Attendees remained positive about the plant; however, after all the excitement, and perhaps due to the national economic downturn starting in 1929, no further mention of the glass factory appeared in the pages of the *Reaper*.

While the proposed glass plant was slowly disappearing from the Sevier County scene, the accomplishments of the Sevier Valley Coal Company were receiving much positive attention. In November 1929 a report in the *Richfield Reaper* reported on an excursion to the area's developing coal mines around Salina: "We saw things that without any exaggeration can be called astonishing," it stated. Rail lines were being laid to the mines; there was a 50,000-gallon water tank that had been "dug out from solid rock"; and a massive physical plant housing offices for mine management, engineering staff, and bookkeeping personnel had been built. The visitors were told that the mine contained at least 15 million tons of coal.[81]

The following month, the Richfield newspaper reported on Salina's Poulson Coal Mine. This venture was also seen as very promising. As soon as necessary preparations were completed at this mine on the south side of Salina Canyon, production of coal would start. It was anticipated that "a large tonnage of coal" would be brought forth from the mine each year. And the mining company hoped to develop another vein on the north side of the canyon in the near future.[82] Sevier County's natural resources seemed to offer great potential for development, and, in the decades to come, mining of coal and other minerals became a significant part of Sevier County's economy.

By the end of the 1920s, with the improved roads and highways, Richfield had emerged as an important regional commercial center, serving much of central Utah. The development of roads and the improvement of bus service after World War I began to reduce the number of railroad passengers. On 2 January 1930 railroad passenger service was briefly discontinued in the county; but, due to public pressure, it was reinstated in June of that year. By 1947, however, both passenger and freight revenues were below operating expenditures for the Marysvale line. As a result, the Denver & Rio Grande Western requested permission to drop its passenger service in the county. Richfield Mayor Norman J. Holt spoke out strongly against the request. "We of the community provide the company freight income. . . . We do not think the railroad should be permitted to deny us this vital service while retaining the cream of the business."[83] The railroad was granted its request in 1949.

While the natural riches of the region's mines were being successfully tapped for human benefit during the 1920s, the county's businesses and industries were also increasing. At the same time, however, Sevier County's farmers were losing their farms and often were unable to sell their produce for a livable income. The hoped-for glass plant had disappeared into dust, and a depression was on the horizon that would soon have much of the nation in its clutches.

Clifford L. Jones of Monroe recalled the descent of the economic crisis of the Great Depression upon Sevier County in these words:

> During the winter [of 1929] the Depression hit, and prices started to drop. Not just a little . . . but the whole bottom dropped out. Lambs which we had purchased for twelve cents a pound [in 1929] brought six cents in the Spring of 1930. The result was we were barely able to pay back the money we had borrowed from the bank to buy the lambs.[84]

William Bliss Daniels remembered people being discouraged and hungry and unemployment being high in Annabella in the late 1920s. Daniels also recalled that "many were unable to pay their taxes."[85] Area farmers had a preview of the economically troubled times that would face much greater numbers of county residents—and all Americans—in the years of the Great Depression ahead.

## ENDNOTES

1. Sevier County Ordinances Register, 2 December 1901, 13, Utah State Archives, Salt Lake City.

2. Robert Edgar Riegel, *The Story of Western Railroads* (New York: Macmillan, 1926), 3.

3. Sevier Stake Minute Books, 21 May 1898, LDS Archives.

4. See M. Guy Bishop, "Building Railroads for the Kingdom: The Career of John W. Young, 1857–91," *Utah Historical Quarterly* 48 (Winter 1980): 78.

5. Pearl F. Jacobson, compiler and editor, et al., *Golden Sheaves from a Rich Field: A Centennial History of Richfield, Utah* (Richfield, Utah: Richfield Reaper Publishing Company, 1964), 268.

6. *Richfield Reaper*, 6 March 1902.

7. Ibid.

8. *Official Freight Shippers Guide and Directory of the Denver & Rio Grande Western Railroad*, 36, Utah State Historical Society.

9. Irvin L. Warnock, compiler and editor, *Thru the Years: Sevier County Centennial History* (Springville, Utah: Art City Publishing Co., 1947), 72–75.

10. Ibid., 73.

11. Ibid.

12. Sevier Stake Minute Books, 2 September 1899.

13. *Richfield Reaper*, 6 March 1902.

14. *Richfield Reaper*, 6 May 1902.

15. Sevier County Ordinances Register, 2 February 1903, 14; 3 August 1903, 15; and 3 April 1911, 37; Utah State Archives.

16. Jacobson, *Golden Sheaves*, 267.

17. Ibid., 88–92, 96, 104.

18. See Jacobson,"*Golden Sheaves*, 233, 242–43. For an excellent study of the Richfield United Order see Feramorz Y. Fox, "Experiment in Utopia: The United Order of Richfield, 1874–1877," *Utah Historical Quarterly* 32 (Fall 1964): 355–81.

19. Jacobson, *Golden Sheaves*, 242–43.

20. Ibid., 280.

21. Ibid., 257.

22. Ibid., 272–73.

23. Ibid., 92–93.

24. Wilford Murdock and Mildred Murdock, *Monroe, Utah: Its First*

*One Hundred Years* (Monroe: Monroe Centennial Committee, 1964), 30, 37.

25. See Jeanne Dastrup, "The Sigurd Story," typescript manuscript, 7, 13, Utah State Historical Society.; Warnock, *Thru the Years,* 450; Murdock and Murdock, *Monroe,* 61.

26. *Third Report of the Superintendent of Public Instruction of the State of Utah, 1900* (Salt Lake City, 1901), 334.

27. Ibid., 393.

28. *Fourth Report of the Superintendent of Public Instruction of the State of Utah, 1902* (Salt Lake City, 1903), appendix 11.

29. Ibid., 237.

30. *Sixth Report of the Superintendent of Public Instruction of the State of Utah, 1906* (1906), 139.

31. *Seventh Report of the Superintendent of Public Instruction of the State of Utah, 1908* (1909), 360.

32. Ibid., appendix 21.

33. The normal school was part of the University of Utah and today is called the College of Education. Those receiving scholarships for the 1909 school year were: Dan Baker, Vivian Bellon, Marvel Bloomquist, Earl Buchanan, Lottie Cornwall, Leo Christensen, Philo Farnsworth, Vance E. Frandsen, Lewis Jones, Sidney Ship, and Alma Sorenson.

34. *Third Report of the Superintendent of Public Instruction,* 282.

35. Warnock, *Thru the Years,* 57.

36. Ibid.

37. Jacobson, *Golden Sheaves,* 199.

38. Sevier County Clerk's Office Records, Minute Book A, 1 July 1901, Utah State Archives, Salt Lake City; *Richfield Reaper,* 6 May 1902; Jacobson, *Golden Sheaves,* 120.

39. William Bliss Daniels, interview, 5, typescript, LDS Archives.

40. Golden R. Buchanan, interview, 20, typescript, LDS Archives.

41. Clifford L. Jones, interview, Monroe, Utah, 20 August 1976, 18, LDS Archives.

42. Sevier County Ordinance Register, 6 January 1919, 49.

43. For more information about the local press see J. Cecil Alter, *Early Utah Journalism* (Salt Lake City: Utah State Historical Society, 1938).

44. *Richfield Reaper,* 20 March 1920.

45. Cynthia Jane Sturgis, "The Mormon Village in Transition: Richfield, Utah, as a Case Study 1910–1930" (Master's thesis, University of Utah, 1978), 130–32.

46. *Richfield Reaper,* 8 April 1920.

47. *Richfield Reaper,* 21 November 1929.

48. Ibid.

49. Donald Worster, *Rivers of Empire: Water, Aridity, and the Growth of the American West* (New York: Pantheon Books, 1985), 210–11; Norris Hundley, Jr., *Water and the West: The Colorado River Compact and the Policies of Water in the American West* (Berkeley: University of California Press, 1975), 184–85, 192–93.

50. *Richfield Reaper,* 18 November 1920.

51. Ibid.

52. *Richfield Reaper,* 25 November 1920.

53. Ibid.

54. Ibid.

55. Ibid.

56. Warnock, *Thru the Years,* 78, 339.

57. Kenneth L. Cannon II, "Deserets, Red Stockings and Out-of-Towners: Baseball Comes of Age in Salt Lake City, 1877–79," *Utah Historical Quarterly* 52 (Spring 1984): 140.

58. *Richfield Reaper,* 7 April 1921, 1; 14 April 1921, 31 March 1922.

59. *Richfield Reaper,* 2 June 1922, 5.

60. *Richfield Reaper* 3 July 1922, 12.

61. See Thomas G. Alexander, *The Rise of Multiple Use Management in the Intermountain West: A Forest History of Region 4 of the Forest Service* (Washington, D.C.: U.S. Forest Service, 1987), 20.

62. Revo Morrey Young, *Ten Penny Nails: Pioneering Sevier Valley* (n.p., n.d.), 54; J. Cecil Alter, *Utah: The Storied Domain,* 3 vols. (Chicago: American Historical Society, 1932), 2:236–37.

63. Iva Lee Sorensen and Kaye S. Bybee, *Founded on Faith—A History of Glenwood, 1864–1984* (Glenwood: Daughters of Utah Pioneers, 1984), 108–9.

64. Murdock and Murdock, *Monroe,* 62.

65. Sturgis, "The Mormon Village," 87.

66. See Sevier County Commission Minutes, Book A, 3 December 1906, Sevier County Clerk's Office, Richfield, Utah. The author wishes to express his gratitude to deputy county clerk Jean Miller for her assistance in locating appropriate county records.

67. Sevier County Commission Minutes, Book A, 1 April 1907.

68. Ibid., 237, 253, 256, 259.

69. Sturgis, "The Mormon Village," 66.

70. Warnock and Warnock, *Sevier Stake Memories,* 51.

71. Ibid.

72. Sturgis, "The Mormon Village," 20–21.

73. *Sixteenth Report of the Superintendent of Public Instruction of the State of Utah, 1926* (1926), 134, 160.

74. *Eighteenth Report of the Superintendent of Public Instruction of the State of Utah, 1930* (1930), 222.

75. Ibid., 49.

76. *Seventeenth Report of the Superintendent of Public Instruction of the State of Utah, 1928* (1928), 68.

77. Alter, *Utah: The Storied Domain,* 3:217–18.

78. 1 *Richfield Reaper,* 24 October 1929.

79. *Richfield Reaper,* 21 November 1929.

80. *Richfield Reaper,* 19 December 1929.

81. *Richfield Reaper,* 12 November 1929.

82. *Richfield Reaper,* 2 December 1920.

83. Warnock, *Thru the Years,* 324; *Salt Lake Tribune,* 2 March 1947, quoted in Robert G. Athern, *Rebel of the Rockies: A History of the Denver and Rio Grande Western Railroad* (New Haven: Yale University Press, 1962), 345.

84. Jones, interview, 18.

85. Daniels, interview, 26–27.

6

# Troubled Times: Sevier County, 1930–1949

In December 1930 the *Richfield Reaper* reported the results of the 1930 U.S. Census for the county. The population of the state of Utah numbered 507,847, an increase of 58,451 (13 percent) from 1920; however, Sevier County's 1930 population stood at 11,199, a decrease of 0.7 percent from the 1920 enumeration. This most recent figure represented a population density of 5.1 persons per square mile for the county.[1]

The county seat of Richfield had 3,067 persons, down from 3,262 in 1920. Of the other incorporated cities in the county, Salina was the second most populous, with a count of 1,383 (down from 1,451 in 1920); Monroe ranked third at 1,247 residents (from 1,719 in 1920). The farming communities of Elsinore, with 654 residents (a decline of 189 people from 1920); Redmond, 577 people (649 in 1920); Aurora, 568 inhabitants (no figure for 1920); Glenwood, 350 people (a decrease of fourteen persons); Koosharem, 319 residents (no figure for 1920); Joseph, 243 inhabitants (224 in 1920); and Annabella, 180 people (no figure for 1920).[2] Of all Sevier County's communities, only Joseph showed a population increase (nineteen persons) from

1920 to 1930. It would seem that the farm crisis of the 1920s with its falling agricultural prices and resulting farm sales was starting to scatter the county's population to more promising lands.

This out-migration from the countryside during the 1920s and 1930s was not unique to Sevier County or to Utah. In the decade between 1930 and 1940 over 90,000 residents of Utah relocated; some, but of course not all, were farmers. Most Utahns moved to California or adjoining western states. The Great Depression hastened the exodus from country to city. However, as historian Charles S. Peterson has noted, referring to John Steinbeck's novel about the midwestern dust bowl of the 1920s and 1930s, "the Utah experience was not *The Grapes of Wrath*." It was far from a rout, being more of an "orderly withdrawal."[3]

The fourth decade of the twentieth century for Sevier County began almost the way the third one had ended. The overriding issues of water rights, modernity, and the rapidly developing Great Depression still dominated the thoughts of the local people. The big story of the early 1930s was, without a doubt, the ever-worsening economy. The tax issue was crucially involved in the problems which wreaked havoc upon American farmers during the Great Depression. An indication of the hard times the Depression brought to Sevier County can be found in the county tax sales conducted between 1929 and 1934.[4] Tax sales, brought about when a property owner was unable to meet his or her taxes, was the dread of the farmer during the Great Depression. Farmers, by the very nature of their profession, are forced to exist on anticipated income from future produce and/or livestock sales. However, when they suffer from a greatly reduced income from that anticipated, many farmers simply cannot make ends meet.

Judging from the property tax records for Sevier County in 1929, the property tax ranged between $7.00 and $140.00 for a farmer in the county, depending upon the amount of acreage owned. Often a "compromise settlement" between the treasurer's office and the farmer averted a tax sale; at other times, delinquent properties were "redeemed" by friends or relatives. Sometimes, for a variety of reasons, the taxes were "cancelled." But, sadly for some, the treasurer's ledger regularly had the words "PROPERTY SOLD FOR TAXES BY

THE BOARD OF COMMISSIONERS" stamped in big red letters across the property tax entry.[5]

Fourteen Sevier County farms were sold on account of unpaid taxes in 1929. This number increased to twenty-four farms by the following year. The numbers declined slightly in 1931 and 1932; but 1933 was a disaster for Sevier County farmers—that year alone 103 farms were sold for taxes. By 1934, when the farm policies of the new president, Franklin D. Roosevelt, were beginning to have some effect, farm tax sales in Sevier County declined to only thirty-five.[6] Not all of Sevier County's farmers suffered equally during the Great Depression, however. Walter B. Daniels was doing well enough that at one point in the period he actually bought eighty acres of pasture land for $800 at a tax sale.[7] Most county residents, however, suffered in those bleak days.

The following advertisements by the Salt Lake City office of the Federal Land Bank of Berkeley, California, appeared in the *Reaper* in 1930:

> FOR SALE Ninety acres irrigated land at Joseph, Sevier County, Utah. Property has home, electric lights, city water. $8500.00. Small cash payment necessary and balance can be carried for 20 years at 6%.
>
> Thirty acres irrigated land full water right, located between Elsinore and Monroe on the main highway. Farm now growing alfalfa and grain crops. Price $3,000.00. 10% down and balance in 20 equal annual installments with interest at 6% per annum.[8]

These sale offerings by the land bank were followed by many others and illustrate the severity of the Great Depression upon the rural economy of the county. The above advertisements offer a glimpse of the engaging attributes of farm property in Sevier County—irrigated land with full water rights, a house on the site, electricity, city water, and good location. However, on many Sevier County farms life was bleak. While the post–World War I depression hit the farmlands somewhat later than it struck manufacturing and mining, the blow has been called "sharper and more lasting."[9] Farmers commonly took a mortgage on their property to produce the necessary cash to carry them until harvest time. As the Depression deepened and agricultural prices fell, individual farmers became increasingly hard-pressed financially.

The signs of farm unrest were everywhere in Sevier County. The Depression brought what has been called a "hurricane of catastrophe."[10] This was certainly true in Sevier County. On 2 October 1930 an opinion on a proposed state income-tax amendment was voiced in the pages of Richfield's newspaper by Charles L. Bean, the son of Sevier County explorer and pioneer George W. Bean. The younger Bean, exhibiting more than a trace of farm-city rivalry, caustically wrote:

> The farmers have quite a different [tax] proposition. They know that these amendments will necessarily mean more money must be collected to take care of extra expenses. . . . The question is, who is going to pay the extra money? . . . It is suggested that $1000 be allowed a single man and $2000 to a married man, with a further exemption of three or four hundred dollars for each child before any income tax is collected, which will practically eliminate all salaried people [from paying income taxes]. But how about the farmer? If he happens to own a few acres of ground and maybe a cow or two, does he get any exemptions? Not on your life![11]

The incensed Bean railed on about the farmer's plight, "They soak him for the value of his property whether he makes a dollar out of it or not." For Charles L. Bean, and likely for many other county farmers, this was as much a concern about a rapidly disappearing way of life as it was about taxes.

In many important ways, the Great Depression did not affect those living in small farming communities as harshly as it did those in urban areas. While some city dwellers appear to have survived and possibly even prospered during the Great Depression, while others struggled. Farmers sometimes faced the possibility of losing their land; but, barring that disaster, farmers were able to keep working (although often for less gain), and continued to provide sufficient food for their families by growing it themselves. The Monroe Creamery Company plant was sold in 1930 to Pet Milk Company, which was able to add an addition to the plant in 1937 for making butter and powdered milk.[12]

Salina's business district, January 1938. (Utah State Historical Society)

Leila Oldroyd, who grew up in Koosharem during the Depression, remembered that her father, a farmer, worked at a sawmill in the mountains during the summer months. He was also a "pretty good" carpenter. He had his own milk cows, pigs, and chickens, Mrs. Oldroyd recalled. As economic times became increasingly more difficult in the early 1930s, the family simply lived off of what the farm produced. For non-farm products, such as clothing or other store items, they either shopped at the Grass Valley "Merc" or ordered from a catalog.[13]

Much of the *Richfield Reaper* edition for 12 October 1930 centered upon local politics. In fact, the platforms of the Republicans and the Democrats filled the front page of this edition. The Sevier County Republicans had had minor troubles in 1920 over the appointment of a replacement for deceased commissioner A.K. Hansen of Richfield. The county G.O.P. remained alive and well, however, in the rural and conservative county. Its platform promoted the principles set forth by the national and state party organizations:

"We believe that the policies of the present [Hoover] administration will result in the economic stability of our state and nation," the county Republicans professed.[14] This continuing support of Herbert Hoover's increasingly unpopular policies would come back to haunt the Republicans of Sevier County two years later.

On the other hand, the 1930 platform of Sevier County's Democrats voiced continuing endorsement of Governor George H. Dern. The Democrats, in an undisguised effort to court the county's farm vote, noted in their platform the primacy of agriculture to Sevier County's economy. The Democrats, seeming to foresee Franklin D. Roosevelt's 1932 strategy, condemned the Republican platform as being "inadequate for the distress which prevails throughout farming communities." They also went on record in favor of an old-age pension, promoted by Francis Townsend of California, which had passed the Utah state legislature during the previous session.[15] This was a precursor of the later national social security system.

By 1932 the escalating discontent of the people of the United States led to the repudiation of the policies of Herbert Hoover in the hope of new ideas. Americans chose Democrat Franklin Delano Roosevelt to succeed Hoover in that year's presidential election. Whatever its merits, Hoover's conservative, pro-business plan to pull the country out of the economic crisis simply had not worked.

Franklin D. Roosevelt had been elected on a platform calling for change. Nationally, Roosevelt defeated Hoover soundly, and in Utah Roosevelt captured 116,750 votes to 84,795 for Hoover. Four years earlier, Hoover had carried Utah by some 15,000 votes, winning Sevier County by a two-to-one margin. But in Sevier, a farming county with severe economic problems, Roosevelt's promise to help "the forgotten man" played quite well; still, Hoover won in the county by 78 votes (2,303 to 2,225).[16]

In the senatorial races that year, Democrat Elbert D. Thomas defeated Utah's incumbent Republican senator Reed Smoot by more than 30,000 votes. In Sevier County, Thomas won by 2,303 votes to Smoot's 2,220, a much closer contest than it was across the state.[17] Locally attractive features of Roosevelt's promised "New Deal" fol-

The Redmond Clay and Salt Company building, an important business in northern Sevier County. (Allan Kent Powell)

lowing his election included the Agricultural Adjustment Act, a plan to aid struggling farmers and help stabilize America's farms.

Most of the nation clambered aboard Franklin D. Roosevelt's Democratic bandwagon throughout the 1930s, and Sevier County generally followed suit. Four years after his 1932 landslide, Roosevelt was again victorious in the presidential election. In Sevier County, the Democratic avalanche helped elect two Democratic county commissioners—Chariton Seegmiller defeated Republican Adolf Nielson by over one thousand votes for the four-year commission seat, while another Democrat, Delbert Hansen, captured the two-year slot by defeating his Republican challenger Edwin Sorensen 2,505 votes to 2,251. Democrats won all other county offices in 1936 as well.[18]

By the end of 1930 Sevier County was allocating $6,500 for the next year's poor fund, an increase of $1,300 over the previous year's allotment.[19] The county's fearful expectations for 1931 were not unfounded. There were various hard-pressed individuals across the county; hence, relief for the impoverished people of Sevier County was much needed. In December 1930, to list but one example, a Mr.

Roundy of Richfield appeared before the county commissioners to request "financial support [since] he was unable to obtain work."[20]

For the most part, local businesses seemed to survive the Depression. Some small businesses, such as cafes and soda shops, struggled during the Depression since people simply had less money to spend on nonessentials. Many retail stores such as Christensen's Department Store in downtown Richfield continued operations, albeit with declining profits. At Christensen's, price markdowns were frequently necessary in the early 1930s in order to sell merchandise to hesitant consumers. The department store had only opened its doors in March 1929, just seven months before the great crash of the following October. Store owner Alten Christensen had no way of comparing the situation with business fluctuations from an earlier era.[21]

In 1930 Soren Christiansen renamed the Richfield Furniture Company the Christiansen Furniture Company. This was Richfield's first furniture company, founded in the 1880s by H. P. Hansen. Through the difficult economic times of the Depression, the Christiansen Furniture Company survived and expanded to other towns in the county and also to Salt Lake City. In 1964 Ralph H. Christiansen became the owner of the furniture stores and changed the name to Christiansen Furniture and Carpet Company.

The automotive service businesses of Richfield weathered the storm of the Great Depression fairly well. In 1931 Malicotte Motor Company and Utah Service and Garage consolidated into the Sevier Car Market of Richfield. Competition for business was keen and the new company offered inducements, including 100 gallons of free gasoline with each car purchase, to attract customers.[22]

The New Deal programs of the Franklin D. Roosevelt administration began to appear in Sevier County by the summer of 1933. The "Blue Eagle," which symbolized a company's support of the National Recovery Administration (NRA), was very evident in the upper right-hand corner of every front page of the *Richfield Reaper* throughout the Depression years. The National Industrial Recovery Act (passed by Congress in June 1933) placed wage, labor, and price controls on businesses. The blue eagle symbol told consumers that the business was complying with the legislation. The National

Recovery Administration, which implemented these controls, has been called "the New Deal's greatest effort."[23]

In August 1933 Frank G. Martines, a former mayor of Richfield and later a candidate for governor of Utah, was appointed by Governor Henry Blood to represent Sevier County in the local district of the National Recovery Administration (NRA) to aid in the implementation of the National Industrial Recovery Act. Martines was to "consult state administrative officers of the NRA in regard to the program to be carried out here." The primary functions of the district NRA officers were to "contact every employer and urge the signing up and strict maintenance of the [National Industrial Recovery Act] code as it applies to them and to see that the various groups adhere to a policy of fair competition."[24]

By 1933 Sevier County was making plans to accommodate a Civilian Conservation Corps (commonly known as the CCC) unit near Fish Lake. The CCC sought to employ young men from needy families, forming them into military-type units to work on conservation and road construction projects. The intent of the Civilian Conservation Corps was two-fold: to provide work and to build or repair the nation's roads, watersheds, and campgrounds. One of the most popular and successful of the New Deal programs, the CCC employed several thousand young men in Utah between 1933 and 1941. The initial quota of CCC workers for Sevier County was forty-eight men. They were housed in forest camps and were paid a dollar a day plus food and shelter for the labor they performed. Much of their effort went toward repairing the damage done to mountain watersheds by overgrazing. By October 1933 the U.S. Forest Service had established camp F-25 at Richfield to work solely on erosion control.[25]

During the winter of 1933–34, plans were laid for the young men of the Fish Lake, Sevier County, CCC camp and the Grover, Wayne County, CCC camp to relocate to Richfield. The Fish Lake camp (officially known as F-12) served the needs of the U.S. Forest Service. Seven miles north of Fish Lake, another Forest Service unit (F-13) was established in a tent camp near a spot known as the Frying Pan.[26] Like other CCC camps assigned to the Fish Lake National Forest, the men worked on flood-control projects, road repair, campground maintenance, and erosion control. Both Fish Lake camps established their winter quarters at the Richfield fairgrounds. Later, the location for the barracks was changed to the Richfield airport. This plan further aided the community's economy when a $14,000 barracks was erected which was to be "turned over" to the city when the Depression had ended.

"The establishment of the camp here for the winter," the *Reaper* noted, "will be an advantage to Richfield, as it will employ forty carpenters, four plumbers, four electricians and other skilled labor for at least thirty days and after the camp is fully established it will mean an expenditure of $80 a day locally for commissary, in addition to bringing a payroll to the 200 boys who will be enlisted in the camp for the winter."[27] Many of these young corpsmen hailed from either Sevier or Wayne counties. A number of young men from outside the state were assigned to other CCC camps in the county. Some stayed and married local girls, establishing businesses in the county. Although the CCC men were required to send most of their pay back home to their families, the five dollars a month they were allowed to keep provided a valuable and much-desired economic boost to the merchants of the towns, including Richfield, in which they spent their money.

Another New Deal agency which impacted Sevier County was the Works Progress Administration (WPA). The WPA provided federal financing for a number of public projects in Utah between 1935 and 1942. WPA workers built dams and canals, did highway construction and maintenance work, and built or renovated dozens of public buildings. Leila Oldroyd, who was about eleven years old at the time, recalled a unique WPA project at Koosharem:

> They came through and they, well, at that time almost everyone had an outdoor toilet, because there wasn't too much indoor plumbing at that time, during the depression, and I remember the WPA very, very well, that's what they did. They came in and they built everybody an outdoor toilet.[28]

She also recalled that "a couple of our girls just a little bit older than I was married WPA workers."

Another WPA project in Richfield during 1936 was the improvement of the old pioneer cemetery located at the county seat. "The purpose of the project," the *Richfield Reaper* reported, "is to bring the cemetery grounds into harmony with the adjoining campus, and to insure its permanent care."[29] Richfield residents who died between 1864 and 1880 were buried in this cemetery. The $1,000 project was sponsored by the city at the request of the Richfield camps of the Daughters of Utah Pioneers.

P.F. Peterson, who managed the Sevier County office of the national employment service, a nationwide job-search network implemented by the Roosevelt administration, was a busy man in 1933. Approximately 700 unemployed men enrolled during the first few months of the office's operation. The Morrison-Knudsen Construction Company, which held a contract to build a road linking Marysvale in Piute County with Sevier County was hiring about 160 men to do the work. Other workers were needed to assist with the construction of the CCC barracks in Richfield. Peterson observed to the *Reaper* that the national employment service was intended as "a service to the employer as well as the unemployed." Probably its strongest selling point during those hard times was that "it is free to both."[30]

Construction projects sponsored by the federal government began to stimulate Sevier County's sagging economy by the fall of 1933. The newspaper reported on the construction activity for the CCC winter quarters:

> The busy sound of hammers and saws at the Richfield airport is music to the ears of some 20 Sevier county carpenters who will have employment at $6 a day for approximately three weeks in the construction of winter quarters for the C.C.C. camp which is to be stationed here until spring.[31]

The frame barracks would house 200 men during the winter months. Besides the sleeping quarters, the airport site eventually included a mess hall and an administration office. One group of CCC workers was to be engaged during the winter months building a "wood road" running twelve miles into the west mountains toward Fillmore. Another group would string telephone lines to give the Fish Lake area a direct connection with the rest of Sevier County.[32]

Richfield High School, January 1938. (Utah State Historical Society)

A New Deal program of great interest in Sevier County was the Agricultural Adjustment Act (AAA). Passed by the "Hundred Days" Congress on 12 May 1933, the "Triple-A" endeavored to create scarcity in order to raise prices of agricultural produce by urging farmers either not to plant or to plow under existing crops. The program confused and angered many Americans struggling against hunger, as its long-range goals were not immediately evident to hungry Americans who heard the news of perfectly good food being destroyed. Said Secretary of Agriculture Henry Wallace of Iowa, "I hope we shall never have to resort to it again. To destroy a standing crop goes against the soundest instincts of human nature."[33] The program never achieved the results or popularity of the CCC, but it did help establish a practice of federal farm supports and subsidies that still exists at the present time.

Farmers received a good deal of federal attention in the aftermath of Roosevelt's inauguration in 1933. In December 1933, farm homes in Sevier County were being surveyed by representatives of the government as to the need for improvements. Over 1,500 homes in the county were surveyed during late 1933 and written reports were submitted to the government. S.R. Boswell, the Sevier County farm agent, was in charge of the surveys locally. An engineer was to draw up plans for identified improvements and the necessary work was to be overseen by state officials.[34]

In the spring of 1934 four Sevier County men—H.B. Crandal, S.E. Tanner, Irvin L. Warnock, and Charlton Seegmiller—were appointed to the state farm adjustment committee by Governor Henry Blood, who had been swept into office with the Democratic landslide of 1932. This committee was organized to assist both local debtors and creditors in an effort to reach "friendly, sensible and fair" solutions to debt problems. "It is expected," read the words of the *Richfield Reaper,* "that their efforts will tend to settle many problems that heretofore resulted in unnecessary foreclosure."[35]

The repercussions of the economic plight went beyond the farmstead. In November 1933 A.J. Ashman, the superintendent of Sevier County's public schools, announced a plan to assist unemployed school teachers. According to word received by Ashman from the federal government, teachers might be employed to do any of the following types of school work:

> First, to continue rural schools which would otherwise close or be greatly curtailed due to lack of funds; second, to teach adults unable to read and write English; third, to give vocational training to the unemployed to qualify them to enter employment; fourth, to give vocational training to adults who are physically handicapped; fifth, to give general training to other adults to help them become more effective citizens.[36]

According to Superintendent Ashman, the relief agencies were "anxious" to get the classes organized in the district.

The following month, the *Reaper* announced the commencement of adult-education classes "under the federal government plan to furnish employment to unemployed teachers."[37] Courses of instruction included bookkeeping, taught by W.L. Ashby, and English grammar and twentieth-century literature with Ila Dastrup. Sophia

Goldbranson offered penmanship, letter writing, and spelling; sports, health, and recreation classes were taught by Thelma Dastrup.

During what must have been for some a very bleak Christmas of 1933, local advertisements urged Sevier County residents to shop early and to be sure to buy from local merchants, who deserve "100 per cent of your patronage." Excerpts from a tongue-in-cheek take-off of "T'was the Night Before Christmas," entitled "It's Days Before Christmas," published in the *Richfield Reaper,* likely told an accurate story of that beleaguered Christmas as viewed through the eyes of a struggling parent:

> It's days before Christmas and in our small cot
> The kids are all dreaming of what Kris has got;
> They hope he has skates, some trains and great dolls
> And even bright nothings and such fol-der-ols.
>
> I tell them that Kris is a practical guy,
> That worthless old gim-cracks he never will buy;
> He may bring a sweater, some socks, or a hat,
> Or mittens or cord'roys and such stuff as that. . . .
>
> By gum, we'll get busy and we'll do our stuff;
> We've got our two eyes and our hands—that's enough.
> I'll get my knife busy, my saw and my plane—
> Why that solves our problem—I'm happy again!
>
> My Mary can make jest the swankiest tricks
> That ever was dreamed of—No toys? Fiddlesticks!
> We'll cut and we'll fit and we'll paint and we'll draw
> Such stuff as we'll have no Kris ever saw![38]

During the 1930s America was a country concerned with protecting community morals; not surprisingly, Sevier County lawmakers seem to have concurred. In 1932 the county commissioners, declaring that an unspecified "emergency" existed, established closing times for dance halls at 1:30 A.M. (Sunday closure being mandatory). During the same years, a county ordinance called for the licensing of dance halls, confectioneries, barber shops, soft-drink parlors, and hot-dog stands. The licensing fee ran from twenty dollars a year for hot-dog stands to $150 a year for dance halls.[39] Some licensing was no doubt intended to raise revenue more than to regulate

The old North Sevier High School Building in Salina, now the North Sevier Junior High School. (Allan Kent Powell)

public morals; but, on the whole, county residents were generally law-abiding and attentive to their own concerns. The great social experiment of Prohibition was repudiated in 1933, the Utah legislature casting the deciding vote in the matter, and it can safely be assumed that many in Sevier County as elsewhere were relieved to reduce government interference in their affairs even if most were not longing to legally sip alcoholic beverages.

Occupying considerable space in the *Richfield Reaper* during 1933 and 1934 was the public discussion about building a new hospital for the county. The Richfield Lions Club led out in this community movement. "The chief topic of discussion at the meeting of the Richfield Lions club Wednesday evening was the proposed county hospital building and the commitment of the members was overwhelmingly in favor of this project," the *Reaper* reported on its front page for 26 October 1933.

At the meeting of the county commissioners the following month, the erection of a county hospital in Richfield was a matter of some discussion. Committees representing the Venice Farm Bureau, the Sevier

County Taxpayers League, and the Business and Profession Women, a women's club in Richfield, as well as concerned individuals from Glenwood and Richfield appeared before the commissioners to voice their opinions. Some supported the proposed hospital—which could be built with federal assistance—while others stood in opposition because of the money that would still be required from local citizens.[40]

By January 1934 a group that the newspaper termed the "representative citizens of Richfield" was mobilizing to push for the construction of the hospital. These leading residents of the county seat vowed before the Richfield City Council "to exhaust every resource before they will submit to a verdict against the establishment of a county hospital here while funds are still available from the public works administration on such generous terms." Designated to lead this fight for their fellow residents were Mayor W.L. Warner, Mrs. J.L. Sevy, and Mrs. W.S. Greenwood.[41]

The pro-hospital forces hoped to qualify for New Deal funds to assist in the construction of the structure. A comparison was drawn with a hospital recently built at Cedar City in Iron County. Richfield doctor D.B. Gottfredson, who had visited the Cedar City facility, judged the two sites to be very similar. A hospital in Richfield would, Dr. Gottfredson believed, "serve a greater territory and really should have better support than the one at Cedar City owing to the more diversified resources of this community." In fact, the *Richfield Reaper* quoted Dr. Gottfredson as saying, "There is no other community in the state or perhaps any other state which has greater need of or is more entitled to a hospital than is Sevier County."[42] While Dr. Gottfredson might have been thought by some to be self-serving in this statement, he likely voiced the opinion of most residents of Richfield and, perhaps, even of the county.

Gottfredson also argued the economic benefits of the hospital. Turning once more to Iron County's hospital, he said that the "total sum" which this hospital had cost that county annually in the several years of its existence was only $7,000. This expense represented, he observed, "about the amount budgeted by [Sevier] county for its indigent expense." Furthermore, according to the doctor, "the four [current] Richfield physicians would be willing to rent offices in the hospital which, if they paid at the rate they now pay elsewhere, would mean an added revenue to the hospital of approximately $1,200 a year." Finally, it was noted that at Richfield "the federal government was spending $15,000 a year for the maintenance and upkeep of the armory and a unit of the national guard." Furthermore, the government was expected to "plan hospitals for certain areas."[43] Sevier County, like most other counties, was not averse to calling upon the government to help with its needs.

On 16 November 1933 the Sevier County Commission heard the arguments in favor of the Richfield hospital. The Richfield Lions Club, initially the driving force behind the hospital movement; the Richfield Parents-Teachers Association; the Richfield Study Club; the Monroe Lions Club; the Business and Professional Women's Club; and the Richfield Business Men's Association all went on record in support of the hospital. But the *Reaper* went on to note that "there have been several committees from the north end of the county who have appeared before the commissioners in opposition to this proposed hospital and also some local groups have presented arguments against it."[44]

An article the following week gave more specifics about this opposition. "Various units of the Farm bureau have filed protests," it was reported, "and also, the Sevier County Taxpayers league opposed the matter." Commission chairman Moroni Jensen admitted that at the present time "the opposition appears to outweigh the element that favors building a hospital" and stated that the commissioners (Jensen, Edwin Sorensen, and G.A. Staples) were only desirous of serving the public." Hence, although all commissioners were in agreement that "there is a great need for such an institution here," and admitted that

> there will probably never come a time again when it could be built upon such easy terms as the government is offering during this emergency work program [Public Works Administration], yet he added that the main and perhaps deciding factor is the matter of financing a hospital, both as to its original cost and as to its maintenance.[45]

Falling back on the caution often exhibited by politicians, and observing that the county already had some "heavy obligations" elsewhere, consideration of a county hospital for Richfield was suspended. The commissioners stated on 23 November 1933 that "they had not reached a decision on the subject although delegations had come from Salina, Redmond, Aurora, Annabella and Monroe with protests against building it."[46] Thus, the hospital proposal was put on hold by the county commission.

Supporters of the hospital in the city of Richfield remained resolute, however. After the county commissioners "failed to take favorable action . . . due to determined opposition from the north end of the county and various other communities and organizations who feared an increase in the tax levy," Richfield's project supporters, refusing to give up the plan, turned elsewhere for the needed support. Furthermore, city attorney Henry F. Beal told the *Richfield Reaper* that "this hospital will not cost the city or taxpayers of Richfield or Sevier County one cent in the way of taxes."[47]

A source of opposition to the construction of a new hospital in Richfield came from Salina and the other northern communities in the county. The residents of Salina already had a private hospital, which had been completed in 1917 just before the outbreak of the Spanish influenza epidemic, and the multistory building provided the northern part of the county with excellent medical services.

Dr. Margaret Ann Freece was one of the physicians who attended to the sick and injured of Salina, Aurora, and Redmond and was one of the county's fine physicians. Born in Scipio, she attended the Presbyterian school in Scipio and Wasatch Academy in Mt. Pleasant. She continued her education by attending Northwestern University Woman's Medical College in Chicago, Illinois, where she received a medical degree. At the turn of the century, she returned to Salina where her mother and other members of her family were living. She began her medical practice working from a small office in her home. Dr. Freece was the first woman elected vice-president of the Utah Medical Association. The community thought highly of her. "We did not think it was strange to have a woman doctor, we were just grateful for her," commented a resident of Salina.[48] According to her biographer, Freece was also involved in the Community Church of Salina, a director of the Sevier Valley Coal Company, a director of the First

State Bank of Salina, and a stockholder in the Salina Grain and Milling Company.

The city of Richfield went directly to the Public Works Administration (PWA), seeking a loan to build the desired hospital. In March 1934 Mayor Warner and City Attorney Beal informed the public, "Richfield's application for a $55,000 loan for the construction and equipment of a thoroughly modern hospital was acted upon [favorably]." Definitive plans for the hospital were announced in 1936 when it was reported that "appropriation for a three-story, fire proof brick hospital in Richfield" was finalized.[49] As the *Reaper* had noted two years before with faintly disguised smugness, now "Sevier County will have to pay for hospitalization of their indigent cases, just as outside counties to the east and south of here will have to do," because "this is to be strictly a Richfield hospital."[50]

The hospital was very much needed. In 1934, for example, only 10.5 percent of the babies born in the county were born in a hospital. The state average for hospital-born babies that year was 35.8 percent—the lowest percentage was in Carbon County, with 3 percent, and the highest percentage was in Grand County with over 90 percent of its babies born in a hospital.[51] That year, a public health nurse was appointed for Sevier County, followed in 1935 by a district health office. The county in the early 1930s was fortunate to have at least seven physicians living in the county who assisted in delivering babies at home. In 1936 the private Sevier Valley Hospital and Clinic was opened in Richfield to help serve area medical needs.[52]

A city hall was built in Monroe in 1934. That city also had many active civic groups, including a local Lions Club, formed in 1927, a literary club, Daughters of Utah Pioneers (DUP) chapter, and an American Legion post. Salina and other area towns also were served by their citizens, who joined church, civic, and service organizations to serve their communities. Salina too had a Lions Club and DUP camp, one of numerous DUP camps in the county. The lack of specific mention of these groups in this history is not meant to slight their importance. It is the individual citizens and their often uncelebrated efforts, after all, which constitute the heart of any county. A municipal building was constructed in Salina in 1936–37 with the assistance of the WPA, which paid 50 percent of the building's cost.

Built in 1934 with funding from the Federal Emergency Relief Administration, the Monroe City Hall initially housed city offices, a jail, a courtroom, public library, and an assembly room. (Allan Kent Powell)

An airport was also built in Richfield as a WPA project in 1936–37 with the assistance of a $30,000 federal grant.

Based on statistics compiled by the Utah Emergency Relief Program for the period from 1 April 1934 to 31 December 1935, about 24 percent of the county's population received some kind of public relief assistance. Similar percentages of relief assistance were found in neighboring counties: Sanpete, 25.2 percent; Emery, 37 percent; Millard, 31.9 percent; Piute, 28.4 percent; and Wayne, 14.3 percent.[53] For the same reporting period, Sevier County received $60.26 per capita in assistance in the form of direct relief, surplus commodities received, drouth relief, reservoir construction or repair, sanitation assistance, and other relief programs.[54] A wide variety of civil works projects including sidewalks, improvements of roads and bridges, pest control, airport improvements, nursing, nutritional and health care assistance, flood and erosion control, culinary water lines installed or repaired, pit privies constructed, and other projects accounted for the $60.26 per capita assistance.

Floods were once again a part of life in Sevier County during the

The Richfield Post Office, February 1938. (Utah State Historical Society)

1930s. They impacted the life of the county's farming villages in ways other than just damaging crops and ruining a season's hard work. As a 8 August 1934 report from Monroe depicts, the ruin could affect domestic life as well:

> The city is without culinary water and power today as a result of a flood in Monroe Canyon last Monday (2 days ago). The fields south of town were covered by floodwaters, rocks, and other debris. Damage was estimated at several thousand dollars.[55]

Within eight days (on 14 August) Monroe was struck once again. This time the deluge caused even greater damage. Waters rushing out of the nearby canyons resulted in "heavy damage" to a pipeline which had just been replaced since the disaster of the previous week. "This time 200 feet washed out," observers noted, "compared to 60 before." Monroe Canyon roads were washed away by the rapidly moving floodwaters. The farmland south of Monroe "received an additional covering of mud and debris."[56]

This same August storm also wreaked havoc upon Richfield. The downpour nearly resulted in a loss of life when floodwaters pouring from nearby canyons overtook a fleeing family in a farm wagon. "The occupants of the wagon had a narrow escape," it was reported. Eleven days later a torrent of water from Flat Canyon west of Richfield discharged sand and rubble throughout the Richfield area. The streets in the northern part of the city were filled with water and mud. Floods continued to worry the people of the county through the 1940s.[57]

Due to the success of President Roosevelt's New Deal programs, the once eagerly anticipated glass factory, which had seemingly died nine years earlier, sprang to life again in the fall of 1938. The *Richfield Reaper* alerted the public to this new development with the following news:

> Renewed hope that Richfield may yet have the plate glass factory which has been considered, is inspired by the announcement in the Salt Lake papers recently to the effect that the Western Plate Glass Co. has filed application with the state securities commission to sell stock for a factory to be located in Richfield, Utah.[58]

By 1938, the financial crisis had all but run its course and Western Plate Glass seemed ready to move forward. The company intended to manufacture 6.1 million square feet of plate glass annually at the envisioned Richfield plant. O.U. Metcalf, director of the company, was reported by the *Reaper* to have "been in Richfield a number of times just recently." Sevier County's abundant supply of the natural resources required for glass production—gypsum, silica, and salt—had attracted the eastern corporation to Richfield. "It is this fact," said Dr. T.R. Gledhill, "and this alone which is bringing this glass factory to Richfield." There was no large plate glass factory west of the Mississippi River, reported the *Richfield Reaper*. Since it cost $2.20 a ton in freight charges to transport the necessary raw materials to the company's plant near Pittsburgh, Pennsylvania, Western Plate Glass had decided to build a plant nearer to the resources. It was estimated that in Sevier County the required silica could be mined and shipped to the plant for under $2.00 per ton.[59]

The anticipated economic benefits that the county could hope to derive from the glass factory were great. The construction of the new

100-acre plant would employ scores of local men. Mining the natural resources would permanently employ many more. It was anticipated that $5 million would be expended on construction and employment within Sevier County.[60] In the wake of the worst economic downturn in the nation's history, this was, indeed, a rosy picture for county residents to envision.

Further agreement on the use of Sevier River irrigation water was reached in 1938. A pact between Sevier, Piute, and Garfield counties was signed which, the newspaper reported, "may be considered the end of the [water] difficulties which have for years confronted the users along the river." Irrigation companies from Joseph, Monroe, Elsinore, Richfield, and Annabella, now legally known as the "Miscellaneous Sevier Valley Morse Decree Users," would be "entitled to the [full] use of the waters decreed to them and their predecessors." From 15 April to 15 October "in each and every year, to the extent that the water is hereafter available in the Sevier river . . . they shall have the right to the use of the same during said period of time by direct diversion or by storing the same or any part thereof."[61] Those farmers in the southern portion of the county, who enjoyed the spring runoff first, could not store water until October. The Sevier Valley Canal Company, located in the northern portion of the valley, received the Sevier's flow last, but it enjoyed the privilege of diversion and/or storage during the first fifteen days in April when the river's flow generally was the greatest. Additionally, those companies which supplied water for culinary use and stock watering "shall only be entitled to such quantity as is reasonable for said purposes."[62]

As the Great Depression was weakening in 1939, Arch McKinlay and his son, O.R. (Bob), purchased Martinez Motors, which had started doing business in Richfield in 1916, renamed it McKinlay Chevrolet, and began selling cars in Sevier County. Six years after the McKinlays opened their dealership, Chevrolet introduced a sports car, the Corvette. However, with a price tag around $1,800, no Corvettes were sold in Sevier County at that time. Along with McKinlay Chevrolet, Richfield was also the home during the Depression and war years of 1930 to 1945 to Whiting Motors, a Buick and GMC dealer, and Pearsons, which sold Pontiacs, Cadillacs, and Ramblers.[63]

Richfield Business District, February 1938. (Utah State Historical Society)

By 1938, old political loyalties appeared to be making a comeback. One Democratic commission candidate, W.W. Sylvester, defeated Republican Lawrence W. Jones by only two votes (2,604 to 2,602); in the other race, Republican Ray H. Buchanan beat his Democratic rival by 600 votes. From that point on the return to a traditional Republican majority in the county was all but complete. In 1940, although Franklin D. Roosevelt was elected to an unprecedented third term and received a large majority of votes in Utah, Republican challenger Wendell Wilkie outpolled him 2,695 to 2,500 votes in Sevier County. Incumbent Democratic Senator Abe Murdock did slightly outpoll his Republican challenger, Philo T, Farnsworth, by thirty votes. In 1944, although Roosevelt won a fourth term, he was again outvoted in Sevier County by his Republican challenger, Thomas Dewey, 2,401 votes to 2,163. All other Republican nominees for major offices also received a majority of votes in Sevier County, although all lost in their statewide races.[64]

Water continued as one of the county's most valued yet difficult resources to manage. It seemed that either there was too little or there was too much. In the latter instance, flooding, usually short in duration, had created serious problems in various communities, especially on the east side of the county. The people of Salina, Monroe, and Annabella especially had periodically witnessed flood damage to their communities. Due to the work of the CCC and other New Deal projects to control runoff, flooding after the 1930s was generally a result of brief but violent summer thunderstorms.

In late July 1939 flooding of Monroe, Main, and Sand canyons caused damage to roads and private property; south of Annabella, flood waters washed out part of the local canal.[65] Four years later, almost to the day, a sudden summer thunderstorm flooded parts of Monroe and the city cemetery, causing an estimated $80,000 in damage. On 5 August 1943 a second thunderstorm caused even more damage, this time an estimated $120,000 in damages, leaving the city of Monroe without electricity for two weeks.[66]

Having fought the local battle over the construction of a new hospital, within the next decade Sevier County residents, along with the rest of the nation's citizens, would fight more deadly enemies during the Second World War. The first allusions to the imminent world war started to appear in the *Richfield Reaper* in 1939. At that time, the newspaper started publishing a syndicated series from the Western Newspaper Union called "Weekly News Analysis by Henry R. Porter." The first installment was on the mounting crisis in Poland. "In a desperate effort to avert the holocaust of war which threatens to engulf Europe," the summary began, "President Roosevelt appealed directly to Chancellor Adolf Hitler of Germany . . . to refrain from hostilities for a 'reasonable and stipulated period' and attempt to settle their difficulties" through negotiation.[67]

But to the horror of the world, Hitler would not talk. The headline of the next report from Porter stunned many county residents: "Germany Opens War on Poland."[68] This occurred on 1 September 1939, just two days after President Roosevelt's appeal for peace. Apprehensive residents of Sevier County and the rest of Utah began to fear that the United States would become involved in war; and, in fact, within two years the United States would become entangled in a war not only with Germany but also with Japan.

Although he had already served two terms as president, Franklin D. Roosevelt chose to break with American tradition and seek a third term in 1940, believing that the increasingly ominous worldwide situation demanded a continuation of his leadership. Again the people of the country voted to return him to the White House. In the 1940 presidential election, county voters opposed Roosevelt's bid for another term, casting the majority of their votes for Republican Wendell Wilkie. Sevier County voters also went against the political current in the nation and in the state in the 1944 presidential elections: in Utah, Roosevelt received 150,088 votes and Thomas Dewey garnered 97,891; in Sevier County, Dewey received 2,401 votes to Roosevelt's 2,163.

An account of the human impact of the Second World War upon the south-central region of Utah can be illustrated through the recollections of local people. Betty Olsen Erickson of Venice recalled the feeling that the bombing of Pearl Harbor on 7 December 1941 brought: "I remember this Sunday night at seven o'clock. The radio announcer broke into the regular program and said, 'Pearl Harbor has just been bombed by the Japanese.' We were all in shock."[69]

Four days later, the weekly *Richfield Reaper,* in announcing the attack, wrote of "treachery in the Pacific." Summing up the events of the past several days, the paper communicated emotions which must have been almost universally felt across Sevier County and the United States:

> Into this community, as into every other community in America, there has stalked the grim visage of war and there has come a sense of direct and kindred loss as those ties that know no bounds of time or space link all America to the men whose lives were lost at the hands of treachery last Sunday.[70]

The *Richfield Reaper* went on to notify Sevier citizens that by a joint resolution of the Senate and the House "the state of war between the United States and the imperial Japanese government . . . is hereby formally declared."

Pearl Harbor brought great personal tragedy to two young men from Monroe, Keith Taylor and Dean Larsen. Taylor, an anti-aircraft gunner on the *USS West Virginia,* was killed when the Japanese

The Utah National Guard Armory in Richfield, October 1947. (Utah State Historical Society)

attacked on 7 December 1941. Twenty-five-year-old Dean Larsen of Monroe was a musician who was also aboard the *West Virginia* when it was sunk. Larsen was first listed as "missing-in-action."[71]

Gus Erickson remembered those unsettling days of early December 1941, stating, "We knew we'd be in a war which we'd been hoping to avoid." Nevertheless, the local people rallied to the cause. Erickson depicted the scene at Venice as one of "flag waving" and other "gallant things." He felt nervous, but willing, about going off to fight. "I think everyone was hoping against hope that something would come up and we wouldn't have to go," he said.[72] In March 1942 Gus Erickson joined the Marine Corps and within days was on his way to San Diego for boot camp.

During the course of the war, Erickson saw action at Tulagi, near Guadalcanal, in the Solomon Islands. As the Marines were preparing to land on the morning of 7 August 1942, the U.S. Navy was shelling the island. Erickson reported that "you could actually see the shells flying through the air." They found the landing on Tulagi "fairly easy." The ease which Erickson and his comrades experienced may have been due to the fact that the Japanese on the island were surprised by the Marine assault.[73]

Gus Erickson later served on Guadalcanal, where he experienced heavy enemy shelling, which he later recalled as feeling like he was "being hit on the helmet with a hammer."[74] This experience left a lasting impact upon him. For years later, after he and his wife, Betty, were married, she reported that "when I would go up to him and touch him or he would get kicked in the middle of the night, he would react as though he were in battle again."[75]

By the spring of 1942, Sevier County men were either volunteering for service or being inducted into the military. On 10 April 1942 an article in the *Reaper* reported: "Another Group of Selectees Will Leave Soon for U.S. Army." The names of the fifteen men slated for conscription in May were published in the newspaper. Some 1,200 men from Sevier County were inducted into the service during the war years.[76]

County citizens supported the war effort through rationing programs and war bond drives. The Richfield Culture Club, founded in 1939, was one of many county groups and school classes especially active in the various war bond purchase campaigns over the years. Betty Erickson remembered life on the home front in Sevier County:

> [W]e were doing all we possibly could in order to support these guys. . . . I remember that they let school out early in April to make it so that the kids that were still home could get out and work in the fields with their dads to raise more food for the war effort. The war effort was the main thing.[77]

She said that on the home front they rationed gasoline, meat, sugar, and various other items. "The girls didn't have stockings because that was before nylons came," she recalled, "so we all went bare legged," since silk came from the Orient.

Wilford J. Barney, Jr., of Richfield tried to go directly into the military as soon as he graduated from high school in 1943. But he was blind in his right eye, so the draft board initially rejected him. But Barney was determined to serve. After several more tries, he found a recruitment officer who, when challenged by Barney to a shooting match to prove he could do the job, told him that if he wanted to go that badly he would let him in.[78]

Wilford Barney originally was enlisted as a clerk typist, but he later volunteered for a special, dangerous assignment. Barney was selected to be a part of the first wave to land at Normandy on D-Day (6 June 1944). Once in France he was assigned to guard German prisoners of war. For more than twenty years after the war's end he continued to correspond with one of the prisoners.[79]

The war also provided some unexpected reunions for Sevier County soldiers. On the Pacific island of Okinawa, brothers Gordon and Leland Duffin of Richfield, along with Leo Brienholt of Venice, discovered one another. Gordon, a marine second lieutenant, and Leland, a sergeant in the army, had not seen each other for nearly three years. They, along with Brienholt, were reported to have had "a wonderful reunion" in the midst of the war.[80] For the marines, Okinawa was a costly campaign—more than 35,000 soldiers killed or wounded.[81]

War brought death. By the summer of 1943, as some of Sevier County's finest young men fell victim to war, the need of local activities such as the "Victory Corps" to boost morale was great. One war tragedy was that of Captain LeGrande Frank of Richfield, who died in a Japanese prison camp. Before being called into active service by the Army Reserve in September 1940, LeGrande Frank had served as bishop of the Richfield LDS Second Ward. At the outbreak of war in 1941 Captain Frank was stationed in the Philippines. He took part in the famous siege of Bataan and was probably captured by the Japanese when they overwhelmed the U.S. forces at Bataan early in 1942. Captain Frank had been listed as "missing in action" for more than a year before word of his death arrived back home to his wife, the former Ruth Ence, who had not received a letter from him for nearly one year.[82]

The same edition of the *Richfield Reaper* which bore the news of LeGrande Frank's death carried an advertisement which gave a glimpse of the growing animosity and even racial hatred that was sweeping the county. The ad, probably produced by the federal government and captioned "SPEAK JAPANESE," told readers:

Tell them slant-eyes in the only language they understand—the language of shells and bullets! You can do it—by turning in used cooking grease for gunpowder. Rationing needn't stop you. The government doesn't want your fats until all cooking good is gone. Then, every drop is desperately needed. Just one tablespoon full will fire five machine gun bullets. Even with rationing you can save at least that much every day. Rush each canfull to your nearest dealer.[83]

Each edition of the *Reaper* from 1943 until the war's end carried a column of the front page entitled "Fightin' Talk." The apparent goal of the section was to offer positive news from the war fronts regarding the activities of the local men. For example, the 17 June 1943 edition told Sevier County readers that Private Billy Carter, then stationed at Camp Cook, California, had received a medal honoring his marksmanship and that Chester L. Fuellendbach of the U.S. Navy had left for "overseas duty." It even told about the sons of Mr. and Mrs. E.E. Thurston, "former residents of Richfield." Readers were informed that Ivan Thurston, a sergeant, was serving with the Army Air Corps in North Africa, while Kimball Thurston, a first lieutenant, was stationed in Iran.[84] Reports on the county's soldiers were solicited by the newspaper's reporters from the families and friends of the men.

The impact which the war was having locally escalated with time. In June 1945, when the war was almost over and the fighting was very intense, the sad news of two more battle deaths was printed in the *Richfield Reaper*. One of the dead was Pfc. Wayne De Leeuw of neighboring Wayne County. He had heroically "crawled out of his fox hole to help an injured comrade" when he was killed fighting in Germany in April 1945. Funeral services were also held for Second Lieutenant Alden Fillmore of Richfield in the Sevier LDS Stake Tabernacle during June 1945.[85]

A national wartime activity which was eagerly adopted in Sevier County was the "Victory Corps." The purpose of this program was "to bring the high schools of the nation into the war effort and provide a program whereby they may contribute their full share to the cause of democracy." A Richfield High School War Council was launched in December 1942, and the paper reported that the goal of this council was to "make all conscious that we are engaged in a war

Some of the 250 German prisoners of war sent to Sevier County in 1945 to work in the sugar beet fields. (Courtesy Shirley Probert)

for survival." The war council hoped to establish favorable attitudes among high school students toward military needs.[86]

Wartime brought a sense of excitement as well as of tragedy to county citizens. On 8 April 1943 the *Richfield Reaper* declared that a simulated air raid was to occur the following Monday: "At 12:00 noon on Monday April 12, Civil Air Patrol planes will fly over the business district dropping leaflet shaped bombs," the newspaper announced. This "action" was to promote the upcoming "Liberty Loan" war-bond sale. The following week the newspaper reported that the "raid" had been a great success. "Under the direction of the Civil Air Patrol," reported the *Reaper,* "Richfield along with nine other Utah cities staged a mock air raid . . . furnishing a sensational start for the April $50,000,000 war bond drive."[87]

Salina got an even closer look at the war beginning in June 1945 when 250 German prisoners of war (POWs) were sent to the community to aid farmers with the sugar-beet harvest and to perform other agricultural work on local farms. This camp was one of twelve across Utah. The Beehive State became the temporary home for more than 8,000 German POWs between January 1944 and June 1946. The Salina prisoners had been sent north from a POW camp at Florence, Arizona.[88]

Tragically, the Salina situation turned to one of trouble. Shortly after midnight on the 9 July 1945 many of the town's 2,000 residents were awakened by the sound of gunfire. Had the POWs overpowered their army guards at the old CCC camp east of Salina's Main Street? some wondered. It was well known that the internees were experienced veterans of North African and European battlefields. It was not, however, the prisoners who were doing the shooting; it was an American guard.[89] Private First Class Clarence V. Bertucci of New Orleans opened fire with a 30-caliber machine gun on the tents of the sleeping prisoners. Six Germans were killed at the scene, three others died later of their wounds. The attack drew national and international attention to Salina.[90]

Whether one was concerned about the future due to the horrors of war, had suffered the loss of a loved one on the battlefield, or just longed for peacetime, certainly all residents of Sevier County were elated by the news in August 1945 that at last the war was over. While the Germans had surrendered in May 1945, the war with Japan dragged on for three more months. The joy felt locally at the cessation of hostilities was recorded in the *Richfield Reaper*:

> When the news that Japan had accepted the peace terms offered by the United Nations came over the air at 5 P.M. on Tuesday, it was raining in Richfield but that did not seem to dampen the spirits of anyone so the weather man soon gave up and let the people have their fun.[91]

In "nothing flat" the joyous word was said to be all over town, and much of the city's population was celebrating on Main Street. When the men and women of the armed forces finally returned home, the local newspaper claimed, "the celebration will really be complete." More than 1,200 Sevier County men served in the military during World War II. Twenty deaths were reported from this group.[92]

After the war's end, the "Fightin' Talk" newspaper column was replaced by "Peace Talk," a similar update on men in the armed forces. But now, of course, the news was generally better.[93]

Postwar Sevier County was a beehive of activity, what with the revived economy and the cessation of hostilities. It seemed that Franklin D. Roosevelt's depression-era maxim, "Happy Days Are Here Again," was more true in 1945 than at any other time since the 1920s. Prosperity had come once more to Sevier County. Worries over loved ones fighting far from home were gone. A return to life as it had been so long ago was desired more than ever.

An advertisement appearing in the *Richfield Reaper* early in September 1945, likely the creation of local businessmen, stated in no uncertain terms that it was now time to resume life as it had been before the war—it was time to reap the rewards of wartime sacrifices. "Farmers want new machinery; housewives want washers, refrigerators," read the advertisement. The notice claimed that Mr. and Mrs. John Q. Public wanted a new car and a new radio.[94]

The wartime Office of Price Administration (OPA) was now targeted. The OPA had been created in 1941 as a wing of the War Productions Board, whose duty it was to closely scrutinize all manufacturing and sales in wartime America. It had been OPA quotas which made life on the home front more difficult for many Americans. By the fall of 1945, with the war over and better times on the horizon, many Americans, including people of Sevier County, saw no further need of the OPA. For the sake of the war effort, merchants had tolerated the price ceiling of 30 percent above 1939 prices and rationing. Now that the conflict was over, why allow the restrictions to continue? Speaking of the Office of Price Administration's actions, this Richfield advertisement blasted the OPA: "Created to maintain necessary price control in wartime, it refuses to recognize the practicalities of peace."[95]

Wartime price controls on civilian goods remained in place even after the formal surrender of Japan on 2 September 1945. Neither the nation's businesses nor consumers in Sevier County were happy with President Harry Truman's policy to maintain the system of price controls; however, President Truman and others were fearful that inflation would create an unstable economy, similar to economic conditions which followed World War I. Political pressure mounted on President Truman and Congress to remove price controls, and by the end of 1946 price controls on all consumer items except rents, sugar, and rice were lifted.

At Richfield in July 1945 construction started on the Dixon Packing Company's new meat-packing plant. This $50,000 factory, being built just south of the Sevier County Fairgrounds, was expected, upon completion, to process up to two hundred head of lambs, pigs, or beef weekly. According to its directors, who were all Utahns, "the new meat processing plant will fill a need that has long existed in Sevier County to process for market animals that have been grown and fattened locally."[96] This local economic development generated a great deal of pride among county residents.

Farther to the north, Salina was able to attract a turkey-processing plant in 1946 that was moved from Richfield, where it had opened in 1938. This became the start of a major industry for Salina. In April 1948 announcement was made of the Salina Lions Club's efforts "to induce industrial leaders to investigate their community." Besides being one of the nation's leading shipping points for range cattle, it was observed that Salina is "on three major highways, is served by a major railroad and has a modern airfield under construction."[97]

The Lions Club's efforts to promote the Salina airport were somewhat weakened by plans in 1946 for a new Richfield airport. In 1946, the Salina airport, later changed to the Salina-Gunnison airport, received a Class-1 classification by the state and was listed as a landing field. During the next several years, the state, using funds received from the Civil Aeronautics Administration, made improvements to the airport, grading the landing strip and making other improvements.[98]

The war's end brought other changes to life in Sevier County. "Because of the lifting of gas rationing," the *Richfield Reaper* announced, "the Sevier stake presidency in cooperation with the stake auxiliary boards has planned a stake Union meeting."[99] A complete schedule of LDS stake priesthood and leadership meetings commenced once more in September 1945. Such had not happened in quite some time as people from outlying communities simply could not afford to use their rationed gas during the war years for such activities.

At the end of the war, the Produce and Marketing Administration took over the duties which until 20 August 1945 had fallen under the auspices of the old Agricultural Adjustment Administration (AAA). This new agricultural agency was intended, just like the AAA, to oversee farm loans, crop insurance, and subsidy payments to farmers. The federal government did not want to see America's farmers slip back into the quandary they had faced in the 1930s.

An August 1945 headline in the *Richfield Reaper* which certainly caught readers' attention announced "Higher Taxes for Sevier County." Taxation always had been a testy issue in the county, as elsewhere, and had been especially disliked by many since the 1930s. This particular property tax increase was to fund school expenditures. As Sevier County Clerk J.L. Despain explained, the "Sevier county schools upped the levy from 13.5 to 14.5 mills, [while] the state school levy jumped 1.10 mills." It was, Despain argued, the actions of the Utah State Tax Commission in raising real estate values in Sevier County by 10 percent which really forced this local tax increase, over the protests of the Sevier County Commissioners.[100] County residents had to grudgingly face the fact that growth and increased or improved services still had to be paid for.

In April 1946, arrangements for "a new airport to be constructed in a new location about 2 miles east of Richfield on the Glenwood road" had been finalized by city officials.[101] The new airport was to be constructed through the cooperative involvement of Richfield City, the state of Utah, and the federal government. The location was chosen after several months of study. After taking into account "air currents and the proximity of the natural hazards of the surrounding mountains," it was determined that this site was the only feasible one available. The new field reportedly would be "capable of handling not only mainline passenger service, but also heavier transport planes for freight traffic." A sidebar story announced that Western Air Lines had been authorized to stop at Richfield. The Sevier County community was to serve as "an intermediate point on the Salt Lake–Las Vegas–Los Angeles route along with Cedar City and St. George." This new air link, "with fast mail, express and passenger service," would help to mark Richfield as a commercial center and regional hub. The airport was built; however, the greatly expanded Salt Lake City

Part of the wagon train commemorating Richfield's centennial of settlement in 1964. (Utah State Historical Society)

International Airport and the growth of Cedar City and St. George have dimmed the dream of making Richfield a commercial and regional hub for air service. Use has been mainly for local passenger and freight service.

In January 1947 the Richfield Chamber of Commerce was organized to promote the area. Later that year, the county's first radio broadcasting station—KSVC—was started. Also in 1947, on 30 October, area Catholics dedicated St. Elizabeth's Catholic Church in Richfield. The structure filled a long-held dream of the region's Catholics to have a formal place of worship. The first services were conducted by the Reverend Leo Halloran, who served until his death in 1950.[102]

In 1947, as well, Sevier County began to lay plans to celebrate the Utah Mormon pioneer centennial with the publication of a "Centennial History of Sevier County." A local committee led by Sevier LDS Stake President Irvin L. Warnock and his wife, along with Mr. and Mrs Arthur C. Lundgren and A.C. Willardsen, mayor of Salina, took the lead in organizing the county's celebration. It was contemplated that 2,000 volumes would be printed. Prospective purchasers were advised to subscribe for the book early.[103]

The local camp of the Daughters of Utah Pioneers pledged its support to the county's centennial committee. According to the *Richfield Reaper,* the volume would be "an invaluable source of factual information." It was to contain the early (pioneer) history of the county; a short history of each town; lists of all war veterans from the Spanish American War through World War II; and a listing of all city and county officers with pictures. The final product, *Thru the Years: A Centennial History of Sevier County,* edited by Irvin L. Warnock, was published in December 1947. As promised, it was "chock full of interesting stories."[104]

Warnock's career as a historian was far from over. In 1948 the Sevier LDS Stake decided to organize a homecoming to celebrate the stake's seventy-fifth anniversary on 24 May 1949. Stake President and Mrs. Irvin L. Warnock were placed in charge of the event. About 2,000 invitations were sent to former members of the stake, inviting them to participate in the celebration. To commemorate this anniversary, the Warnocks co-authored *Memories of the Sevier Stake,* published in 1949.

Human tragedy struck Richfield, Annabella, and Sevier County twice within two weeks during the spring of 1948. On 4 March, Richfield's mayor, Howard B. Mendenhall, who had been elected one year before, was killed instantly when a train struck his car. Then, on 18 March, Sevier County Attorney D.C. Winget, along with Annabella town councilman Reed Watson, died in a plane crash near Levan in Sanpete County. On 1 April, Norman Holt was sworn in as Richfield's mayor to fill the unexpired term of Mendenhall.[105]

On a lighter front, in January 1948 Richfield's young women were offered the chance to attend a charm school, "something new for Richfield." The school's operator, Frances Peterson, planned to

The Western Gypsum Company at Sigurd. (Utah State Historical Society)

offer instruction in "the many phases of charm that are so necessary in each girl's life." Mrs. Peterson would also offer the girls direction in poise, posture, how to apply make-up, the care of the skin, and several other feminine concerns. According to the instructor, charm will help young women in the business world as well as in "regular life."[106] Such an addition to the local scene speaks loudly about the rapidly changing world of Sevier County and about the evolving roles of women in the United States.

Other items in the *Reaper* reflected the tumultuous postwar world. In May 1948 *Deseret News* correspondent Vivian Meik spoke to the people of Richfield about the dangers of communism. Meik told listeners that "the international communistic movement was continuing and unrelenting in its drive to force capitalism into decay."[107] Soviet communism came to be viewed with trepidation across much of the United States during the next decade, and Meik likely did much to escalate this worry among Sevier County's residents.

Industrial expansion was taking place throughout Sevier County during the postwar years. The Western Gypsum Company opened a new facility at Sigurd in 1948. The plant, said to be "one of the most modern and one of the largest integrated plants of its kind in the country," represented the county's largest industrial enterprise to date. The gypsum company promised to provide "a steady pay roll in the future." Speculation suggested that nearly five hundred tons of rock per day would be removed from the Sigurd site.[108]

The Sigurd deposit of gypsum was one of the world's finest, and the word about Sevier County's abundant natural resources was getting out. The following month, United States Gypsum Company moved to Sigurd to also mine and package the chalklike mineral used for plaster of paris and plaster board. Home building was soaring in post–World War II America as suburbs began to spring up all over the nation, making plaster (with its required gypsum component) in great demand. The editor of the *Richfield Reaper* along with the citizens of Sigurd and Sevier County realized quickly that with two competing plaster companies at Sigurd, "the economy of Sevier valley should be greatly improved."[109]

County voters displayed their displeasure in part with Truman's and the Democrats' policy of government managing the economy during peacetime. In 1948, county voters rejected President Truman's bid for election. The county tally for Truman was 1,943 as contrasted with 2,791 votes for Republican nominee Thomas Dewey; Utahns in 1948 voted 149,151 for Truman, while Dewey received 124,402 votes.

By 1949 Sevier County displayed a sound economy and was optimistic about future industrial growth. New industries, such as Sigurd's gypsum mines and plaster-manufacturing concerns, gave Sevier County a sense of vibrancy. The people of the county had faced economic calamity as well as human tragedy during years of depression and war. Yet, after all of the trials, the residents of Sevier County, like most of their fellow Utahns and other Americans, looked hopefully toward the future.

ENDNOTES

1. *Richfield Reaper,* 4 December 1930, 1.

2. *Richfield Reaper,* 11 December 1930, 1.

3. Charles S. Peterson, *Utah: A History* (New York: W.W. Norton & Company, 1977), 149.

4. Sevier County Treasurer, Tax Sale Records, microfilm no. 014031, Utah State Archives.

5. Ibid.

6. Ibid., microfilm no. 014034.

7. William Bliss Daniels, interview, 21, typescript, LDS Archives.

8. *Richfield Reaper,* 2 October 1930, 2.

9. Dean L. May, *Utah: A People's History,* (Salt Lake City: University of Utah Press, 1987), 173.

10. Peterson, *Utah,* 175.

11. *Richfield Reaper,* 12 October 1930, 8.

12. Wilford Murdock and Mildred Murdock, *Monroe, Utah: Its First One Hundred Years* (Monroe: Monroe Centennial Committe, 1964), 37.

13. Liela Oldroyd, interview by David Oldroyd, 24 March 1988, copy at Richfield City Library.

14. *Richfield Reaper,* 12 October 1930, 8.

15. Ibid.

16. Dan E. Jones, "Utah Politics, 1926–1932" (Ph.D. diss., University of Utah, 1968), 305, 306.

17. Ibid., 309.

18. "Biennial Report of the Secretary of State," *Public Documents, 1936* 3 vols. (Salt Lake City: State of Utah, 1936), 3:30, copy at the Utah State Historical Society.

19. *Richfield Reaper,* 25 December 1930, 1.

20. See Minute Book A, Sevier County Clerk's Office, 1 December 1930, 543, Utah State Archives.

21. Alten Christensen, interview by Alan Thompson, 5 January 1988, copy at Richfield City Library.

22. Mike Brown, "The Automobile Industry in Sevier County," 4, paper, 1988, copy at Richfield City Library.

23. William Manchester, *The Glory and the Dream: A Narrative History of America, 1932–1972,* 2 vols. (Boston: Little, Brown and Company, 1973), 1:104.

24. *Richfield Reaper,* 31 August 1933, 1.

25. Kenneth W. Baldridge, "Nine Years of Achievement: The Civilian Conservation Corps in Utah" (Ph.D. diss., Brigham Young University, 1971), 23, 81.

26. Ibid., 47.

27. *Richfield Reaper* 5 October 1933, 1; 12 October 1933, 1.

28. Oldroyd, interview, 3.

29. *Richfield Reaper,* 15 October 1936, 6.

30. *Richfield Reaper,* 19 October 1933, 1.

31. *Richfield Reaper,* 26 October 1933, 1.

32. Ibid.

33. Manchester, *The Glory and the Dream,* 1:102–3.

34. *Richfield Reaper,* 28 December 1933, 1, 6.

35. *Richfield Reaper,* 5 April 1934, 1.

36. *Richfield Reaper,* 6 November 1933, 6.

37. *Richfield Reaper,* 7 December 1933, 1.

38. Ibid.; and 14 December 1933, 1.

39. Sevier County Ordinance Register, 13 May 1932, 63; and 22 July 1932, 66.

40. *Richfield Reaper,* 9 November 1933, 1.

41. *Richfield Reaper,* 18 January 1934, 1.

42. Ibid.

43. Ibid.

44. *Richfield Reaper,* 16 November 1933.

45. *Richfield Reaper,* 23 November 1933, 1.

46. Ibid.

47. *Richfield Reaper,* 1 March 1934, 1.

48. Quoted in Vicky Burgess-Olson, *Sister Saints* (Provo: Brigham Young University Press, 1978), 408.

49. *Richfield Reaper,* 29 November 1936.

50. *Richfield Reaper,* 1 March 1934.

51. D.C. Houston, and Rey M. Hill, *Health Conditions and Facilities in Utah, 1936* (Salt Lake City: Utah State Planning Board, 1936), 89.

52. Pearl F. Jacobson, compiler and editor, et al., *Golden Sheaves from a Rich Field: A Centennial History of Richfield, Utah* (Richfield, Utah: Richfield Reaper Publishing Company, 1964), 115, 120; Houston and Hill, *Health Conditions and Facilities in Utah,* 99. This study indicates that in 1930 there were seven physicians in the county. Those seven physicians provided medical care to 11,199 residents. Daggett County had no physicians and Wayne, Rich, and Grand counties had one physician each. In 1935 the county had six dentists, one of the higher number of dentists in the rural counties in the state.

53. *Statistical Summary of Expenditures and Accomplishments, Utah Emergency Relief Program* (Salt Lake City: Utah State Advisory Committee on Public Welfare and Emergency Relief, 1936), 6, copy at Utah State Historical Society.

54. Ibid., 8. The highest per capita was Tooele County, which received $92.33; the lowest was Box Elder County, which received $37.20 per individual. Of all the counties, Tooele experienced the most severe drought in Utah during this period.

55. Max R. Keetch, comp., *Sevier River Basin Floods, 1852–1967* (Salt Lake City: United States Department of Agriculture, Economic Research Service, U.S. Forest Service, U.S. Soil Conservation Service, 1971), 80, copy at Utah State Historical Society Library.

56. Ibid., 81.

57. Ibid., 80–81, 87–88.

58. *Richfield Reaper,* 23 October 1938, 1.

59. Ibid.

60. Ibid.

61. Ibid.

62. Ibid., 4.

63. Ibid., 3–4; O.R. McKinlay, interview by Dave Brown, 6 January 1988; Sylvester, "Business History of Richfield, Utah," 247.

64. "Report of the Secretary of State," *Public Documents, 1938,* 3:33; "Report of the Secretary of State," *Public Documents, 1950* 3: 26; copies at Utah State Historical Society.

65. See *Richfield Reaper,* 3 August 1939; and Butler and Marsell, "Developing a State Water Plan," 51.

66. Butler and Marsell, "Developing a State Water Plan," 55.

67. *Richfield Reaper,* 31 August 1939, 6.

68. *Richfield Reaper,* 7 September 1939, 6.

69. Betty Olson Erickson, interview by Ryan L. Stone, 27 March 1988, Venice , Utah, 1, copy at Richfield City Library.

70. *Richfield Reaper,* 11 December 1941, 1.

71. Ibid.; and 25 December 1941, 8. By December 1941 Larsen's family was living in Logan, so no follow-up information was ever published in the *Reaper.* In Irvin L. Warnock, compiler and editor, *Thru the Years: Sevier County Centennial History* (Springville, Utah: Art City Publishing Co., 1947), 241, Larsen is listed as killed in action.

72. Eric Gustive Erickson, interview by Ryan L. Stone, 27 March 1988, 2, copy at Richfield City Library.

73. Ibid., 5; regarding the invasion of Tulagi, see Thomas B. Allen and Norman Polmar, *Code-Name Downfall: The Secret Plan to Invade Japan and Why Truman Dropped the Bomb* (New York: Simon & Schuster, 1995), 51–52.

74. Eric Erickson, interview, 5–6.

75. Betty Erickson, interview, 14–15.

76. *Richfield Reaper,* 10 April 1942, 1; Warnock, *Thru the Years,* 58.

77. Betty Erickson, interview, 17.

78. Jeffery Nielson, "World War II Comes to Rural Utah," 2, paper, 16 January 1989, copy at Richfield City Library.

79. Ibid., 3.

80. *Richfield Reaper,* 14 June 1945, 5.

81. Allen and Polmar, *Code-Name Downfall,* 110.

82. *Richfield Reaper,* 17 June 1943, 1.

83. Ibid., 6.

84. *Richfield Reaper,* 24 June 1943, 1.

85. *Richfield Reaper,* 14 June 1945, 5.

86. *Richfield Reaper,* 24 December 1942, 1.

87. *Richfield Reaper,* 8 April 1943, 1; 15 April 1943, 1.

88. Allan Kent Powell, *Splinters of a Nation: German Prisoners of War in Utah* (Salt Lake City: University of Utah Press, 1989), 223–39.

89. Ibid., 223–24.

90. Ibid., 2.

91. *Richfield Reaper,* 16 August 1945, 1.

92. Warnock, *Thru the Years,* 58.

93. The final column of "Fightin' Talk" had appeared in the *Richfield Reaper* on 9 August 1945.

94. *Richfield Reaper,* 6 September 1945, 2.

95. Ibid.

96. *Richfield Reaper,* 14 July 1945, 1.

97. See Warnock, *Thru the Years,* 401; Jacobson, *Golden Sheaves,* 278; *Richfield Reaper,* 19 February 1948, 11.

98. "Fifth Biennial Report of the Utah State Aeronautics Commission, 1945–1946," in *State of Utah Public Documents,* 1944–1946, Part 3, 12, and "Seventh Biennial Report of the Utah State Aeronautics Commission, 1949–1950," in *State of Utah Public Documents,* 1948–1950, Part 1, 21, Utah State Historical Society.

99. *Richfield Reaper,* 20 September 1945, 7.

100. *Richfield Reaper,* 13 September 1945, 1.

101. *Richfield Reaper,* 4 April 1946. 1.

102. Jacobson, *Golden Sheaves,* 73.

103. *Richfield Reaper,* 16 January 1947, 1.

104. *Richfield Reaper,* 25 December 1947, 1.

105. *Richfield Reaper,* 11 March 1948, 1; 18 March 1948, 1; 1 April 1948, 1.

106. *Richfield Reaper,* 28 January 1948, 7.

107. *Richfield Reaper,* 13 May 1948, 1.

108. *Richfield Reaper,* 15 April 1948, 1.

109. *Richfield Reaper,* 6 May 1948, 1.

7

# CONFRONTING A NEW WORLD: SEVIER COUNTY, 1950–1975

In 1950 the census showed that there were 12,072 people in Sevier County, down slightly from the 12,112 of 1940. These figures seem to indicate that there was basic stability in the county. A closer examination, however, reveals that the rural sections of the county had lost some people; Richfield had grown by more than 600 people during the decade—from 3,584 in 1940 to 4,212 in 1950. Businessmen and civic boosters hoped to continue the growth of the more urban areas, as Americans in general were looking to enjoy post-war prosperity. Nationally, the economy was vibrant. Locally, Republican conservatives were backed by most of the county's residents. Private enterprise was primed to take over from the New Deal. By 1950, with Roosevelt dead and World War II over, the Republican county commission candidates, Edwin Sorensen and Lawrence W. Jones, were unopposed. In 1952, Republicans Jones and Kendrick Harward ran unchallenged as well.[1]

The year 1950 and the dawning of a new decade saw the United States embroiled in another war, however, officially termed a "police action," on the other side of the globe against North Korea. Soldiers

213

again were called from Sevier County. As in 1917 and 1941, the Korean War again reminded the people of Sevier County that it was no longer possible to live an isolated life free of global concerns.

By 1949 United States foreign policy dictated that the spread of communism must be checked and not be allowed to spread beyond its current bounds. This policy, formulated in 1947 by state department foreign-policy adviser George F. Kennan, became known as "containment." By 1950 the North Korean communists were attempting to reunify their country, which had been arbitrarily divided at the 38th Parallel following World War II. On 25 June 1950 North Korean troops launched a surprise attack across this line into South Korea. The United Nations authorized a "police action" against the invaders. United States President Harry S. Truman acted boldly, moving to support the South Koreans. Within six weeks American reservists were involved in the conflict.

The 213th Field Artillery Battalion of the Utah National Guard, including Richfield's Battery A, was one of the units mobilized to fight in South Korea. The hometown newspaper was justifiably proud of the contributions of these local men. "To say that Southern Utah is particularly proud of the members of Battery A would only be a statement of fact which the *Reaper* is glad to emphasize," proclaimed the newspaper.[2] A local member of Battery A, Corporal Vincent D. Harding, was soon contributing articles to the *Reaper* from the battlefront. These reports were published under the same headline as that used during World War II, "Fightin' Talk."

Within two months, local soldiers had firsthand war experience. Shortly after arriving in Korea, while still supposedly behind the lines, some members of the 213th got their first taste of combat duty.[3] A month later, these same local soldiers were in fierce combat that won the praise of their commanding general. The *Richfield Reaper* reported in June 1951:

> Men of Southern Utah's 213th Armored Field Artillery Battalion, including Richfield's Battery "A," were cited today by their commanding general for acts of courage which they displayed in recent heavy fighting on the road to Kapyong.[4]

Specifically, the commendation noted that "large numbers of well armed Chinese [allies of the North Koreans] opened fire at close range on 'A' Battery of the 213th AFA Battalion." The Richfield men successfully repelled the attack with small-arms fire from their gun positions. Enemy troops were said to have been within twenty feet of overrunning their position when they were turned back.

Earlier, in September 1950, Colonel Joseph H. Buys of Richfield had earned the Bronze Star for "heroic achievement" in Korea. While Colonel Buys's command post was under heavy enemy fire, he had refused to withdraw. Instead, in total disregard of the intense hostile fire, "he went forward and personally reconnoitered the situation [where] he remained in an exposed position in order to better observe enemy disposition and supervise the supporting fire of his battalion."[5]

Near the end of the Korean hostilities, a Salina man, Infantry Sergeant Dan A. Burns, a much-decorated soldier, was honored for rescuing an American patrol from annihilation by enemy forces in Korea. Sergeant Burns's bravery occurred on 4 July 1953 when he offered to help save a patrol which was pinned down by heavy enemy fire. As a result of Burns's action, the entire patrol evacuated to safety. Another Salina soldier, Pfc. Don H. Nielson, received a Purple Heart for wounds received in November 1952. While recuperating in Tokyo, Private Nielson received an unexpected visit from movie actor Cary Grant.[6]

The Korean War was less costly in human life to Sevier County than the Second World War had been; still, county men were in heated combat in Korea, and eight were killed.[7] On 27 July 1953, an armistice, which actually satisfied no one, was agreed upon. North Korea lost limited territory, and a new boundary between North and South Korea was drawn at the 38th Parallel. Communism continued in power in the north while the U.S.-supported government remained in the south.

The Cold War continued unabated through the 1950s as the United States and the Soviet Union sparred for ideological control of the world. In 1953, civil defense officials from four southern Utah counties—Sevier, Sanpete, Iron, and Piute—met at the Sevier County Courthouse to discuss their various needs. Plans were formulated to accommodate refugees from the hypothetically bombed cities of Salt

Sugar beets under irrigation in Sevier County. (Utah State Historical Society)

Lake City and Ogden as well as people from the two northern counties who were in transit to southern Utah. The plans called for Joseph to house and provide food for 1,500 refugees; Elsinore, 1,000 refugees; Monroe, 2,000; Richfield, 10,000; Aurora, 500; Salina, 5,000; Redmond, 500; and Grass Valley, 500 refugees.[8]

Gordon Hansen of Richfield, a World War II veteran employed by the U.S. Soil Conservation Service, was named as the county director of civil defense. Hansen immediately announced that a civil-defense school would be held beginning the next Monday at the Sevier County Courthouse. Community leaders were "especially urged to attend the meetings." All attendees were required to sign a "loyalty oath." They then viewed civil defense films and listened to lectures from military personnel and civic leaders. Hansen told the *Reaper*'s reporter, "Lectures and movies on some phase of civil preparedness will be interspersed throughout the training program."[9]

Interest in civil defense was strong across the United States during the 1950s. "World War II's civil defense program had been something of a joke," historian William Manchester wrote, "the oceans had been too wide for Axis bombers to constitute a real menace." But, in the 1950s, with Soviet intercontinental nuclear missiles aimed at the U.S. interior, civil defense was taken quite seriously.[10] Hence, Gordon Hansen and his civil-defense school were a significant addition to community events in Sevier County in 1953.

The South Central Utah Knife and Fork Club of Richfield periodically hosted speakers who discussed various aspects of the Cold War. For example, John Morley, a foreign correspondent, author, and former director of the U.S. military intelligence campaign against spies in the War Department during World War II, spoke in April 1953 on the role of food in the Cold War. "There is only one thing the hungry people of the world understand," observed Morley, "and that is food." Criticizing the Voice of America program, an attempt to penetrate the air waves of Iron Curtain countries, Morley brought up an issue easily understood by Sevier County's conservative residents—the wasting of tax dollars.[11] Nationally, the arch-conservative senator Joseph McCarthy was enjoying his greatest influence, and the speech by Morley indicated that the conservative movement could find an audience in Sevier County.

Atomic hysteria was on everyone's mind during the 1950s. The benefits and the threats of the nuclear atom were discussed at a later meeting of the Knife and Fork Club. In March 1957, Dr. Gerald Wendt, advertised as "the world's leading interpreter of science to the layman," addressed the club on the subject of "new aids for better living" brought about in the age of nuclear energy. Wendt discussed the latest inventions in science such as the two-way radio, the telephone, radar, and the atom bomb.[12] County residents attended such lectures in an attempt to keep pace with the rapidly changing age.

Many county residents wholeheartedly supported the U.S. government's testing of nuclear weapons during the 1950s and 1960s in nearby Nevada, unaware that they were downwind of the radioactive fallout from many of the tests. In later years, health problems of a number of county residents would be blamed on this cause as people throughout southern Utah would seek redress from their government. However, at the time, considering themselves to be patriotic citizens, conservative county residents regularly supported U.S. policies during the Cold War as well as private attempts to expand the nuclear industry, not believing that government or business leaders would knowingly but silently expose them to danger.

The *Richfield Reaper* kept county residents abreast of local happenings as well as some national and international affairs. It reported LDS mission calls and the marriages of local couples along with the news of births, deaths, and unrest in the world. Its articles attested to the county's continuing agricultural economic focus. There were also misdeeds and crimes to report, For example, a 1951 notice reported that two Aurora men had been sentenced to prison for an old Western crime—cattle rustling. On a more positive side, in February 1951 the *Richfield Reaper* gave notice of two new LDS wards being created in Richfield.[13] Other religious news in Sevier County during 1951 was the call of a local man, Golden R. Buchanan, as the president of the LDS church's Southwest Indian Mission. Buchanan was instrumental in the shaping of the Mormon church's Indian Placement Program in 1948, and for the previous three years he had served as the coordinator of Indian affairs for the LDS church.

Continuing anxiety over an adequate water supply led Sevier County to join with neighboring Millard County in an effort to employ the latest in modern technology to bring additional rain to the region. By the 1950s county officials subscribed to the scientific attempt to modify the weather by artificial means. A March 1951 story in the *Richfield Reaper* told of a project to artificially bring rain to the Sevier River Valley. The two counties were intending to participate in the purchase of a "rainmaking machine," a "gadget which throws minute crystals of the chemical [silver iodide] into the clouds."[14] A consortium known as the Southern Utah Water Resources Development Corporation, which initially included Beaver, Garfield, Iron, Millard, Piute, Sevier, and Wayne counties, was involved with the rainmaking scheme. Each county was expected to participate in funding the rainmaking venture.

The same report, however, rather embarrassingly observed that only Millard and Sevier counties, once the "two sparkplugs" in the project, had "not as yet, presented their respective checks to help finance the project."[15] This may have been the first time Sevier

A storage facility along side an irrigation canal west of Monroe. (Allan Kent Powell)

County officials wavered on a water project due to cost, but it would not be the last. Forty years later the county would withdraw from the Central Utah Project (CUP) for similar reasons.

By April 1951 the "first appreciable rainfall in many months" brought much-needed water to the sun-baked soil of the region.[16] Uncertain whether the moisture came as the result of oft-spoken prayers, of silver-oxide cloud seeding, or from normal weather patterns, the local people nonetheless were elated with the rain. Within three weeks, more than 0.27 inches of "precious precipitation" had fallen in Richfield alone. While less than one inch may not seem to many like much rain, Sevier and the neighboring counties were historically very dry.

Before the rains came, the south-central region of Utah had experienced eight months of drought. Now, the farmers in adjoining Wayne County were predicting "good range conditions." In Sanpete County the reservoirs were said to be "bulging." More importantly to the people of Sevier County, Piute County to the south reported that the rainshowers had swollen the northward flowing Sevier River.[17]

This was good news indeed. Always near the forefront of many county residents' thoughts was water. Most residents of Sevier County still kept a constant eye on weather conditions and moisture predictions.

The silver iodide–dispersing generators had been placed across southern Utah at the communities of Beaver, Antimony, Blanding, and Ferron. The most common method of distributing the silver iodide particles in a mountainous area like south-central Utah was through the use of ground-based generators. Upon release from a ground generator, the very small silver iodide particles spread skyward much like smoke from a chimney, and, in fact, the resulting cloud was called "blue smoke." Conditions are most favorable for seeding when a storm is approaching. For the greatest impact, the silver iodide particles were released on the windward side of a mountain barrier.[18]

By May 1951 twelve southern Utah counties were participating in the cloud-seeding project. At that time the *Reaper* reported favorably on the rainmaking venture:

> All counties are pleased with the project thus far and more rain has been received during this year's April than during all other months of 1950 and '51 . . . although Sevier County remains one of the least affected counties in the project membership.[19]

Why the county received less rain than other participating counties was unclear. While listing the total April rainfall for each of the others, the *Richfield Reaper* surprisingly gave no total for Sevier, but the newspaper had reported rain in Richfield on 5 April and 27 April. Fortunately for area farmers, even if the rain was not falling in large amounts in most areas of the county, the Sevier River was running high and the promise of adequate water for farming seemed evident.

Interest in cloud-seeding was strong enough in the area by February 1953 that Richfield hosted the annual meeting of the Southern Utah Water Resources Development Corporation. Dr. Irving P. Krick, head and founder of the corporation, spoke at the meeting held in the Sevier Stake tabernacle. He was joined by Dr. J. Vern Hales of the meteorology department at the University of Utah and Dr. Vincent Scharfer of General Electric Corporation, "one of the discoverers of weather modification."[20]

As hopeful as cloud-seeding had appeared from 1951 to 1953, by mid-decade, with no unequivocal evidence of the program's success, some detractors of the idea were beginning to appear in parts of the county. In a letter to the editor printed in the *Salina Sun* in March 1956, Conrad Frischknecht wondered whether or not a reevaluation of the technique was needed. Frischknecht quoted an article in a recent farm publication which stated, "Cloud seeding, by releasing silver iodide smoke from ground generators, gives results which are not [only] spectacular or breath-taking, but which can be very important to the water economy of the nation." He believed it would be best, however, to enlist the federal government in the effort, hoping the government could be induced to participate "percentage wise" to assist drouth-striken areas in "bearing the cost of this new type of water conservation."[21] Like many other Americans, though they might like less involvement from government generally, county residents' hands were always open to receive aid for specific projects that could benefit them.

Two years later, the *Salina Sun* printed a report of research conducted by the meteorology department of the University of Utah which questioned the benefits of cloud-seeding. "Cloud seeding conducted in Southern Utah since 1951," the report read, "has shown no detectable increase in precipitation during that period." The paper quoted the university's Dr. J. Vern Hales as saying, "In our opinion, this report shows quite clearly that the cloud seeding has not produced any changes by the most sensitive measures which we could devise."[22] There was doubt in the minds of at least some Sevier County residents about the wisdom of using county monies to fund what to them seemed a project of questionable value.

There were, however, significant rains during the period. In August 1952 "heavy rains" rushed from Denmark Wash near Aurora in the form of "a muddy current" which swept onto farms and over U.S. Highway 89. The following year "intense rain" caused a discharge of 2,650 cubic feet per second to pour down Salina Creek. Three weeks later, Salina Creek roared again following a heavy storm. At Salina on the evening of 15 August 1955 a "cloudburst" in Salina

Canyon quickly "raised Salina Creek to floodstage," threatening damage to lowlands and the local highway (Utah Highway 10). On 1 August 1959 Salina was struck again when a cloudburst expelled waters down Denmark Wash and Salina Creek. Areas were flooded both west and east of the town.[23]

Still, even with the rain, water always was a pressing concern in the county, which remained predominantly agriculturally oriented, although the decade saw the beginnings of what would become a decrease in the amount of land farmed and used for other agricultural purposes. In April 1953 the benefits of irrigation was the focus of an article in the *Richfield Reaper*. While forecasts were favorable for an adequate water supply during the upcoming summer's farming season, the outlook for those who depended solely upon stream run-off was less promising. Figures released by the local office of the federal Soil Conservation Service predicted a "severe drouth" due to below average snow measurements in the mountains. Flow from the Sevier River northward to the San Pitch River was expected to be about 85 percent of normal. However, the article noted that storage reservoirs had retained a "considerable amount of water from last year." Important holding reservoirs of the Sevier Valley were Rocky Ford near Sigurd, built in the early twentieth century; Three Creek Reservoir near Clear Creek; the Koosharem Reservoir; and the Rex Reservoir on the west slope of the Fish Lake Mountains.[24]

The *Richfield Reaper* reported interesting items of local news during 1953. In February, J. Elliot Cameron, the principal of South Sevier High School, was chosen to succeed A.J. Ashman, who had retired from his post as superintendent of the Sevier School District after thirty-five years of service. That same month, the *Reaper* noted the opening of the Sevier Banking Company. This new bank was to be directed by Morris B. Nielson, former assistant cashier with the Richfield Commercial and Savings Bank.[25]

Salina's annual city budget was publicly released in January 1953, with projected revenues of $71,218. The city council hoped to get through the year with distributions totalling $64,423, topped by $33,350 for water works and $23,400 for public safety. Other anticipated expenses were for streets, parks and cemeteries, irrigation expenses, the library, and operation of the Salina hospital.[26] With some variation in detail, this budget was representative of that of other county towns of the period.

Water projects were a major concern for all Sevier County communities, particularly expansion and improvement of culinary water supplies. Over half (52 percent) of Salina's annual budget was earmarked for water projects, and about 36 percent went for public safety—police and fire departments. Thus, water and public safety projects combined accounted for about 88 percent of Salina's annual expenses in 1953. Increased expenditures were signs of a growing community.

A facet of modern technology that took Sevier County by storm in 1953 was television. A main attraction for county fairgoers in August 1953 was the unveiling of "TV." The first television service offered in Sevier County was very limited. A preview of this new attraction was reported by the *Richfield Reaper* in May 1953:

> The plan calls for a high tower to be erected on some peak near Richfield where a television signal from Salt Lake City can be picked up. From the tower the signal would be transmitted to Richfield by coaxial cable and distributed to subscribers like a public utility distributes electrical power. There would be a charge for hook up to the system and a monthly charge to subscribers.[27]

This first county TV service was much like later cable networks, with paid subscribers and programs emanating from a distant source. Richfield residents wishing television could expect to pay $150 or more for the hook-up service. Then a monthly service charge would be applied. The world of the early 1950s held bright promises, although at a cost, for county residents.

A proposal by the federal government to construct a dormitory for Navajo students at Richfield (known locally as the "Indian School") emerged in late January 1953. The "long sought" Indian school promised to bring additional income to the area. Local people not only would make money in construction work but also some would have the chance to obtain employment at the school. The action which brought the school to Richfield was, in the words of the *Richfield Reaper,* the culmination of "two years of work by the people of Richfield."[28]

Baseball grandstand in Aurora. (Allan Kent Powell)

Measles and juvenile delinquency also concerned Sevier County residents in the early 1950s. The state of the community's health was examined during the spring of 1953 when a measles outbreak "of major proportions" swept Richfield. Local children who contracted the disease were required to secure permission from Dr. T.R. Gledhill, Richfield physician, before returning to school. During a ten-day period at the height of the epidemic, the city physician "made 40 visits to homes, made about 100 telephone calls and issued 76 permits to return to school." By 16 April the school principals of both the Richfield high school and the elementary school were reporting "a decrease in the number of absences because of the disease."[29]

School absenteeism due to the measles was not the only concern for parents during the mid-1950s. In August 1953 at a meeting of the three LDS stake presidencies covering the county—the Sevier Stake (headquartered at Richfield), the North Sevier Stake (Salina), and the South Sevier Stake (Monroe)—methods for "controlling and rooting out juvenile delinquency in the county" were discussed. Local ward bishops, juvenile authorities, and law enforcement representatives joined the stake presidencies at the meeting in the Sevier Stake tabernacle to discuss the "extent and possible causes" of the county's juvenile problems. William Bliss Daniels, president of the South Sevier Stake, was in charge of the meeting. A.C. Prows, the mayor of Salina, charged that "honky tonks operating throughout the county had been selling whiskey and beer to juveniles." Prows urged that efforts be made to close these establishments down, a plan reminiscent of the early years of the twentieth century when the county community was also fearful of crime, alcohol abuse, and delinquency.

A committee of eight, including the three LDS stake presidents, was empaneled to "study the question more thoroughly."[30] Although the committee may have come up with some worthwhile measures, delinquincy, as might have been expected, was not eradicated. County youth, then as always, found amusements that their elders disapproved of, but all county residents were seeking ways to enjoy themselves. Many pursued traditional entertainments, but activities such as bowling and drive-in movies were attracting increasing numbers of county residents. Automobiles were becoming central to entertainment as well as most other aspects of life. Movies were another vital part of the entertainment scene in the 1950s and beyond. Sports remained important to many, and the county's high school teams increasingly became the focus of local sports enthusiasts. Although for every winner there was at least one loser, success came to area high schools, beginning especially in the 1950s when the South Sevier High School boys baseball team won two state championships to accompany a third gained in 1949, while the school's boys basketball team won the state crown in 1951 and 1954. The county's other high schools would also find similar success in large measure in later decades.

The Sevier School District faced other concerns beyond juvenile delinquents during the 1950s. It confronted problems regarding funding and space. Superintendent J. Elliot Cameron brought these matters before a meeting of the Richfield Parents-Teachers Association in October 1953. The district, he claimed, was faced with a shortage of teachers, a steadily increasing number of students, a lack of physical facilities, and lowered purchasing power. The combination of these factors was proving critical for education in the county. "While Utah ranked forty-seventh in the United States in its ability to pay for education," stated the superintendent, "it has more students in elementary school per capita, more high school graduates, and more students in college than any other state." Yet the average teacher's salary in Utah during the 1952–53 academic year was only $3,325—next to the lowest in the Intermountain West. Utah's teachers, according to Cameron, were leaving the profession for other fields because they were underpaid—especially Utah's rural educators. While all in attendance agreed with Cameron that greater equity was needed, "no concrete motion was adopted."[31] Like their fellow Americans elsewhere, county residents wanted improved services and facilities; however, they often balked at increasing their own taxes to help make this possible.

In November 1953, county residents went to the polls to elect local officials. As usual since the mid-1940s, they voted predominantly Republican. Much to the surprise of the *Richfield Reaper*, Salina, which had been "heavily Democratic" for many years, turned Republican that year. According to the Richfield newspaper, Salina went Republican in two out of three city races in 1953. In Richfield, the third-party candidacy of write-in mayoral aspirant O.R. McKinlay brought "one of the most exciting elections in recent years." This alternative choice was created by some dissatisfied local voters who challenged the incumbency of Mayor J.N. Stacey, the choice of both the Republican and Democratic parties. The last-minute entry of McKinlay was promoted aggressively through radio advertising to the point that the Richfield newspaper called his campaign "a machine." Civic leaders "lept to the defense of the mayor" to bring victory. Nevertheless, McKinlay's challenge brought a "record turnout" for the election.[32]

Two years later, the *Salina Sun* published the results of voting in north Sevier County: the Republican candidates for city councilman in Salina—H. Othello Madsen, John O. Olsen, Jr., and Harold Peterson—won by a 178-vote margin out of 1,212 votes cast. This time "Redmond and Aurora deviated from party lines, while Salina stuck to one party and named all councilmen from the Republican side."[33] Sevier County elections during the early 1950s could be both predictable and unpredictable. Republican candidates were the winners most frequently; but occasional surprise candidates, like O.R. McKinlay, kept things more lively.

In 1956 the *Salina Sun* predicted water woes once more. The March 1956 snow survey of the Gooseberry and Farnsworth Lake snowfields showed a below average snowfall. The measurements at Gooseberry revealed an average snow depth of 31.9 inches, nearly fifteen inches less than it had been in 1955. For the past six years the average depth in March had been more than 37 inches of snow. The Farnsworth Lake area, at the head of Sheep Creek, had an average snow depth of 49.5 inches, compared to 56.35 the year before. The four-year average at this site was 51.31 inches.[34] For Sevier County, as in much of the region, the yearly precipitation could vary greatly.

Cloud-seeding may have brought increased precipitation to the county. Between 1950 and 1960, when active cloud-seeding was occurring, Sevier County, especially Salina, suffered a higher number of cloudburst-produced floods than it had during the previous eleven years—almost twice as many, in fact.[35] Many people may have concluded that cloud-seeding was to blame for the floods.

In 1959 the Salina newspaper reported improved snow pack measurements. However, when the amount of snow above Salina was measured near Farnsworth Lake, it was determined that while "February storms improved the water outlook, it is still poor." The water outlook for the spring reportedly had "brightened considerably as a result of the storm pattern through February"; however, future water conditions remained at only about 60 percent of the average. Sevier County farmers employing irrigation were in good shape since reservoir storage was "above average," but farmers relying upon direct flow were likely to have less water come summer.[36] As had been the case since settlement years, local farmers were at the mercy of nature. Modern technology had helped in the control of the resources but could not significantly change the area's general climate.

The *Salina Sun* reported on different conservation efforts underway at Glenwood near Richfield. This project, "one of the first of the small watershed projects completed in Utah under Public Law 566," attempted to kill with pesticides all "undesirable" range plants which were "competing for moisture and suppressing the desirable range grasses and palatable deer browse." These selective chemicals killed

The Fish Lake Lodge, constructed between 1928 and 1932. At 360 feet long and 80 feet wide, it was considered the largest wooden structure west of the Mississippi River at the time of its completion. (Allan Kent Powell)

sagebrush but did not harm bitterbrush and grasses which were foods of choice for both game and livestock.[37]

Along with local news, the *Richfield Reaper* began covering another war, this one waged against the crippling childhood disease polio. Sevier County joined with the rest of Utah and the United States in the fight against this horrendous disease which had come powerfully to the forefront of American consciousness during the 1930s when it became known that President Franklin D. Roosevelt had been afflicted by the disease. By the mid-1950s, the public crusade against polio received ever-increasing attention in Sevier County and in Utah.

A 1957 editorial in the *Richfield Reaper* urged local residents to continue the fight: "1956 was a year of great achievement in the long fight against infantile paralysis," the editorialist observed. "Tens of millions of American children were inoculated with Salk vaccine."[38] The annihilation of polio, it was claimed, could now be seen on the horizon. This source of "extreme fear" was gradually being removed from local lives, according to the newspaper. Polio officials in the county were urged to remain vigilant and not let "apathy" set in now that the fight was being won. The Salina Lions Club spearheaded the yearly March of Dimes drive in northern Sevier County. At Monroe, Neal Jones, also of the Lions Club, whose son suffered from polio, announced that the polio drive was "progressing very well." At Redmond, Lamar Rasmussen was appointed the local polio drive chairman. In 1956 Utah had had the highest increase in polio cases of any state in the nation—up over 150 percent. By 31 January the annual March of Dimes drive in Sevier County was over. County chairman Hansen announced that over $1,300 had been collected.[39]

Seven months later, polio was again in the Richfield news. A countywide survey was announced to assess the needs of all those who had contracted polio. The purpose of this survey was to compile a roster of polio cases of all ages in the county.[40]

Modern applied science came to play an ever-increasing role in the county during the 1950s. The vaccine to combat polio and the technology to artificially produce rain and to bring to residents the electronic wonders of transistor radios, dial telephones, and television sets captured the attention of the county's people to varying degrees during the 1950s. Still there was the need to wrestle with a myriad of political, economic, and social problems during the middle decades of the twentieth century. The county was generally economically prosperous during the decade of the 1950s, as increased mining production of coal and gypsum bolstered the general economy. Agriculture remained strong, particularly the livestock industry. The diary industry was also continuing in the county. In 1949, for example, Monroe residents Russell Ware and sons had founded a milk bottling plant—the South Sevier Diary. They sold the successful operation in 1955 to the statewide Highland Dairy company.[41]

A trend was developing in the 1950s towards fewer farms of greater acreage. In 1954 the were 923 farms in the county; by 1959 there were not quite 700, but the average size of a farm had grown from 256 acres to 358 acres. The amount of acres under the plow remained about the same—240,199 acres in 1959. The number of full-time farm operators shrank from 543 to 365 during the period. In 1959 there were 33,371 cattle recorded in the county; 3,156 milk

Hay derricks, like this one south of Richfield, were an important part of the county's agricultural landscape. (Allan Kent Powell)

cows; more than 15,000 chickens; 224,720 dozen eggs sold; and 293,273 pounds of wool sold.[42]

The fear of communism brought some paranoia to Sevier County residents between the 1950s and the 1970s. The Cold War tensions and arms race with the Soviet Union and its allies created stress and worry in Americans. The threat of nuclear weapons was felt even in remote areas like Sevier County, Utah. Conflict erupted in Korea in the 1950s and in Vietnam from the mid-1960s into the 1970s. In the midst of what could be described as a terrifying and confusing world, many county residents must have found a great sense of security and well-being in the pursuit of their time-honored practices of the seasonal planting and harvesting of crops, the rearing of children, church work, and civic activities.

A move toward modernization came to the northern part of the county in 1956. On 12 August 1955, Howard Casey, manager for Mountain States Telephone, delivered the news of plans to install dial telephone service in the Salina area. This meant that individual dial telephones could be connected in each Salina home and business. Lines initially were strung only between Salina and Aurora. Twenty-one early applicants were the first to receive this service. Speaking for Mountain States Telephone, Casey said, "We are especially proud of this new telephone system because it will give our customers in the Salina area telephone service on a par with any other city in the United States."[43]

Another development which interested the residents of the county was the possibility, first discussed in August 1957, of bringing a "translator television system to the county." The Sevier County Commission, led by chairman Kendrick Harward, entertained public discussion of the possibility, but reported that "no official action has been taken thus far." However, the proposed translator plan to bring television signals through the airwaves received the support of the public. Therefore, said Commissioner Harward, if "a good practical and workable system" can be secured, then "we will carry the proposition on further."[44]

Television had been brought to the citizens of Sevier County in 1953; however, this early offering was available only through a rather expensive coaxial cable hook-up plus a monthly service charge, something that was beyond the financial means of many in the county. It was hoped that this proposed "free" television connection with Salt Lake City networks would make TV available to more people in the county. A local group, the Sevier County Citizens for Improved Television, certainly thought so. Gareth Larsen, its chairman, believed it would be possible to raise the funds necessary for the initial installation of the airwave signal translator stations by "public subscription." Once installed, Larsen believed, the system could be maintained by "a levy through the county recreational fund as allowed by statute of the recent legislature."[45]

By October 1957 the issue of a television tax was put to a vote in the county. The vote was on the proposition of whether or not the county should "sell bonds in the amount of $50,000 to finance the building of a television station to broadcast the programs of the three Salt Lake City television stations to the people in the county through an Ultra High Frequency wave range."[46] The "heaviest recorded vote in many years" approved the measure by a three to one margin.[47] The vote was 2,473 in favor of the bond issue, 836 against.

A reading of letters to the editor published in the *Richfield Reaper* just before the election offers insight into the mind of certain county residents on this issue. Ken Isbell, a Richfield teacher, a strong believer in the educational potential of television, wrote the following:

> [Television] should be made available to every possible person at the lowest possible cost consistent with good business practices.
>
> A vote yes is a move in the right direction for this forward step taken by the young men of our area. We can be educated and entertained to new heights by the medium of TV.

However, an anonymous writer, signing his letter "A Taxpayer," blasted the TV bond with these words:

> Of course we want better television and we want it as good as Salt Lake City gets it; no snow and no interruptions. But before we spend $50,000 we certainly ought to have a guarantee from the manufacturer of the equipment backed by a cash bond that we will get good uninterrupted television the year around. . . .
>
> You can bet your bottom dollar not one of the commissioners would spend his own money on such a deal without a bonded-guarantee of satisfaction.[48]

Within two weeks of the public's approval of the TV bond, work began to place the translator equipment in Sevier County. It was to be located on a site high up on an 8,000-foot ridge at the north end of Cove Mountain between Annabella and Monroe. The plan, as explained by Commissioner Harward, called for a "temporary installation" of VHF booster equipment to test broadcast the television signal coming from Salt Lake City.

The television issue stayed at the forefront of Sevier County news until well into 1958. An editorial printed in the *Richfield Reaper* in late 1957 attempted to urge caution in proceeding, although it conceded, "There is no question what the majority of the tax payers want," which was to "pick up Salt Lake City television." Referring to the recent referendum, the newspaper observed, "Seldom is there shown such an overwhelming affirmative vote."[49]

People were impatiently clamoring for television. The county commissioners had been put in the awkward position of striving to answer this public outcry yet doing it in a fiscally responsible manner. The *Richfield Reaper* expressed the editorial opinion that "the commissioners are a group of responsible individuals" and communicated the hope that the public, who, after all, "are going to foot the bill," would show a little "prudence in their demands."[50]

The commissioners had authorized a booster located on Cove Mountain; however, at the end of 1957 the Forest Service ordered the equipment removed from federal land after government officials issued a directive banning any use of said land for "unlicensed equipment." At the same time, Sevier TV Cable Company, owned by T. Collins Jackson, began challenging the legal standing of the booster station. Ben D. Browning of Salt Lake City, attorney for the cable company, met with the operators of the booster station, warning them to "keep the test signal [from the booster] out of the area being served by Sevier TV Cable Company." Browning filed a writ of prohibition against the county-operated booster system with the Utah Supreme Court.[51]

The problem with the U.S. Forest Service was resolved by moving the booster to private property south of the original site. The new location was still on Cove Mountain, some five miles south of Monroe. The legal tangle was yet to be solved, however. In early February, county residents were informed by commission chairman Kendrick Harward that they would receive television on a converted booster system within the next few weeks. "For the present time," said Harward, "the converted booster system will serve the area adequately and at a cost much less than the $50,000 allotted through the bond election." The booster system was to cost only $17,000.[52]

However, just because the commissioners and the public wanted the issue to be resolved did not necessarily make it so. T. Collins Jackson, owner and operator of Sevier TV Cable, brought suit against the county and the commissioners over the television plan. T. Merlin Ashman, then town president of Redmond and later a county commissioner, came out as a private citizen in support of the suit. He stated that he was a taxpaying citizen of Sevier County who was being taxed for TV which he did not want. Later, however, Ashman claimed that he had been "duped" by Jackson and disavowed his previous support of the lawsuit.[53]

T. Collins Jackson, who had more than 600 cable customers, alleged that the county and the commissioners were "threatening to jam or destroy his signal." He also claimed that the county had "no jurisdiction to set up a television station." Jackson asked the courts to rule both the law creating the booster network and the one taxing citizens for the television service to be null and void. Despite this legal action, the county reportedly was still going forward with its plans to construct a converter-booster station.

Jackson found that he had stirred up a hornet's nest in challenging the actions of the county commissioners. He was subsequently ordered by the commission to secure a franchise to operate his community television system. The commissioners stated that Jackson had "failed and refused to secure a franchise land right from the county." The claim went on to note that Jackson "has received no license, franchise, right or proper interest from any town, city or the county."[54] When Jackson's cable TV was the only television available in Sevier County, these requirements were never mentioned, but as soon as he brought suit against the county, licensing became an issue. Two weeks later, Jackson was back in court requesting that the county commissioners be ordered to stop testing on the TV booster. The final court decision left the commission with the power to control television in the county through the ability to place the relay antenna where it pleased.

The people of the county must have wondered if they would ever have the television system which they had voted for the past

November. By April 1958 the installation work on the county's television booster system was about completed. Two pickup and rebroadcast units were to be used in the county. One was to be placed on Carter's Peak near Aurora, while a second unit was to be located farther south in the county.[55] Sevier County residents had their "free" television by the end of the year.

With advanced technological projects developing in the county during the early 1950s, Sevier County commissioners wisely decided to place $20,000 of surplus funds into a "sinking fund" earmarked for the later construction of a new county courthouse. City funds were used to build a modern fire station and a modern sewage treatment plant during the decade. The sewage-treatment plant was finished in 1957 after residents in 1955 approved a $200,000 bond to finance its construction. The city of Richfield also agreed to maintain Lions Park, which was established in 1958 by the Richfield Lions Club.[56]

The *Reaper* also provided insights into the activities of the small but energetic non-LDS religious community of Sevier County. In January 1957 the Richfield congregation of the Jehovah's Witnesses announced the visit of their circuit supervisor, Mr. L. Kraushaar, from Brooklyn, New York. He spoke at Richfield's Telluride Auditorium and all "persons of goodwill" were cordially invited to attend. In February 1958 the Reverend Nathan T. Helms was installed as the new minister of the Richfield Community Presbyterian Church. A local Baptist congregation began in 1957, and by 1959 the congregation had puchased a church building in Richfield. By that time, organized groups of Lutherans, the Church of Christ, and other denominations were established in Sevier County.[57]

The Catholic church also remained an active force in the Richfield community. The Catholic church purchased the Sevier Valley Hospital from owner Dan Manning in 1960. Manning, who had constructed the facility in 1946, had been operating it as a private hospital since that time. However, the hospital was becoming a financial drain to Manning, which led to the sale. Manning had earlier stated that if the hospital were not sold, it would be closed. Contributions from businessmen and private parties had kept the hospital functioning until the Catholic church purchased it. The Benedictine Order of Catholic nuns, looking for a way to serve the community, took over the operation of the hospital. The Benedictine sisters assumed the day-to-day operation of the hospital in mid-April 1960.[58] It was renamed the Sevier Valley Church Hospital in 1963. Also, the private Richfield Clinic was opened in 1961 to serve medical needs of area residents.

In the late 1950s and the 1960s the Baptist church, which had had itinerant ministers serving Richfield since the late nineteenth century, established a dynamic, if small, congregation in Salina. In April 1959 the Salina Baptists held a weeklong series of revival meetings in the county. By the end of the 1960s the congregation was able to purchase a new chapel in Salina.[59]

As the legal storm over television in the county was subsiding, the northern portion of the county was hit by severe windstorms. "Terrific winds of tornado proportions blasted through the towns of Redmond and Salina last Wednesday at about 5:30 P.M.," the *Richfield Reaper* reported on 15 August 1957. Trees were uprooted, roofs were blown off houses, power and phone services were disrupted, and TV aerials were tangled. In 1958 Utah Power and Light Company formally purchased the Telluride Power Company holdings and officially provided electric power to Sevier County residents.

As a result of the recurrent summer flooding, the county office of the United States Soil Conservation Service (SCS) was asked to provide assistance in solving this problem. The SCS administered a program of small watershed projects and flood and erosion control which was established in 1954. Its program called for co-sponsorship from local communities; Monroe and Annabella residents were willing and anxious to participate in the general project, which had a total estimated cost of over $8 million. In 1963 the Monroe-Annabella portion of the SCS project was begun.

A flood basin and earth-filled dam was constructed early in 1971 by Strong Construction Company of Springville. This element of the Monroe-Annabella Watershed Project cost more than $300,000. The residents of Monroe applauded the project: "While federal funding of many projects hits a sour note with many," observed the *Richfield Reaper*, "this is one type of project in which federal funds can be used to the greatest advantage and perhaps with the least doubt of the good it will do."[60] The work and funds from the SCS have helped solve and reduce many flood and soil erosion problems in the county. Glenwood residents, for example, were saved from extensive damage from floods on Labor Day in 1960 due to earlier SCS work on a project for their town approved in 1955.[61]

Since the beginning in September 1954 of the "Indian integration program" placing Navajo students in public schools, the students had been temporarily housed in a former dance hall and bowling alley located on Main Street in Richfield. A new dormitory, expected to be completed by the 1958–59 academic year, would house 125 students. Henry A. Wall, director of Navajo schools for the government, was in Richfield in late January 1953 to confirm the news. Work on the dormitory progressed on schedule and by March 1958, after nearly five years of living in makeshift quarters, 120 Navajo students in Sevier District schools moved to their new home, a $217,000 dormitory. Fourteen local people worked at the new dormitory, and several Richfield firms, including Ideal Cleaners and the Richfield Shoe Shop, held contracts to provide services for the students. The cost alone of feeding the students infused over $3,000 a month into the local community. While the students, nine through seventeen years of age, lived at the Richfield dormitory, they attended public schools in Richfield, Monroe, Elsinore, and Sigurd. All of the original Navajo children at the dormitory were from Tuba City, Arizona.[62]

Both the community of Richfield and Navajo tribal leaders were pleased with the project. Dillon Platero, tribal chairman of education, wrote Ken Adams, principal of the Indian dormitory:

> I have just reviewed the very fine report submitted by Messrs. Walter Collins and Marcus Kanuho following their visit to the Richfield Dormitory on January 16. I was impressed by the very fine things they had to say about the dormitory program there and the integration of the Navaho boys and girls in the Richfield and other public schools.[63]

Efforts of the LDS church helped bring this project to Richfield. Apparently the Indian School was, in general principle, much like the church's Indian Placement program. The Richfield site was being assisted through the efforts of the LDS Relief Society Social Services and the Child Welfare Department of the Mormon church. Sevier

Stake president Alton B. Christensen as well as Stake Relief Society president Beth B. Anderson were also involved with the program.[64]

In November 1958 the county voted for a United States senator, a congressman, a county commissioner, and several other local officials. In Utah the 1958 senatorial race included an independent candidate, J. Bracken Lee, former mayor of Price and a true political maverick.[65] Lee was a very conservative Republican, but when that party failed to give him its senatorial nomination in 1958 he ran as an independent. Lee was an outspoken opponent of income tax and many government and education programs.

J. Bracken Lee carried the senatorial vote of Sevier County in 1958, receiving 1,684 votes. He defeated Arthur V. Watkins (R) with 1,447 and Frank E. Moss (D) with 1,054 votes, respectively. Statewide, Moss was elected to the U.S. Senate, but, as the *Richfield Reaper* observed, "Completely reversing the state trend, J. Bracken Lee, Independent candidate for the U.S. Senate was high man in the county."[66] The vote revealed the depth of the county's conservative base as much as it did any kind of mandate for J. Bracken Lee. The issues Lee ran on, such as his opposition to the federal income tax, big government, and less money for education, appealed to the majority of voters in the county and indicated that they were even more conservative than others in an increasingly conservative state.

County livestock men like their counterparts throughout the state were becoming increasingly opposed to federal regulation of public lands, in their case grazing fees and permits to run livestock on national forest and Bureau of Land Management (BLM) administered land. The BLM was created in 1946 to manage public lands and a district office was established in Richfield. The district extends beyond Sevier County and manages over 2 million acres of public domain land in the region. In 1964, with the passage of the national Classification and Multiple Use Act mandating various management and conservation policies, the agency has come under increasing fire from many conservative rural residents who have seen their traditional livelihoods threatened by more restrictive land policies. In the years to come, many in Sevier County as elsewhere in the West would come into increasing conflict with more liberal conservationists, as public lands became a political battleground.

Livestock shipping corrals and facilities, like this one south of Richfield, were important for the county's sheep and cattle industry. (Allan Kent Powell)

In November 1964 Democrat Lyndon B. Johnson was overwhelming elected president over conservative Republican Barry Goldwater. But in Sevier County Johnson had no landslide. Still, Utah's Democratic senator Frank Moss, in the words of the *Salina Sun,* "handily defeated" his conservative Republican challenger Ernest Wilkinson in the county. "All state offices went to Democrats," the newspaper noted. On the local level, however, Republicans fared much better: former county commissioner Kendrick Harward won a seat in the Utah state senate, Republican Lawrence W. Jones was reelected as state representative, and both Republican county commission candidates, Virge N. Brown and Arnel T. Dastrup, were elected.[67]

The Vietnam conflict that rapidly escalated during this period was an almost invisible struggle, if one judges it from the pages of the *Richfield Reaper.* Between 1968 and 1972, when the war was at its hottest, Vietnam-related material appeared only a handful of times in the newspaper. Although this war was tearing apart the fabric of American society, one might think that it was being overlooked in

Sevier County. However, this perhaps indicates instead how thoroughly integrated into the national mainstream the county had become. County residents now looked to national television and radio for news of the world, and the larger Salt Lake City newspapers were subscribed to by county residents for national and international news. Local issues were the focus of the county newspapers.

President Johnson became increasingly unpopular nationally as the Vietnam War dragged on. He chose not to run for reelection in 1968, thus opening the door for a Republican successor—Richard M. Nixon. From January 1969 to August 1974, Nixon occupied the White House. This fact alone helped make any contention about or debate of the war in highly Republican Sevier County less likely. In a letter to the editor of the *Richfield Reaper* in 1971 regarding the Vietnam War, Sunnie Thompson expressed one opinion: "Like the weather most of us have something to say about the Vietnam war," Thompson wrote, "yet nobody seems able to do anything about it." This letter, in contrast to what was happening across much of the nation in 1971, was openly pro-Nixon.[68] Student unrest was sweeping across U.S. college campuses at the time. At Kent State University in Ohio four protesters had been shot by fearful National Guardsmen in May 1970; two other student protesters were killed soon afterwards at Jackson State College in Mississippi. Yet the conservative reaction, likely reflective of that of the majority of Sevier County's residents, comes through in Thompson's letter. The writer criticized the contemporary anti-war movement: "I do not believe it is necessary to be bearded and barefoot or that riot makes right."[69] Anti-war activism was not part of the Sevier County scene.

The majority of references to the Vietnam War found in the *Richfield Reaper* either were reports of gallantry or appealing popular interest stories. Unlike some newspapers elsewhere, there was no discussion of the war or lengthy editorials as there had been with World War II or the Korean conflict. The column "Fightin' Talk" or some such equivalent was nowhere to be found during the Vietnam War. Still, the region had its share of military heroes and victims during the Vietnam War—some came from Sevier County. In 1968, for example, U.S. Army Sergeant Glen Earl Christensen of Richfield received the bronze star for heroism during ground hostilities near Bien Hoa, Vietnam.[70]

An upbeat local story related during the Vietnam War was the 1968 account of an Annabella woman's efforts to help her soldier sons find each other halfway across the world. Private Lloyd L. Bybee was a clerk serving with the U.S. Army in Vietnam, while his brother, Donald E. Bybee, age nineteen, was with the Navy Seebees stationed at Cam Ranh Bay, South Vietnam. Neither man knew the whereabouts of the other. Their mother looked at an atlas and discovered the men were stationed only two miles apart. When she informed her sons of their geographical immediacy, they were soon able to spend some off-duty time together.[71]

Between 1958 and 1968 the people of the county benefited from the linking of Interstate 70 from Denver to Cove Fort. In an economy struggling to tap into Utah's and the nation's exploding tourist industry, this development was a real bonanza for the county. On 20 January 1958 Senator Wallace F. Bennett had announced that the new freeway, made possible by the Highway Act of 1956, would use a Denver to Cove Fort route as part of the east-west running I-70, with north-south-running Interstate 15 being routed near the Beaver County/Millard County line just west of Sevier County.[72] The lengthy construction of the project helped the local economy of the county, and once the freeway was completed county residents and businesses looked forward to increased traffic to and through the county. Residents forgot their general antipathy to federal government spending projects when they could directly benefit from them.

By 1971 the recorded use of the I-70 link from Emery County across Sevier County was very promising. This stretch of the highway had nearly a 25 percent higher usage than the Department of Highways had projected. The "annual average daily traffic" for the section was 727 vehicles. Several years earlier it had been projected at 550 vehicles per day. Of the 727 vehicles, only 8.4 percent were Utah cars. Nearly 60 percent were out-of-state passenger cars and nearly 31 percent were light trucks and heavy commercial trucks.[73] For Sevier County these figures meant increased tourist trade, food and lodging revenues, gasoline and automobile service income, and tax revenues—all that highway boosters and county and state officials had hoped for.

Almost all county communities experienced growth from 1900 to mid-century. However, during the next twenty years, the county's population dipped to its lowest level since 1920—there were 10,565 people in the county in 1960 and only 10,103 in 1970. Many communities of the county—Annabella, Central, Joseph, Koosharem, Redmond, Richfield, Salina, and Sigurd—had generally experienced similar population increases after 1900. However, Redmond (641), Koosharem (375), Joseph (297), Central (282), and Annabella (351) peaked in 1940, dropping in population during the next several decades. Annabella dropped to 177 people by 1960; it then experienced a steady growth. Central continued to loose population from 1940 onward. Joseph, Koosharem, Redmond, and Sigurd also lost population after World War II, reaching lows in 1970. Only Richfield experienced an uninterrupted increase of population throughout the period.[74]

Many county young people left to pursue brighter employment prospects and economic opportunities outside the county and region, leaving many area residents increasingly anxious to keep their traditional economic industries, even in the face of increasing government, economic, and conservationist pressures. Between 1964 and 1969 the number of county farms decreased by more than 13 percent, and was down to 514 total.[75] Small farmers were being forced out of business by larger agribusiness concerns and an increasingly worldwide commodities market. This was true in Sevier County as elsewhere, and although many farmers sought to place the blame on government regulations or environmentalists, in great part they were becoming victims of worldwide economic market forces beyond the simple control of any agency. Livestock raisers were faced with an increasingly vocal and conscious citizenry of the state and nation that was crying for increased protection of public lands and decrying what they saw as the subsidizing of ranchers at public expense through the low fees ranchers paid for livestock grazing permits.

County leaders attempted to attract new industries and businesses to the county, while other boosters looked to tourism and the increased leisure recreational lifestyles of urban residents to boost the economy and the local population. Efforts to boost the region grad-

Part of the gypsum board plant complex in Sigurd. (Allan Kent Powell)

ually worked, especially when coupled with the general growth of the population of the state of Utah through both its high birth rates and rates of in-migration and the increasing desire of many in recent decades to retreat from urban areas. Like most Utah counties to one degree or another, Sevier County has been a beneficiary of these trends. From population figures in 1970, many county communities and the county itself have experienced a steady increase of population, which has continued to the present and is expected to continue in the immediate years to come.

Educational needs were vital during the 1960s and early 1970s. Even without enrollment increases, facilities needed to be upgraded and maintained. In 1961, for example, Richfield High School had a new building, and other schools were built or remodeled throughout the period. A vocational education program was also begun in Richfield in 1961. By the early 1970s enrollment was beginning to increase in areas of the county, necessitating new school expenditures. The general trend of moving to the more urban areas of the county also led to increased enrollments in some schools, especially in Richfield and Monroe.

The county's high schools continued to have success in athletic competition. South Sevier High School in Monroe added three new boys basketball state championship trophies to its trophy case between 1964 and 1970, and North Sevier in Salina won the boys basketball championship in 1971.

In 1975 there was an effort by the Utah High School Athletics Association (UHSAA) to realign regional athletic competition classifications. Protests arose from practically every affected area. Residents of Richfield submitted a petition bearing 555 signatures opposing the realignment. The problem arose from the changing enrollments at the high schools in question. The designation mandated by the UHSAA placed schools with up to 199 students in Class 1-A; those with from 200 to 599 students in 2-A; those with 600 to 1,399 students in 3-A; and those with more than 1,400 students in Class 4-A.[76]

Enrollment at South Sevier High School, for example, had increased to 425, which now qualified it to compete in Class 2-A rather than its previous 1-A category. To the great displeasure of local sports fans, longstanding intracounty sports rivalries would fall victim to the realignment. North Sevier High School, a 1-A school, would no longer play league games against South Sevier. An editorial in the *Richfield Reaper* was strongly opposed to the new plan. Calling the current realignment the "most ridiculous" ever devised by the UHSAA, the newspaper contended it would "kill" the competition between schools, thus eliminating a good deal of fan interest in high school sports.[77] The athletic success of all three county schools in the years to come, however, would help maintain a great deal of interest in high school sports throughout the county.

Many residents of the county, like others elsewhere across the state, were always interested in the development of the area's natural resources. In 1975 the *Richfield Reaper* reported on plans for the potential development of geothermal steam on public lands.[78] Such wells were reportedly being increasingly considered as a major source of energy. It was hoped that the geothermal sites could be leased to outside developers. The idea for such a scheme may well have migrated to Sevier County from Kane County, where residents had high hopes of exploiting local coal to power a generator to produce electricity to be exported to southern California. The Kane County plan was often discussed in Sevier County, perhaps as a good general idea for local consideration.

An energy-producing consortium led by Southern California Edison, a Los Angeles–based power company, proposed building a large coal-fired power plant on the Kaiparowits Plateau. The Environmental Protection Agency, urged on by environmental groups, held a series of meetings across the American West to solicit public input on the Kaiparowits project. One such meeting took place in Richfield on 19 October 1974. At the meeting, Robert Currie, of Southern California Edison and project director for Kaiparowits, admitted that the "full expected impact" of the project "is still rather vague." Currie advised attendees at the Richfield meeting that "Sevier County's biggest, immediate role [in the Kaiparowits project] will probably be in . . . having heavy pieces of machinery and equipment move through the area." It was expected that the completed project would "vastly change the complexion of both the economy and the lifestyle of southern Utah."[79] Just how Sevier County might be expected to benefit was not discussed in any great detail at the meeting. While the Kaiparowits project was eventually cancelled due to escalating costs and increased pressure from the environmental movement, Sevier County's plan to market geothermal energy may well have taken its lead from this much larger project.

The first geothermal well in the state of Utah was drilled in 1967 at a site twelve miles north of Milford in Beaver County. Other geothermal wells were later drilled in the same area in 1974 and 1979. The outlook for geothermal energy in south-central Utah "appears to be favorable," according to a report issued in 1982.[80] Sevier County's geothermal resources were included in the Five County Association of Governments' economic plan. Locally, preliminary plans to use geothermal energy were developed, but no further steps were taken when such use proved to be economically unfeasible.[81]

County residents approached the national bicentennial with a mixture of frustration, hope, and apprehension. Many were frustrated that large projects had been blocked in recent years and that the world was changing in ways they could little predict or control. A conflict was brewing between traditional users of the land and those in the environmental movement, many of whom were in urban areas; and most Sevier County residents were worried that their traditional lifeways were increasingly threatened by the "outsiders." Still, the county was not overly dependent upon any one economic industry, and so it had avoided any great economic bust, even though it also had not enjoyed the boom that goes before such an event. Hopes for growth continued to be held by most as they looked forward to 1976.

## ENDNOTES

1. "Report of the Secretary of State," *Public Documents, 1952* 3: 25, copy at Utah State Historical Society Library.

2. *Richfield Reaper,* 15 March 1951, 1.

3. *Richfield Reaper,* 31 May 1951, 1.

4. *Richfield Reaper,* 28 June 1951, 1.

5. *Richfield Reaper,* 18 January 1951, 1.

6. *Richfield Reaper,* 23 October 1953, 2C; and 19 February 1953, B1.

7. "Korean War Casualties," manuscript, Utah State Historical Society Library.

8. *Richfield Reaper,* 16 July 1953.

9. *Richfield Reaper,* 20 August 1953, 8.

10. Manchester, *The Glory and the Dream,* 1:704.

11. Ibid.

12. *Richfield Reaper,* 28 March 1957, 1.

13. *Richfield Reaper,* 11 January 1951, 1; and 8 February 1951, 1.

14. *Richfield Reaper,* 5 April 1951, 1.

15. *Richfield Reaper,* 29 March 1951, 1.

16. *Richfield Reaper,* 5 April 1951, 1.

17. *Richfield Reaper,* 26 April 1951, 1.

18. Leo W. Weisbecker, *Snowpack, Cloud-Seeding, and the Colorado River* (Norman: University of Oklahoma Press, 1974), 11.

19. *Richfield Reaper,* 3 May 1951, 1.

20. *Richfield Reaper,* 2 February 1953. 1.

21. *Salina Sun,* 2 March 1956, 4.

22. *Salina Sun,* 9 September 1958, 4.

23. Elmer Butler and Ray E. Marsell, "Developing a State Water Plan: Cloudburst Floods in Utah, 1939–69," Cooperative-Investigations Report

Number 11 (U.S. Geological Survey and Division of Water Resources, 1972), table two, Utah State Historical Society Library.

24. *Richfield Reaper*, 29 April 1953, 8; Revo Morrey Young, *Ten Penny Nails: Pioneering Sevier County* (n.p., n.d.), 52.

25. *Richfield Reaper*, 19 February 1953.

26. *Salina Sun*, 15 January 1953, 5.

27. *Richfield Reaper*, 7 May 1953, 1.

28. *Richfield Reaper*, 31 January 1953, 1.

29. *Richfield Reaper*, 16 April 1953, 1.

30. *Richfield Reaper*, 27 August 1953, 1.

31. *Richfield Reaper*, 8 October 1953, 1, 5.

32. *Richfield Reaper*, 5 November 1953, 1.

33. *Richfield Reaper*, 5 November 1953; *Salina Sun*, 11 November 1955, 1.

34. *Salina Sun*, 9 March 1956, 1.

35. See Butler and Marsell, "Developing a State Water Plan," 4.

36. See *Salina Sun*, 6 May 1959, 1; and 17 February 1959, 1.

37. *Salina Sun*, 9 January 1959, 1.

38. *Richfield Reaper*, 3 January 1957, 12. Dr. Jonas K. Salk was an American physician who developed the first effective polio vaccine, which was named after him.

39. *Richfield Reaper*, 10 January 1957, 1; 31 January 1957, 1.

40. *Richfield Reaper*, 8 August 1957, 5.

41. Wilford Murdock and Mildred Murdock, *Monroe, Utah: Its First One Hundred Years* (Monroe: Monroe Centennial Committee, 1964), 39.

42. *United States Census of Agriculture, 1959, Part 44* (Washington, D.C.: U.S. Government Printing Office, 1961), 122–23, 132, 135–38.

43. *Salina Sun*, 12 August 1955, 1; and 24 February 1956, 1.

44. *Richfield Reaper*, 15 August 1957, 1.

45. Ibid.

46. *Richfield Reaper*, 10 October 1957, 1.

47. *Richfield Reaper*, 7 November 1957, 1.

48. *Richfield Reaper*, 12 October 1957, 12.

49. *Richfield Reaper*, 21 November 1957, 3.

50. Ibid.

51. *Richfield Reaper*, 2 January 1958, 1.

52. *Richfield Reaper*, 6 February 1958, 1.

53. T. Merlin Ashman, letter to the author, 5 October 1995.

54. *Richfield Reaper,* 13 March 1958, 1.

55. *Richfield Reaper,* 17 April 1958, 1.

56. Jacobson, *Golden Sheaves,* 109, 134–35.

57. Ibid., 72–73.

58. *Salina Sun,* 8 April 1960, 1.

59. *Salina Sun,* 10 April 1959, 1; and 1 April 1968, 1.

60. *Richfield Reaper,* 21 January 1971, 4.

61. Pearl F. Jacobson, compiler and editor, et al., *Golden Sheaves from a Rich Field: A Centennial History of Richfield, Utah* (Richfield, Utah: Richfield Reaper Publishing Company, 1964), 228.

62. *Richfield Reaper,* 5 September 1957, 1.

63. *Richfield Reaper,* 6 February 1958, B1.

64. *Richfield Reaper,* 5 September 1957. 1.

65. See Charles S. Peterson, *Utah, A History* (New York: W. W. Norton and American Association for State and Local History, 1977), 179–80; and Dean L. May, *Utah: A People's History* (Salt Lake City: University of Utah Press, 1987), 191.

66. *Richfield Reaper,* 6 November 1958, 1.

67. *Salina Sun,* 6 November 1964, 1.

68. *Richfield Reaper,* 25 March 1971, 4.

69. Ibid.

70. *Richfield Reaper,* 1 August 1968, 5; and 11 February 1971, 2.

71. *Richfield Reaper,* 24 October 1968, 8.

72. *Richfield Reaper,* 6 March 1958, 7.

73. *Richfield Reaper,* 23 December 1971, 5.

74. Allan Kent Powell, ed., *Utah History Encyclopedia* (Salt Lake City: University of Utah, 1994), 433–38.

75. *County and City Data Book, 1972* (Washington, D.C.: U.S. Department of Commerce, 1972), 164.

76. *Richfield Reaper,* 13 February 1975, 1.

77. Ibid.

78. *Richfield Reaper,* 16 January 1975, 1.

79. *Richfield Reaper,* 31 October 1974, 1.

80. Five County Association of Governments, "Overall Economic Development Plan, Planning District Five," March 1982, 127, Utah State Historical Society Library.

81. Max Robinson, telephone interview with author, 28 March 1997.

8

# CONTEMPORARY SEVIER COUNTY, 1976–1995

In 1976, county residents—most of whom were Mormon—saw the placement of full-time LDS missionaries to serve in Sevier County as part of a church decision to create the new Utah Mission. Missionaries were assigned to proselyte in the county, and other LDS church missionaries were assigned to other places in Utah.

In November 1976, Sevier County voters voted overwhelmingly for Republican Gerald Ford for president—3,677 votes to 1,560 for Democrat Jimmy Carter. Nationally, however, Carter defeated Ford to capture the presidency. In the local races, Republicans continued to prevail. Republican Ivan Mills of Monroe was reelected to the county commission, defeating the American party's Wayne Boucher of Elsinore by a very decisive margin, 3,857 votes to 671. In the other commission contest, Elmo Herring, who had defeated incumbent commissioner Dr. David Urie in the Republican primary, won handily over his challengers from the Democratic party (George Platt) and the American party (David Deaton).[1]

Six months earlier, in April 1976, at least some county residents must have been shocked by the news coming from Kane County. The

The old Sevier County Courthouse in 1975 shortly before its demolition. (Utah State Historical Society)

Kaiparowits coal-fired generator project which had been billed by some as the economic savior of southern Utah had been cancelled. Sevier County had seemed destined to play at least a small part as a transportation corridor for heavy equipment. The *Richfield Reaper*, which had kept interested parties within the county updated on the project, reported that the proposed Kaiparowits project had become a dead issue when two of the major power company investors withdrew their financial support.[2] The planners of Kaiparowits finally gave up in 1976 due to increasing expenses and frustrating delays.

People in the West have often wrestled with questions of home rule, and these concerns have been especially evident during the last quarter of the twentieth century. The so-called "Sagebrush Rebellion" epitomized this attempt by some residents of western states to try to recapture what they saw as the lost control over their economic lives.[3]

This movement was centered in the Rocky Mountain West and, though short-lived in name, was powerful and, to some extent, enduring.[4] The sagebrush rebels were largely led by western natural resource users and state politicians who actively and often aggressively opposed federal control of western land and federal land-use policies, even though that land was in the public domain.

Nevada state senator Richard Blakemore, a founder of the movement, said, "While the particular issues on which the Sagebrush rebellion is based are more common to the west, the principles behind the movement are national in scope." The concern raised by the sagebrush rebels was that of regional destiny. "States, local governments, and the people should make more of these determinations and the federal government less," Blakemore and his fellow sagebrush rebels believed.[5]

Judging from the *Richfield Reaper,* the Sagebrush Rebellion did not seem to have captivated Sevier County land users as the movement did in many other rural areas of the West. The sole article published in the *Reaper* which addressed the movement by name appeared in January 1980. "Controversy stirred up by the 'sagebrush rebellion' has improved communication and cooperation between federal land administrators and western land users," the article reported.[6] Yet the Sagebrush Rebellion had a dramatic impact upon federal land policy in the region and helped channel and direct much citizen-based political action. Since more than 70 percent of Sevier County was federally controlled public land, the rebellion impacted county land users as it affected governmental policies.

The attempt to gain effective control of the federal lands within state boundaries was the essence and aim of the Sagebrush Rebellion. Yet, at least for Sevier County and for the state of Utah, the benefits of gaining such control might have proven negligible. As things stood in 1979, Utah already received generous revenue from the federal lands within its borders, yet it had to assume none of the related expenses of upkeep. There was more to the issue, however. As the

The new Sevier County Courthouse, constructed in 1976. (Allan Kent Powell)

above article concluded, "It does not appear, however, that the fiscal balance is the real crux of the issue embodied in the sagebrush rebellion."[7] For some, the "real crux" was unrestricted use of the land for grazing, mining, and timber harvesting with few or no federal rules or limitations. This seemed to have been the real issue as far as some Utahns were concerned, and, understandably, many other citizens throughout the state and nation were not too supportive of the attempt, especially those outside the rural areas of the West, to whom the land also belonged.

Although the majority of Sevier County residents were politically conservative, the region was not a community of rebels. Utah's more fiery sagebrush rebels were found farther to the east and to the south in Grand and San Juan counties, where there were actual acts of defiance against the government. At Moab in Grand County, on 4 July 1980 local county leaders and residents delivered fiery speeches from the back of a flag-draped bulldozer and then the beginning of a road was scraped into an adjoining wilderness study area.

Farther to the south in Utah's San Juan County, the local county commission's unrest over federal control of the public lands also turned to anger. Environmentalists, euphemistically known locally as "backpackers," were viewed as the archenemy by many residents out of fear that they would bring the county to its knees economically.[8] The San Juan County Commission, much like that of Grand County, actively opposed federal control of natural resources.

Similar acts never took place in Sevier County. In fact, the very term "sagebrush rebellion" seldom if ever again appeared in the *Richfield Reaper*. However, if one reads between the lines, the revolt was present, although on a much more limited scale. While most sagebrush rebels were inclined to lay the blame for their problems at the feet of the growing environmental movement, there seems to have been little, if any, environmental activism—pro or con—in contemporary Sevier County. In fact, most attacks on environmentalists were imported in the guise of unsolicited letters to the editor of the *Richfield Reaper*.

Cal Black, a county commissioner of San Juan County, who was particularly upset by the loss of the Kaiparowits project in 1976, wrote from Blanding four years later:

> It is fortunate that the mayors of the cities of Utah who are involved in the Intermountain Power Project are finally asking questions that should have been raised during the past two or three years.
>
> By moving the plant from near the coal source, (Salt Wash) the consumers (Utah and California cities) will pay about 20 percent more for electricity from now on.
>
> The so called pollution issue . . . was so much hot (polluted) air spouted by [Secretary of the Interior] Cecil Andrus and other environmental extremists.[9]

A letter addressing the same subject written by Marwood J. Hales of Redmond appeared in the same edition of the *Reaper*. It voiced concern over the additional costs to the Intermountain Power Project because of environmental requirements. However, Hales was also concerned about the water needs of local farmers who used the Sevier River for irrigation. Water for irrigation was more important than the water needs of a power plant in the eyes of at least one county resident. "There has been long standing feelings over water rights of the Sevier River for users. Are we going to stand by and see these rights threatened again?" asked Hales.[10] Some county residents were aware that the limited natural resources of the area—in this case, water—could not support all the development envisaged by some.

In the late 1970s, as previously, Sevier County's economy was heavily based upon the utilization of natural resources. Ranching and mining joined with farming as the primary economic industries across the county. Cattle raising remained a leading enterprise. The 1978 statistics issued by the Utah Department of Agriculture counted 265 farms with cattle in the county. This total included over 36,000 head of cattle and calves. County farms had over 30,000 sheep and lambs as well.[11] Nearly two decades later, in 1993, the Utah Department of Agriculture reported Sevier County farmers and ranchers raised an estimated 49,000 head of cattle, placing the county seventh in the state behind the leader, Box Elder County, with an estimated 82,000 head of beef cattle.[12] The county continues to be a major sheep and lamb breeder. The Utah Department of Agriculture estimated that for the year 1995, sheep men of the county produced 13,000 breeder sheep and lambs; the leading county was Iron, with 37,500 sheep and lambs.[13] The county provides an important livestock market for central and southeastern Utah. Salina hosts one of five livestock auctions in the state, and one of only two south of Spanish Fork, the second being located in Cedar City.

Mining growth was anticipated by many citizens. An article in the *Richfield Reaper* of 13 October 1977 observed that the development of coal mines and coal production in eastern Sevier County within the next ten years "could double the present population and turn the area into one of the state's major coal producing areas."[14] Hopeful words indeed to county promoters.

It was estimated that these coal mines could provide enough employment to add "some 13,240 people" to the county's population. "If the mines should open," the *Reaper* optimistically speculated, "the first year's production is estimated at about half a million tons." The paper continued, estimating "another half to three quarter million tons the second year." Less than two years after the Kaiparowits plan failure dashed the hopes of its Kane and Garfield county advocates,

Sevier County boosters were hoping to develop area coal mining. The newspaper said that these expectations "did not take into consideration the possibility of locating the Intermountain Power Project electricity generating plant in [neighboring] Wayne County." If that should happen, it was assumed that "most of the coal to operate it would come from the Sevier area and would increase the impact on the region even more."[15]

Historically, thirteen coal mines have been opened and operated in Sevier County. By 1989 only one was in operation, operated by the South Utah Fuel Company. It was very important to the county's economy, however, employing more than 250 people in 1989 and producing some 3 million tons of coal that year, out of 19 million tons mined in the state of Utah.[16]

Salt has continued through the century to be profitably mined in the northern portion of the county, and the gypsum mines provide economic stability to the county and valued employment to many county residents through both the mines and the manufacturing plants that have been built to make use of the product. Though they have never dominated the economy of the county, traditional extractive industries have continued to have an important place in Sevier County.

Vocational education came to the county in a major way during the late 1970s. Construction of the new Sevier Valley Technical School had been announced in September 1975. Dewain C. Washburn was to be the director of the school. The facility was to be located on a thirty-acre site about one block west of Richfield High School. Offerings at the new technological school were to include auto mechanics, auto body work, building trades, business, business-machines repair, commercial art and graphics, cosmetology, diesel mechanics, distributive education, drafting, electronics, nurse's-aide training, and welding. The new campus would include administrative offices, a library, audio-visual services, a student center, and food services. The low bid for construction of the new facility—$2,482,407—was submitted by a local firm, American Building Corporation (ABC). This was believed to be the most costly building ever constructed within the county.[17] Classes were held in the new facility for the first time in early September 1977. Nearly two hun-

The Sevier Valley Applied Technology Center. (Allan Kent Powell)

dred students attended the inaugural classes. The students came not only from Sevier County but also from Piute County. In subsequent years hundreds of county residents have benefited from this and other educational programs designed to equip citizens to meet the needs of a rapidly changing job market while preparing to face the challenges of the computer age of the twenty-first century.

The election in 1980 of Ronald Reagan, a self-avowed sagebrush rebel, as president dramatically altered the character of the confrontation between the environmentalists and the developers of the natural resources of the West. Reagan's political ideas meshed comfortably with the Sagebrush Rebellion proponents' belief that government was too restrictive regarding the public lands, thus stifling economic growth.[18] In 1980 presidential candidate Reagan's rhetoric had suggested his support for the opening of public lands to greater mineral exploration and development. This talk found favor with many in Sevier County and throughout the West.

Such talk helped bring Ronald Reagan a sweeping election victory. As the *Richfield Reaper* reported, "Voters in Sevier County joined the nation-wide Republican sweep as they cast ballots in Tuesday's general election." Among county voters, Ronald Reagan won 5,427 votes to Democratic incumbent Jimmy Carter's 1,110.[19] The only Democrat to win the favor of Sevier County's electorate was incumbent governor Scott Matheson, who defeated Republican challenger Bob Wright in a reasonably close local race 3,647 to 3,204, although the incumbent won much more handily statewide.

For at least one year prior to the election of Ronald Reagan, criticism similar to that voiced by sagebrush rebels had been at play within the county. The local issue which triggered public interest at this time was a proposal by the Bureau of Land Management (BLM) to classify 4,000 acres of BLM-managed public land within the county as "wilderness" as part of a comprehensive statewide analysis of possible wilderness lands. An editorial in the *Richfield Reaper* of 1 November 1979 was highly critical of the proposed designation of a wilderness area near Fish Lake. Fishlake Mountain, west of Fish Lake and in the Fishlake National Forest, was recommended to Congress for designation as a wilderness area. Its new status as a candidate for RARE II (Roadless Area Review Evaluation) was opposed by many area residents who feared increased restrictions on federal land within the county's boundaries. The editor of the local newspaper gave voice to the opponents of the plan: "While we agree that a certain wilderness status should be maintained, we disagree that more and more public land should be locked up to anything but the walk-in, walk-out camper and wildlife species."[20] In effect, what the editor seems to have been saying was wilderness is fine if it has few use restrictions, but it is even better somewhere else. The editorial went on to comment,

> Locking up 25,000 acres on Fishlake National Forest doesn't seem like much. And in the case of Fishlake Mountain, there could be some merit. But it also sets a precedent which can, and no doubt will, spread to other mountains, other deserts, other lakes and streams and wildlife habitats.[21]

Even if the term "sagebrush rebel" was rarely used in Sevier County, a similar mindset was clearly present. Residents were increasingly fearful that they would lose traditional economic assets such as public lands, which many had come to see as their own, or at least

The Monroe Pavilion, built in 1907, was the recreational center for southern Sevier County for many years. (Allan Kent Powell)

theirs to use as they wished. They would battle attempts to conserve or protect the very land they prized in their efforts to make sure that they could retain its use for their own benefit, having come to view that use as a right rather than a privilege extended to them in the past by the overseers of the land, the federal goverment, acting for its owners, the American public. That American public, whether in Salt Lake City or New York City, was beginning to be more vocal about what was happening to public land in the West. Environmentalists were making their voices heard.

Other opponents of the environmental movement were evident throughout south-central Utah. Met Johnson of New Harmony in Washington County had been raised in Sevier County and was openly opposed to the ecological safeguards on federal lands demanded by environmentalists. He saw them as economically damaging. To him, environmental activists were shaping federal land-use policies to the detriment of local land users. Johnson and a host of others in southern Utah were strongly pro-development and anti-environmentalist. Simply put, Johnson favored use of the land for agriculture, mining, timber, and other development over preservation of the natural resources in ways advocated by environmentalists.

Letters to the editor written over the years regularly attacked environmentalists, maintaining that "outsiders" (environmentalists and the federal government) were "telling property owners and taxpayers here in Utah, what we may or may not do with our land, our resources, jobs, businesses, etc."[22] In Sevier County, as throughout the entire region, there was a strong anti-environmentalist bias.

A natural-resources issue of interest in the southern part of the county during 1979 was the development of geothermal energy near Monroe. The hot springs located at the base of Monroe Mountain were the only non-sulphurous body of such water within the state.[23] This project had first been contemplated by the community of Monroe in 1975. Four years later, in February 1979, the *Richfield Reaper* announced that a new "$1.5 million geothermal development will be underway immediately" which would make the city of Monroe "the first community in the nation" to employ geothermal energy for public use.[24] Here was an energy development plan which met with governmental approval and most likely would have drawn the applause of environmentalists as well. The development taking place at the Monroe Hot Springs owned by Karl Mecham was initiated by the Sweetwater Drilling Company of Sweetwater, Wyoming.

The company planned to drill down to the 1,500-foot level in hopes of discovering geothermal hot water between 165 and 175 degrees Fahrenheit bearing sufficient pressure to produce around 120 gallons of hot water per minute. It was anticipated that the drilling would be completed around 15 March 1979. The next phase of the undertaking would be the installation of a pump and the laying of water pipes to the first beneficiary of the geothermal energy, South Sevier High School.[25]

These same Monroe Hot Springs had been featured in a very different sort of article appearing in *Newsweek* magazine three years earlier. In 1976, *Newsweek* ran a story on evangelism in America. The article, bearing the title "Born Again," included a photograph of Richfield's Baptist minister, Rev. K. Medford Hutson, baptizing sixteen-year-old Danny Keller of Monroe in the hot springs.[26]

The use of geothermal energy from the hot springs was conceived initially during the administration of Mayor Morris Jensen (1970–78) and was investigated under the leadership of Mayor Duane Nay (1978–80). For the better part of the 1970s, the United States Department of Energy had been funding a wide variety of alternative energy projects in the United States, including Utah, as a result of political and economic turmoil in the international oil market during the decade. Most unsettling was the oil embargo of the Arab nations as a result of the Yom Kippur War in 1973. International oil prices per barrel rose from $2.90 to $11.64 in four months as a result of the Arab-Israel conflict. The overthrow of the Shah of Iran in 1979 made the international oil market even more unstable. The Monroe-Red Hill and Joseph geothermal systems looked promising to state and national energy experts.

The U.S. Department of Energy pledged the city of Monroe a grant of more than $1 million as part of a pilot program to assist municipalities with energy conservation. The Sevier School District also pledged $10,000 to the geothermal project. Part of the money went to drill two geothermal test holes. In addition to providing heat to the school and homes of Monroe, plans called for the heating of local nurseries. There were thirty nurseries in Monroe which, it was hoped, could "provide two vegetable crops per year using hot water from the earth." Furthermore, the water-conservation aspect of the entire scheme was not lost on the local people, since the water used in the nurseries not only helped enhance the vegetable and flower growth but also was then recycled for irrigation purposes. The geo-thermal project appeared to have been a well-conceived endeavor by all involved.

However, even with a more than doubling of oil prices, from thirteen to thirty-four dollars a barrel during the years 1979 to 1981, the geothermal project in Monroe proved to be too expensive. Among the problems related to the project were an unacceptably large draw down of water in nearby springs, concerns from the Utah Water Quality Control Board, and other environmental issues.[27] Since 1987 the geothermal springs have only been used for bathing and swimming, as a privately owned municipal swimming pool uses thermal energy from the hot springs to heat its pool water.

Issues related to grazing and, to a lesser degree, mining were of great economic significance to people in the county. The Bureau of Land Management's Richfield office announced a public meeting for 20 February 1979 to "discuss proposed interior policies and mining regulations on Bureau of Land Management lands."[28] Of this meeting, the *Richfield Reaper* noted,

> An inventory of existing resources and their uses is being compiled for these public lands, called the Mountain Valley Planning Area [Sevier, Piute, and Sanpete counties]. . . .
>
> The final management plan will be completed in mid-1979, with a grazing environmental statement for the Mountain Valley Area projected for completion in 1980.
>
> Preliminary data . . . indicates that adjustments in livestock grazing may be necessary. Other issues being analyzed include . . . the effects of current land use on Sevier River water quality, the protection of endangered plant and animal species in the area and possible future conflicts between wildlife and livestock.
>
> Mining, off road vehicle use, and possible range improvements will also be addressed.[29]

At the county seat a different sort of municipal improvement was in the planning stages in 1979—a project to revitalize Richfield's Main Street. The Utah Department of Transportation (UDOT) had a team of engineers who specialized in road construction in Richfield during January 1979 analyzing the road surface to provide information before Main Street was torn up and a complete new roadbed constructed. According to reports in the *Richfield Reaper,* the UDOT plan called for the widening of Main Street, new curb and gutters, and "possibly" new storm and sanitary sewers. The installation of new water lines was also contemplated. It was hoped that all of this new construction could be completed by late 1980.[30] When it was completed, downtown Richfield, which prided itself as a regional center for south-central Utah, would have a new and improved look.

The city of Richfield and the entire county had experienced tremendous growth in the 1970s. The county's population jumped from the 10,103 residents of 1970 to 14,727 in 1980—a growth rate of well over 40 percent. Richfield went from 4,471 residents in 1970 to 5,482 in 1980. No major industry had fueled the growth, which was in part a result of in-migration, as people from the Wasatch

Front and from other states were attracted to the quiet charm and beauty of the area. This time virtually all area towns and cities shared in the growth, which prompted additional growth in retail and service industries.[31] Unemployment was low, as the economy of the county was basically sound, even booming in a modest way. In 1981 the unemployment rate in the county was 4.5 percent, almost a full percentage point below the state average of 5.4 percent. Out of a labor force of 7,149 people, 6,830 were gainfully employed.[32]

The Richfield road project was successfully completed in 1982. The road was widened to four lanes and resurfaced. Storm gutters were added and drainage of Main Street was improved. Costs of the project were split between UDOT and the city of Richfield, with the state agency paying 80 percent. Richfield city is currently (1997) digging up Main Street again, hoping to improve local sewer services and drainage capacity. This time they are surfacing the street with concrete instead of asphalt.

In January 1980 the water supply as reported by the *Richfield Reaper*, "despite a rather dry fall and early winter," was "only slightly below normal" and the three major storage reservoirs serving the region were "either near or above normal storage for this time of year."[33] Prospects for local farmers, if not exceptional, were at least satisfactory. However, fears were expressed later in January that the location of the proposed new Intermountain Power Project (IPP) plant near Lynndyl in Millard County might bring "repercussions" for Sevier County water users. In fact, there are indications that this project may have had something to do with Sevier County's withdrawal from the CUP thirteen years later. As the *Richfield Reaper* tellingly observed in January 1980:

> Anyone who has lived in either Sevier or Millard counties for more than a week is aware of the water allocation battles and high feelings. The Central Utah Project, basically backs plans to divert water from the Utah County area through a series of canals and viaducts, to Millard County as part of this area's supply allocation of the CUP.[34]

In an arid land, water could easily make enemies of once friendly neighbors.

Improvements at the Richfield airport included paving a 6,600-foot runway, constructing a new hanger, and installing runway lights. By the early 1980s the Richfield airport was accommodating between 100 and 250 takeoffs annually.[35]

In the 1988 general election the county followed its traditional Republican pattern. Voters gave majorities to every GOP candidate on the ticket. Locally, incumbent Jerry Nice of Annabella was overwhelmingly reelected to the four-year county commission seat, defeating Democratic challenger Bill Laird of Austin by more than 3,000 votes. For the two-year slot, Republican Jay F. Garner of Richfield defeated Glenwood's Clair Rickenbach 3,329 votes to 2,692.[36]

In the statewide contests, Norman Bangerter, a Republican, defeated former Salt Lake City mayor Ted Wilson in the governor's race by a 900-vote margin, while incumbent Republican U.S. Senator Orrin Hatch soundly defeated his challenger, Democrat Brian Moss. Voters of the county joined with the majority of their fellows in the nation in voting for Republican presidential candidate George Bush over Democrat Michael Dukakis of Massachusetts by a wide margin (4,740 votes to 1,403). Sevier County voters gave majorities "to every GOP candidate on the ballot."[37]

Improvements for the Fish Lake area roads also took center stage in 1988. The U.S. Forest Service undertook efforts to improve and pave both the Fremont River Road and Utah Highway 72 in the Fishlake National Forest. As Forest Supervisor J. Kent Taylor observed, this project was "just a small part of a statewide effort" to develop the national forests making them more accessible to the general public.[38]

Enhancing outdoor recreation was a primary goal of improving the roads. "The forests haven't been publicized as much as the National Parks," said Mr. Taylor, "but they provide twice the outdoor recreation opportunity." Forest Service officials hoped "that by providing scenic highways through our forests people will want to travel through them and stay in our state longer." Fishlake National Forest was to be the recipient of "several miles of [paved] forest roads."[39] The county's boosters certainly approved of this plan.

Along with improving forest roads, in 1988 the county commission appointed a steering committee to "study the direction of the fair in the future." The previous year, the Sevier County Fair had lost $8,000 on its entertainment programs. Commissioner Jerry Nice, who bore responsibility for the fairgrounds and fair activities, was concerned about the losses. It was not the commission's desire to do away with the fair, only to make it more economically successful.[40]

In naming the committee, Commissioner T. Merlin Ashman said that he hoped they "will be able to come up with some ideas and recommendations" regarding the fair. Questions as to the best dates for the fair and the public's perception of it were to be priorities for the committee. Noting that Sevier County was an agricultural county, it was suggested that the fair could best be held in August when agricultural produce could be viewed following the harvest. If an earlier fair date were to be used, that benefit would be lost.

Rollie Waddell, manager of the county fairgrounds, further noted that it was the same people every year who supported the fair and that a way had to be found to make the fair "more attractive" to others if it was to be successful. Sadly, Commissioner Nice remarked, "We have studied the fair, its attendance and participation and it has been going downhill for several years. Only the demolition derby, sponsored by the Richfield Lions Club, continues to make money."[41] Still, whether or not the county fair operated profitably, the public demand was strong that it be held.

Water continued to be one of the issues of most importance to county residents into the 1990s. In February 1993 the *Richfield Reaper* happily announced that the snowpack in the mountains was 162 percent above the average for the past thirty-three years.[42] The availability and cost of water were issues of great importance to the county. The Central Utah Project (CUP) to bring water to the parched lands of southern Utah had been on the drawing board since the late 1950s, with the county as one of its promoters and major participants. According to former Sevier County commissioner and Redmond-area farmer T. Merlin Ashman, "In the 1950s I was a farmer using water diverted from the Sevier River. In a meeting with the Farm Bureau and CUP officials . . . , the CUP officials explained that it was planned to have three hydro-electric power plants on the Diamond Fork part of the CUP. Funds received from the sale of power would

This building in Redmond was used as a school until 1911 and a church until 1917. The original one-story adobe building was constructed in 1881 and the two story rock structure added to the front in the 1890s. (Allan Kent Powell)

be applied to the irrigation and drainage project costs." It was estimated at that time that water could be delivered to county farmers for "about $2.00 per acre foot." But things did not turn out as planned. "Cost over-runs, inflation, ecological and environmental inclusions, and continual additions of congressional[ly] mandated regulations and requirements," wrote Ashman, "made farmers realize that what emerged from the CUP cocoon was no butterfly." According to Ashman, later engineering estimates found that the CUP would benefit Sevier County farmers by "less than 10%."[43]

By the summer of 1993 both Millard and Sevier counties surprised many by deciding to withdraw from the CUP. Salt Lake City's *Deseret News* noted of the withdrawal of these counties from the project that cost seemed to be the dominant factor in the decision. The newspaper observed that "Sevier is the second of five south-central Utah counties to consider abandoning the CUP after some 25 years in the program."[44] What brought about such a change of direction in regard to the county's water policy?

According to Sevier County Commission Chairman T. Merlin Ashman, the whole project had become a "burden on the farmers," who had initially hoped for reduced water costs.[45] The deadline to withdraw was 1 October. Commissioner Ashman observed in an account published in the *Richfield Reaper* that the county had three options: it could proceed with involvement in the Central Utah Project as it stood; it could schedule a referendum vote of the people on the matter; or it could hold hearings and get further public input. "Currently," noted Ashman, "the county, through taxes, pays CUP $170,000 per year."[46]

The commissioners had recently received a petition signed by 5 percent of county land owners requesting that Sevier County withdraw from the project. The basic purpose of the Central Utah Project was to bring water by pipeline from the Colorado River drainage area to the central part of the state. For Sevier County that would mean transporting the water to the Sevier River Bridge Reservoir for storage. Then Millard, Piute, Garfield, Sanpete, and Sevier counties would share the water.

On 23 June 1993 Sevier County commissioners unanimously supported a motion to hold a referendum and "allow the public to determine the CUP's future in the county." Commissioner Gene Mendenhall then suggested that public meetings be held in the northern, central, and southern portions of the county "to inform voters what the CUP is and how Sevier County is involved."[47] The CUP issue allows one to see grassroots democracy at work in Sevier County.

All three county commissioners were concerned over the continuing cost and the seeming lack of direction shown by the CUP. The latest cost estimates indicated that the total price tag for the county's share of the project could run as high as $86 million. Commissioner Ashman observed that that would result in "another big tax increase for citizens." He further noted that "the original plans of the CUP were to construct power plants along the concourse of the water diversion from the east into the central and southern Utah areas to provide revenue and additional power." However, said Ashman, "That seems to have been forgotten along the way."[48] So, not only was the

CUP very expensive, to many eyes it was also starting to look rather incomplete.

The county commission set 31 August 1993 as the date of a public referendum on the CUP. Law required that a decision be reached by 1 October. So far "the county has put $1.8 million of tax money into the project," the local newspaper noted. The county commissioners were hopeful that at least some of the money would be returned if Sevier County were to drop out of the CUP.[49]

The very day that the referendum was announced, the *Richfield Reaper* gave voice to the editorial opinion that the CUP might not be the answer to Sevier Valley's water needs. When actual construction of the CUP began with the Steinaker Dam near Vernal, Uintah County, in May 1959, it appeared to be a good reclamation project for Utah and for Sevier County. However, it now appeared that the "life-long project which began nearly 30 years ago and could take another 15 to 20 years to completion," could result in little or no additional water to Sevier Valley, according to the newspaper.[50] The initial CUP plans called for 30,000 acre-feet of water to be delivered into the Sevier River Basin. Later, local officials reportedly learned that only about one-third that amount would actually be allotted.

The tide was clearly turning against the CUP in Sevier County. Two weeks earlier, Millard County residents had voted "overwhelmingly" to withdraw from the CUP. Now, the Sevier County Commission had determined that "it was no longer in the interest of the citizens of Sevier County to remain in the Central Utah Water Conservancy District." By pulling out of the project at the time, the county commission felt there "would be a [property] tax decrease equivalent to about four mills."[51]

While water remained a vital concern within Sevier County, the financial drain was apparently more than the people cared to sustain. The question to be asked of voters in the 31 August referendum was, "Shall the Sevier County Commissioners take the necessary steps, including, but not limited to, petitioning the board of directors of the Central Utah Water Conservancy District to exclude all lands within the boundaries of Sevier County, Utah, from the Central Utah Water Conservancy District and the Central Utah Project?"[52] The *Richfield*

*Reaper* offered further guidance for voters in an editorial printed on 25 August, just days before the important vote.

> It has been determined by the Sevier County attorney that the vote is binding, and whatever voters decide will be the direction the county will go. . . .
>
> We urge voters to vote "yes" in Tuesday's election. Yes, to allow the county to end its association with CUP.[53]

When the vote was cast, by a margin of 1,017 votes in favor to 160 opposed, Sevier County voters chose to leave the CUP.[54] While the turnout for this special election was sparse (just over 15 percent of registered voters), perhaps because the outcome seemed to be a foregone conclusion by 31 August, the voting public's opinion was quite decisive—the motion to withdraw won by an 86 percent vote. While he was not surprised with the outcome, Commissioner Ashman said he was "pleased with the vote." It showed, he said, that Sevier County citizens were not convinced that the CUP would benefit the county. According to Ashman, it would still take two more years before the county could actually withdraw under the terms of the original contract.

In the spring of 1995, Sevier County officially withdrew from the Central Utah Project. "After nearly two years of meetings, arguments, attempted persuasion, frustration and negotiations," the *Deseret News* reported, "Sevier County is finally getting out of the Central Utah Project."[55] Judge Boyd Park of the Fourth District Court ruled that Sevier County was to be refunded $530,000 plus interest during the next two years and that all land in the county would now be excluded from the CUP.

According to the *Deseret News* story, Sevier County taxpayers had paid "nearly $3.2 million into the CUP but direct benefits have amounted to $1 million." Sevier County Attorney Don Brown argued that "county taxpayers have paid dearly for the benefits of a few small projects" to bring additional water to Sevier County.[56]

Although Millard and Sevier counties withdrew from the CUP, other nearby counties planned to stay. Sanpete, Piute, and Garfield county commissioners all voiced their continued support of the project. "We're not hitting the panic button," said Sanpete County

Commissioner Robert Bessey. Garfield County commissioner Louise Liston voiced similar thoughts, "We're going to hang with it." As of April 1995, Sanpete, Piute, and Garfield counties had not opted to withdraw from the CUP.[57]

Why did Sevier County leave when its neighbors stayed? County voters were clearly unhappy with the escalating costs of the Central Utah Project and the long delays; also, the local power brokers—newspapers, business leaders, ranchers, and politicians—must also receive at least some of the credit for the collapse of the CUP in Sevier County. The public record clearly shows that the county commissioners came to believe that the project was not in the best interests of Sevier County. The editor of the *Richfield Reaper,* possibly with a sound newspaperman's feel for the local pulse, bolstered that stance. From the nineteenth century, Sevier County's people had always demonstrated some measure of independent thinking.

While the vote on the CUP probably stimulated more local interest, the national, state, and local elections of the preceding year also stirred interest among Sevier County residents. In July 1992 Republican gubernatorial candidate Michael Leavitt, a southern Utah native, paid Richfield a visit. Leavitt and his wife, Jackie, were accompanied by U.S. Senator Jake Garn of Utah and the Republican nominee for lieutenant governor, Olene Walker. Local Leavitt campaign manager Paul Lyman hosted the visit at his home in Richfield. Lyman told visitors, "I know Mike's interests are just as much for southern Utah as for the Wasatch Front."[58]

Leavitt's campaign stop affirmed that Sevier County's vote was still important to state politicians, who could basically be assured of the county's basic conservatism. Not surprisingly, Sevier County voters generally followed the state's Republican voting trend in the 1992 general election—they supported all of the party's candidates except one. County voters cast ballots in support of incumbent Republican president George Bush, who, nationally, lost to Democrat Bill Clinton. In Sevier County Bush won by nearly a two-to-one margin. In fact, independent candidate Ross Perot garnered more presidential votes in Sevier County than did Clinton.[59]

The local voters overwhelmingly chose Republican senatorial candidate Robert F. Bennett over Democrat Wayne Owens (4,485

Elsinore School Building, constructed of native limestone in 1898, is now the community center. (Allan Kent Powell)

votes to 1,654). Mike Leavitt won the governorship. Somewhat surprisingly, given the county's usual Republican voting trend, the voters of the county voted to reelect Democratic Congressman Bill Orton. Representative Orton was a bit of an anomaly in heavily Republican Utah, however. His voting record generally pleased his Republican constituents and, as an incumbent, his popularity was strong even in the face of a overwhelming Republican majority across most of the state. Locally, incumbent county commissioner Jerry Nice of Annabella, a Republican, defeated Democrat Frederick "Rico" Baker of Joseph by a three-to-one margin.[60]

Another concern facing the people of the county during the late twentieth century was more readily identifiable with urban America—illegal drugs. They began increasingly to appear in Sevier

County—especially during the 1980s and 1990s. The routing of Interstate 70 through the county near the highly traveled north-south Interstate 15 route seems to have made this geographically isolated traffic artery an attractive one for drug smugglers. In February 1993 an editorial in the *Richfield Reaper* urged a crackdown on "drug runners."

> For years the stretch of Interstate-70 through Sevier County has been referred to as "Cocaine Lane" because of the many arrests of persons arrested for drug possession.
>
> Sevier County Sheriff's and Utah Highway Patrol officers have a reputation of spotting potential drug runners and hundreds of arrests have been made.[61]

The motivation for such an editorial can be seen within the pages of the local newspaper throughout the period. While local law enforcement officers were vigilant in their attempt to thwart the narcotics traffickers crossing Sevier County, drug traffic was, as police in other areas had found, a very large problem. At times the apprehension of suspected drug smugglers assumed dramatic proportions. In August 1992 Sevier County Sheriff Deputy Phil Barney ended a high-speed pursuit of a pair of fugitives on I-70 in Salina Canyon by puncturing a tire of the fleeing vehicle with a shotgun blast. The occupants had thrown containers filled with PCP, an illegal drug, out of the car as they sped away from police. The two smugglers along with a large supply of drugs were netted by authorities. After being arraigned in Richfield before Sixth District Judge Don V. Tibbs, the pair was bound over to federal authorities to face charges for transporting drugs across state lines.[62]

In another instance the following year, four men, two from Las Vegas, Nevada, and two from Sevier County, were arrested in what was described by Sevier County Sheriff John L. Mecham as a major drug-sales operation. The arrests, made nearly simultaneously in Sevier County and in Las Vegas, stemmed from what had been, in Sheriff Meacham's words, "a year-long investigation into the activities of a large-scale drug organization which has been operating in Sevier County."[63]

In March 1993 a drug runner was nabbed on I-70 with over $30 million worth of cocaine. As in 1992, the vigilant eye of Deputy Sheriff Phil Barney brought about the capture of the suspect. After stopping the vehicle, Barney noticed undercoat paint and sealer and became suspicious. After securing the driver's permission to search the vehicle, the illegal drugs were uncovered.[64]

These instances of criminal activity demonstrated that the county was not immune from the crimes and troubles which were plaguing many other communities across the nation. Much like the mythical heroes of the Old West, Sevier County's lawmen battled a seemingly unending array of outlaws. For the quiet, rural communities of Sevier County, the influx of drugs, whether just passing through on the interstate or originating and being used in Sevier County, brought the contemporary outside world a little closer to home.

Narcotics traffickers were not the only out-of-staters impacting the region, however. A more positive development which greatly affected Sevier County's economy from the 1970s onward was tourism. In January 1976 an editorial appearing in the *Richfield Reaper* urged that now was the time to prepare for the tourist season. Speaking to all local residents, the editorial noted:

> The fact is that practically everyone is in a tourist-related business to some degree, not just the motel, cafe and service station owners. Without the revenue generated in the community by tourism, along with the taxes collected for rooms and all other goods and services, a big gap would appear in local and state revenues.[65]

The editorial observed that over 40 percent of local tourism revenues came in the form of a room tax levied on motel rooms. This so-called "transient room tax" was earmarked for advertising programs both within and outside the state to promote Utah tourism.

Just one week earlier, the *Reaper* had noted the beginning of a new motel being built in Salina: "Groundbreaking ceremonies Friday officially began construction of a new $430,000 motel near the Salina interchange just off Interstate-70," the newspaper reported.[66] The structure was to be owned by two Salina businessmen, Nick and Ellis Shaheen, and would feature forty rooms. The Shaheens already owned a cafe on Main Street in Salina which they had operated for about thirty years.

Yet another example of the county's growing interest in tourism during the 1970s was a workshop to assist "businessmen, community and state leaders, planners and others develop Utah's growing tourist industry" which convened at Richfield's Roadway Inn in May 1976. The focus of the gathering centered upon the promotion of the region now being called "Panoramaland" by Utah Travel Council officials—Juab, Millard, Piute, Sanpete, Sevier, and Wayne Counties.[67]

Tourism is a "growing and vital industry in Utah," John Hunt of the Institute for the Study of Outdoor Recreation and Tourism told the gathering. It was the hope of the workshop's sponsors that those in attendance would be able to improve this industry so that it might become "both an economic and social contributor to the state of Utah."[68] Clearly Sevier County was already becoming aware of the economic advantages of tourism as residents began to posture themselves as part of "Panoramaland" and their area as a gateway to the famed national parks of southern Utah. The growth of tourism brought with it an increase in the service industry and retail sales, and hopes were increasingly put on these things to bring Sevier County to a new level of population and prosperity. By 1979 the trade, service, and government sectors of the economy in the county showed the greatest growth during the decade.[69]

A 1980 report published in the *Richfield Reaper* forecast an 80 percent increase in the county's population by the year 2000. This projection, prepared by the Utah Foundation for the Utah State Planning Office, predicted that within the next two decades Sevier County's population would grow from its present 15,700 to 28,300. The estimates were based on "Utah's rapid population growth," which was "the highest in the nation." The figure for Sevier County assumed continued energy development in the region and ongoing population shifts from urban areas to the more rural West.[70]

The forecast reckoned that the county's population by 1990 would be at 23,850. It was, in fact, however, only 15,431—actually a slight decrease from 1980. Sevier County's immediate hopes of an increasing population seem to have died in 1975 with the Kaiparowits power project and the prospect of regional energy development. Yet the county still had its harsh yet beautiful natural attractiveness with which to draw the much-wanted tourists to the region.

The preservation of nature with its attendant benefits to humans of enjoying natural beauty and fostering personal well-being attracted many people to "environmentalism," or at least to becoming more aware of the importance of the environment to the quality of life in general and recreation opportunities in particular. The search for a "higher quality of living," escape from crowded urban areas, and access to the parks and woodlands of rural America, if only for the weekend or summer vacation, became important in the lifestyles of many Americans. Many in Sevier County realized that they already had what others desired and were seeking.

Recognizing this role, and the citizens' inherent duty to safeguard Utah's treasures, the *Richfield Reaper* editorialized on the "Self Preservation Of Our Little Paradise" in December 1993:

> When it comes to enjoying the great outdoors, we in the central part of Utah live in a paradise.
>
> Recreation opportunities abound in every direction and are easily and quickly accessible to all.
>
> Within a few hours, a person can experience high mountain forests, lakes and streams, desert vistas and slickrock terrain as well as every type of environment in between.
>
> We live in the midst of an incomparable collection of national parks and monuments and have the greatest art collection Mother Nature ever gathered before us constantly.[71]

This editorial to a large degree reflected conservation thinking and contemporary environmental politics. While in the late nineteenth and early twentieth century the desire of a few farsighted individuals to conserve America's natural resources led to the founding of the U.S. Forest Service and the National Park Service, in the years following World War II conservation efforts took more individually oriented and private group forms of environmental activism.[72]

Extolling the natural beauty of the region, the *Reaper* urged greater caution in protecting the public lands of Sevier County from accidental fire damage. Tourists, who "fill our motel rooms, eat in our restaurants and generally play a vital role in our communities," would

Built for Peter Frederick Peterson at the turn of the century, this Salina home was renovated as a bed and breakfast inn in 1983. (Allan Kent Powell)

not come if it were not for the natural beauties the county's public lands had to offer; so local residents were implored to use these lands with caution in their own economic interest. "Blackened rangeland" would destroy the livelihood of the county's ranchers while "blackened forests" would obviously hurt tourism, although the writer still found the traditional industries to be the economic and social backbone of the region: "The cattle and sheep we see grazing on public allotments and the timber and mineral leases" allowed many residents to "live as they want, where they want, away from the hustling, bustling life of the cities."[73] The conservationism expressed in this article was, at least to a degree, motivated by economic self-interest.

Local people were becoming aware of the increased dependence of the region's economy on visitors. They knew that tourists spent money which bolstered the county's economy. Yet, the people of the county also enjoyed their traditional quality of life and wanted to protect it. During the 1970s and 1980s residents of many communities across the nation were expressing concern about the quality of living in their particular locale. Sevier County inhabitants endeavored to protect their traditional quality of life while benefiting from increased outside access to, and use of, the region.

Between 1976 and 1995 county residents faced both drought and flood conditions. If an anticipated drought in 1976 was not enough worry for local people, flash flooding once again visited Sevier County in July 1976. "Southern Utah's first significant rain storm in several weeks roared into the Sevier Valley," the *Richfield Reaper* observed, "dumping nearly half an inch of rain in less than half an hour." This cloudburst resulted in heavy flooding and mud damage. "Yards and gardens in the southwest portion of Richfield received the greatest amounts of mud which covered the lawns and damaged gardens," reported the *Reaper*. The parking lot of the Sevier Valley Hospital was "covered with a thick layer of mud as water rushed out of Cottonwood Canyon to the northwest." The accompanying high winds uprooted a "large tree at the Ariel Parker home in Joseph" and also "lifted" a large shed at the James Hanson farm in Elsinore, carrying it "across a corral, open yard and haystack before it smashed it to the ground a half a block away."[74]

This was quite a different story from that which occurred later, in 1992. That summer the rains were reported as "heavy," but flood damage was minimal. According to the *Reaper,* "a total of .36 inches of rain" fell in Richfield resulting in "only minor flooding." Farther

The Monroe Presbyterian Church and School was constructed of native stone in 1884 and used as a church until 1926. It was renovated as a private residence in 1972. (Allan Kent Powell)

south, near Fremont Indian State Park, however, serious flash flooding occurred in the canyons. The difference was likely due to the more narrow canyons and bottoms near the park; however, the flood abatement efforts in Richfield which had been ongoing since at least the 1960s also reduced impacts in the city.[75]

The search of many for a quieter lifestyle in a pleasant rural setting, along with increasing economic development, began to bring about the earlier projected growth for the county. In the spring of 1993 the community of Salina in Sevier County reportedly was the fastest growing postal zip code area in the state. A report produced by the Utah Tax Commission recorded that Salina's adjusted gross income had grown 88 percent during the previous five years.[76] Ironically, the report also noted that the village of Sigurd, just seven miles from Salina, showed "one of the greatest" decreases in adjusted gross income during the same period, revealing that for Sevier County growth was not universal and was dependent upon many factors.

Also in 1992, eleven former members of Company 479, Camp 32, of the Civilian Conservation Corps who were stationed at Salina during the 1930s returned to that community for a reunion. Coming from as far away as Mississippi and Montana and as near as Monroe, nine out-of-town CCC veterans joined with Salina's Ellis Shaheen and Henry Squires to remember their Depression-era efforts at Salina. The group had a banquet and other activities in Salina, traveled to Fish Lake "to view the site selected for a commemorative sign" lauding a CCC work site, and made plans for the placement of a plaque marking the CCC camp site at Salina.[77]

A gathering at Richfield in August 1992 was not expected to be as harmonious as the Salina CCC veterans assembly. The Utah Wildlife Board was to hold a day-long meeting at Richfield High School on 13 August to hear public input on the management policies regarding cougar, bear, and other wild mammals. At least three groups had been "loudly expressing their concerns" regarding any changes in cougar and bear management, reported the *Richfield Reaper*. One, the Wildlife Board, advised the Division of Wildlife Resources (DWR) on all regulations regarding hunting seasons (dates), quotas, and so forth. One opponent to any changes, Richfield's Paul Niemeyer, president of the Sevier Wildlife Federation, urged interested parties to be sure to attend the meeting. Fears were rampant among local hunters that "anti-groups have chartered buses from the Wasatch Front to come down and attend this meeting."[78] Such outside intrusion into what was considered a local matter was unwanted by Sevier County hunters.

"Make no mistake," Niemeyer warned, "hunting, trapping, or almost any other consumptive use of our forests or wildlife is under direct fire by over zealous preservationist groups, antihunter groups and animal protectionist organizations. If we are to continue to hunt, fish, or use our forests, we must become organized, we must become united, we must become vocal."[79] It would appear that pro-hunting groups like the Sevier Wildlife Federation were now using the tactics so successfully employed by environmentalists—strong grass-roots organization, public unity, and a loud voice. Conservation or land-management measures that threatened to curtail traditional uses and practices were rejected by the majority of county residents.

Paul Niemeyer's statement also had the familiar ring of the earlier Sagebrush Rebellion. His reference to "our forests or wildlife," claiming a public resource as a private county reserve, echoed the words of the sagebrush rebels of an earlier day. Remnants of that rebellion had clearly not passed from the county scene.

Wildlife has often been viewed by humans as either good or bad, useful or useless. To many it exists to be used or used up.[80] The 1992 meetings in Sevier County and in the state of Utah over a new DWR policy on the hunting and trapping of fur-bearing animals provide a good example of such differing viewpoints. On the one hand, there was the DWR, whose duty it was to manage natural resources, including cougars, bear, and the like, in what it perceived as an eco-logically sound manner as part of a general conservation scheme and philosophy. On the other hand, there were local hunters and trappers like Paul Niemeyer who were afraid that their traditional practices would be curtailed and perhaps even ultimately banned. Like other western issues at this time, many Sevier County residents seem to have considered such matters to be local issues best decided by local people, even though the resources were public property under state or federal management.

Some interesting social demographic statistics for Sevier County were printed in the *Richfield Reaper* in July 1992. The county's birth rate of 16.2 per 1,000 population for 1990 was significantly lower than the state average of 21 per 1,000, but the county's death rate of 8.9 per 1,000 was notably higher than the state average of 5.2. By comparison, Piute County had a birth rate in 1990 of 11.2 per 1,000 and a death rate of 9.6, and in Wayne County it was 9.6 births per 1,000 population and 8.4 deaths. The cumulative totals for the region, which also included Sanpete, Millard, and Juab counties, was 17.7 per 1,000 births and 8.1 per 1,000 deaths. Regionally, Sevier

County was below the average in births and above the average in deaths. Overall there was a natural increase of 113 persons in Sevier County at the end of 1990 from the number in 1980.[81] Sevier County's demographic make-up seemed to show that many younger people were leaving the area for better employment and/or increased social opportunities elsewhere, while older people—either long-time residents or older retirees from outside the area—were remaining in the county or moving to it to live out their retirement years.

The economic conditions of the county during the last quarter of the twentieth century were mixed. An important new economic development has been tourism and recreation. Gross taxable room rents have steadily increased since the mid-1970s. For example, the taxable hotel and motel room rents in 1994 was almost $4.8 million, up 58.1 percent over the tourist year of 1984 when room rents reached a little over $3 million.[82] During that ten-year period, Sevier County enjoyed the highest gross taxable room rents collected in the six-county region of Juab, Millard, Paiute, Sanpete, Sevier, and Wayne counties.

Several factors have accounted for the growth of tourism in the county. Regional tourism districts and the state tourist council have promoted recreation and tourism. Equally important to the growth of tourism in the county has been the construction of Interstate 70 through the county, a major highway link between southern California and Denver, Colorado, and the creation of Fremont Indian State Park. Since its opening in 1987, the park has witnessed a steady increase of visitors—many from outside the county—from 20,767 in 1987 to over 109,000 in 1994.[83]

As tourism has grown in importance, agriculture has slipped slightly in economic importance in the county and in the state as a whole. Between 1982 and 1992 the number of farms shrank from 477 to 406, while the county lands in farms decreased from 171,772 acres in 1982 to 158,189 acres in 1992. The average size of a farm increased by thirty acres during the period. Value of products sold was up more than $3 million in 1992 over the $27 million total of 1982.[84] Even adjusting for inflation during the period and the decline in the amount of land farmed and fewer farms, it must be concluded that many farmers and ranchers in the county still find agriculture to be

A mechanical irrigation system, typical of those found throughout the county, in operation during the summer of 1997. (Allan Kent Powell)

economically viable. Fewer acres being farmed suggests that Sevier County farmers are farming more intensively and more economically than were farmers of past generations.

The average value of farm products sold by county farmers in 1992 was $75,507 per farm, compared to the state average of $53,636. In comparison, eighteen years earlier, county farms on average produced $31,259 of product value and the state average per farm was $27,795.[85]

Since 1975 the number of manufacturing plants in the county has fluctuated between twenty-one in 1975 and twenty-eight in 1980. In 1994, the most recent data available, there were twenty-three manufacturing plants in the county.[86] Sevier County and Sanpete County are the two strongest manufacturing counties in the central region of the state.

Sevier County during the last decade of the twentieth century has remained the center of retail commerce for the south-central region of the state. However, county retailers have faced stiff competition for the consumer dollar in the county and the central region of the state with the construction of the large University Mall in Orem very early in the 1970s and improved highways through the region making relatively distant urban shopping centers and professional and service businesses closer in time. The number of retail establishments in the county was 107 in 1972, with $26.6 million in sales; ten years later the number of retail businesses in the county increased by seventy, with total retail sales in 1982 amounting to nearly $67.6 million. In 1992 there were 188 retail establishments in the county, with slightly over $106 million in sales.[87]

Unemployment is another important indicator of the county's economic vitality. In 1977 the county unemployment rate for civilian workers was 5.7 percent, which was the same as that for the state and nearly two percentage points below that of the central region of the state. During much of 1977 the national unemployment rate exceeded 6.5 percent. In 1994 the county's unemployment rate was 4.8 percent; the state unemployment rate was 3.7 percent; and in the central region of the state it was 5.2 percent. A year earlier, the national unemployment rate was at 7 percent. The county experienced a high unemployment rate in the mid-1980s, reaching 7.9 percent in 1986, which exceeded the state unemployment rate of 4.3 percent but was below the central region of the state, which stood at 10.2 percent.[88]

South Sevier High School in Monroe. (Allan Kent Powell)

In 1992 the future of housing and educating Navajo students in Sevier County was called into question. The status of those programs for students from Indian reservations in Arizona who had been housed in Richfield dormitories and educated in Sevier schools since 1957 was now threatened. While some elements of the Navajo tribe were still supportive of the Richfield program, continued federal funding from the Bureau of Indian Affairs (BIA) was now in doubt, as some people began a move to have the students study closer to their homes. According to program director Duane Bresee, "Many reservation roads are now paved and school buses have four-wheel drive capability. Reservation schools are only two-thirds full, but we still have tribal support for the dorm."[89]

The Richfield dorm situation was apparently a popular choice with Navajo students and their parents, since a waiting list existed for the opportunity to come to Sevier County. It was hoped that the uncertain situation would be resolved soon. By April 1993 it was announced that, following talks with Navajo tribal officials, funding for the Richfield residential hall had been approved at least through 1994.[90]

Sevier County's schools have continued to educate the young

people of the county, and their concern to provide a quality education is important to all parents and most other county citizens. The county's high schools have also achieved athletic success in great measure—all three have won state championships in boys basketball since 1975: South Sevier in 1984; Richfield in 1977, 1980, 1985, 1987, and 1988; and North Sevier in 1990, 1991, 1996, and 1997. Boys baseball crowns have gone to South Sevier four times during that period and to Richfield in 1992. The state football title in 1984 was also won by Richfield High School. Girls basketball teams of South Sevier have won two state championships—in 1981 and 1982—and Richfield girls won the title in 1985. Many other team and individual titles have been won by county high school students, including numerous cross country crowns for both boys and girls.[91] Certainly in sports county residents have had much to cheer about through the years. Though the accomplishment on playing fields gather more headlines, many in Sevier County are at least as proud of those students who continue their education, many with high academic honors.

Even with a relatively sound economy, county officials have continued to promote more industry and commerce. In August 1992 many Richfield leaders and citizens had hoped to become the site of a planned and "highly sought-after" Wal-Mart Distribution Center for the region. Other competitors for the center included the Hurricane-St. George area and Cedar City. Hurricane was eventually chosen as the new site.

Even without the hoped-for Wal-Mart Distribution Center, the county's economic picture was basically strong in 1993. Another important contributor to the county's economy was construction, which generally provided more high-paying employment opportunities than did the service and retail industries. During the first quarter of 1993, twenty-five new dwelling units were approved, including twelve single-family dwellings and thirteen mobile homes. The single-family structures were to be built mostly in Richfield, with two others to go up in Annabella. New non-residential building permits were issued for four stores or restaurants, two public projects, and "many" garages and carports.[92]

Along with the good economic news of 1993, however, came some local protests. Residents of Monroe opposed a local construction project which, it was believed, threatened the serene nature of the town. Ryan Cashin of Monroe and his California business partner, Allen Newman, planned to construct six multi-unit apartment complexes in Monroe. When their plan was presented to the Monroe City Council in April 1993, an "overflow crowd" of more than 150 persons attended the meeting. In fact, so many Monroe residents came that the meeting, usually held in the basement of the city hall building, had to be moved to the South Sevier Middle School to accommodate all who wished to attend.[93]

The plan drew what the *Richfield Reaper*'s reporter termed "bitter opposition" from all but two of the persons who offered verbal testimony. Opponents were almost unanimously concerned about the number of people who would reside in the units. Others were disturbed by what they perceived as the "inability" of Monroe City to handle the waste water and sewage that the housing project would generate. Others were bothered by the federal government's role in the project.

It is interesting to note that in 1979 Monroe residents willingly accepted federal help in regard to thermal energy development, but now many were unwilling to have federally-subsidized housing in their community. As was often the case throughout the West, citizens would receive federal funds with one hand while holding up a protest sign with the other, depending on how they felt the particular project would immediately affect them. While Monroe's zoning law would allow for a "conditional use permit" in such an instance, the city council was concerned about having never received a complete set of plans from the developers, therefore, the council decided to delay a decision until seeing such plans and until it received official approval of the plans from the Utah State Health Department.[94]

By the end of 1993 most economic signs indicated that Sevier County was a growing, vital place. New homes and businesses were being constructed. The county's economy was benefiting from the increased tourism brought by the completion of Interstate 70 and the national growth in the travel and recreation industries. With growth also came problems, however, including drug smuggling and increased crime.

The county remained a conservative, Republican party stronghold throughout the latter part of the twentieth century. Many of the policies of Democratic presidents Jimmy Carter or Bill Clinton have been anathema in Sevier County, while those of Ronald Reagan and, to a lesser degree, George Bush seem to have been extremely popular in the county. In recent times, Republicans have tended to favor industrial and business expansion and oppose increased regulation and the expansion of the federal bureaucracy.[95] In Sevier County, and probably across Utah, the term "conservative" is likely a more descriptive political tag than Republican or Democrat. The majority of the people of Sevier County have proven themselves to be truly conservative.

Water in both its beneficial and destructive aspects continued to concern local residents. Although they sometimes supported the use of modern technology to bring more water, as with their willing experimentation with cloud-seeding, they could also reject advances that could have brought more water, such as the 1993 vote to withdraw from the Central Utah Project, an undertaking which, though expensive and plagued by delays, seemed to offer Sevier County and the rest of south-central Utah access to vast amounts of water. Was the choice to pull out of the CUP a wise one for Sevier County? Local voters overwhelmingly thought so. And while time will eventually allow people to judge the soundness of this decision, in a democratic referendum when the people speak, the decision is made.

Development was a leading aspect of Sevier County during the last quarter of the twentieth century, for which the farming community of Monroe serves as an example. In 1979 Monroe eagerly began a project to tap its hot springs for geothermal energy. Fourteen years later, in 1993, the citizens of Monroe rallied to try to block the proposed construction of multi-unit apartment complexes in the community. Both projects offered the potential of economic development for Monroe; but one was embraced and the other rejected when it was feared that it would cause the lifestyle of Monroe residents to deteriorate.

By 1995, according to census estimates, there were 17,166 residents of Sevier County—a healthy growth from the 15,431 of 1990. Sevier County appears to be in a relatively rapid growth phase, as was predicted years ago. The economy is varied, which can be seen as a

Saint Elizabeth's Catholic Church south of Richfield. (Allan Kent Powell)

sign of health and protection from economic busts. In the mid-1990s Sevier County residents and boosters were continuing to strive to become more modern, more progressive, more like the outside world. Yet the county was hampered, to some extent, by its limited funds and resources. A major question facing the people of Sevier County in the mid-1990s was how to preserve their "little paradise." Many favored material progress while still endeavoring to retain the natural beauty and rural lifestyle of their little portion of the American West.

Contemporary Sevier County remains predominantly Mormon, with four stakes in the county and numerous wards—at least one in every town, with some cities like Monroe, Salina, and Richfield being divided into many more. There is also increasing religious diversity, with many non-Mormons establishing congregations within the county. The regional phone book of 1996 listed among the county's religious congregations an Assembly of God, First Baptist Church, Richfield Bible Church, Valley Community Church, St. Elizabeth's Catholic Church, St. Jude's Episcopal Church, Good Shepherd Lutheran Church, and Jehovah's Witnesses congregation in Richfield, in addition to the Faith Baptist Church in Salina. Increased tolerance and understanding fostered by the diversity help make Sevier County a more pleasant place to live for all its residents.

In June 1993 Sevier County joined with the other twenty-eight Utah counties in laying plans to commemorate the 1996 Utah statehood centennial. Representatives from Sevier and Wayne counties met with Statehood Centennial Committee representative Linda Sappington at the Sevier County Courthouse to begin organizing centennial celebrations in the local area. Sevier County committee members included Trish Bumgardner, chairman; C. Howard Watkins, vice-chairman; Elaine Woodward, Frank Biagi, Neal Busk, and Barbara Oldroyd.[96]

Commission members have been "encouraging celebration at the local level in order to involve as many people as possible." Sevier County planned a number of contests to begin celebrating the centennial, including a photograph contest of old-time art, a "best old-time outfit contest," and a centennial float contest. The Sevier County centennial committee also designed a logo and planned to print and sell T-shirts with this centennial logo.[97] Sevier County embraced the centennial celebration of Utah statehood with open arms. Residents of Sevier County have contributed greatly to their communities and to the state as a whole; some, like artist LeConte Stewart, have achieved national and international recognition for their accomplishments. There is much for Sevier County to celebrate.

The 1996 statehood centennial and the sesquicentennial in 1997 of the first arrival of Mormon pioneers to Utah have provided opportunities to gather information about and reflect upon the county's history—the struggles and accomplishments of its residents in a sometimes harsh but always beautiful land. It is to be hoped that this increased awareness will help county residents as they prepare to meet the challenges of the future.

ENDNOTES

1. *Richfield Reaper,* 4 November 1976, 1.

2. *Richfield Reaper,* 15 April 1976, 1.

3. See R. McGreggor Cawley, *Federal Land, Western Anger: The*

*Sagebrush Rebellion and Environmental Politics* (Lawrence: University Press of Kansas, 1993).

4. C. Brant Short, *Ronald Reagan and the Public Lands: America's Conservation Debate, 1979–1984* (College Station: Texas A & M University Press, 1989), 10, 12.

5. Cawley, *Federal Land, Western Anger*, 72.

6. *Richfield Reaper*, 17 January 1980, 7-B.

7. Ibid.

8. Robert S. McPherson, *A History of San Juan County* (Salt Lake City: Utah State Historical Society, 1995), 360.

9. *Richfield Reaper*, 28 February 1980, 2.

10. Ibid.

11. *Utah Agricultural Statistics 1978* (Salt Lake City: Utah Department of Agriculture, 1978), 87, 88.

12. *1995 Utah Agriculture Statistics and Utah Department of Agriculture Annual Report* (Salt Lake City: Utah Department of Agriculture, 1995), 105, 115.

13. Ibid., 107.

14. *Richfield Reaper*, 13 October 1977, 1.

15. Ibid., 2.

16. Revo Morrey Young, *Ten Penny Nails: Pioneering Sevier Valley* (n.p., n.d.), 47.

17. *Richfield Reaper*, 25 September 1975, 1.

18. Short, *Ronald Reagan and the Public Lands*, 42.

19. *Richfield Reaper*, 6 November 1980, 1.

20. *Richfield Reaper*, 1 November 1979, 1–2.

21. Ibid.

22. *Richfield Reaper*, 22 January 1976, 2.

23. Irvin L. Warnock, compiler and editor, *Thru the Years: Sevier County Centennial History* (Springville, Utah: Art City Publishing Co., 1947), 39.

24. *Richfield Reaper* 1 February 1979, 1.

25. *Richfield Reaper*, 15 February 1979, 1–2.

26. *Newsweek*, 25 October 1976, 68–70.

27. *Salt Lake Tribune*, 18 April 1980; Jeffrey B. Hulen and Susan M. Sandberg, *Exploration Case History of the Monroe KGRA, Sevier County, Utah* (Salt Lake City: Earth Science Laboratory, University of Utah Research Institute for U.S. Department of Energy, 1981), 3.

28. *Richfield Reaper*, 15 February 1979, 1.

29. *Richfield Reaper*, 22 February 1979, 2.

30. *Richfield Reaper*, 18 January 1979, 1.

31. Allan Kent Powell, ed., *Utah History Encyclopedia* (Salt Lake City: University of Utah Press, 1994), 433–37.

32. *Utah Statistical Abstract, 1983* (Salt Lake City: Bureau of Economic and Business Research, University of Utah, 1983), iv-11.

33. *Richfield Reaper*, 17 January 1980, 1.

34. *Richfield Reaper*, 24 January 1980, 2.

35. Bureau of Economic and Business Research, Graduate School of Business, University of Utah, "Profile of the Richfield/Salina Labor Market Area," August 1982, 5; Wayne L. Wahlquist, ed., *Atlas of Utah* (Provo: Brigham Young University Press, 1981), 242.

36. *Richfield Reaper*, 16 November 1988, 1.

37. Ibid.

38. *Richfield Reaper*, 7 September 1988, 6-C.

39. Ibid.

40. *Richfield Reaper*, 19 October 1988, 1.

41. Ibid., 3-A.

42. *Richfield Reaper*, 3 February 1993, 1.

43. T. Merlin Ashman, letter to the author, 5 October 1995.

44. *Deseret News*, 22–23 July 1993, B–11.

45. T. Merlin Ashman, telephone interview with the author, 6 March 1995.

46. *Richfield Reaper*, 16 June 1993, 1

47. *Richfield Reaper*, 23 June 1993, 1.

48. Ibid., 3; Ashman, interview.

49. *Richfield Reaper*, 14 July 1993, 1; Ashman, interview.

50. *Richfield Reaper*, 14 July 1993, 2.

51. Ibid.

52. *Richfield Reaper*, 25 August 1993, 1.

53. Ibid., 2.

54. *Richfield Reaper*, 8 September 1993, 1.

55. *Deseret News*, 9 April 1995, B–3.

56. Ibid.

57. *Richfield Reaper*, 8 September 1993, 8; *Deseret News*, 9 April 1995, B–3.

58. *Richfield Reaper*, 22 July 1992, 1, 3.

59. *Richfield Reaper*, 11 November 1992, 1.

60. Ibid.

61. *Richfield Reaper*, 24 February 1993, 2.

62. *Richfield Reaper*, 19 August 1992, 1; 26 August 1992, 2.

63. *Richfield Reaper*, 24 February 1993, 1.

64. *Richfield Reaper*, 17 March 1993, 1.

65. *Richfield Reaper*, 22 January 1976, 2.

66. *Richfield Reaper*, 15 January 1976, 5.

67. *Richfield Reaper*, 29 April 1976, 8–B.

68. Ibid.

69. *Utah Statistical Abstract, 1983*, iv-13, iv-15.

70. *Richfield Reaper* 4 September 1980, 2.

71. *Richfield Reaper*, 31 December 1993, 2.

72. Samuel P. Hays, *Beauty, Health and Permanence: Environmental Politics in the United States, 1955–1985* (New York: Cambridge University Press, 1987, 1989), 3.

73. *Richfield Reaper*, 31 December 1993.

74. *Richfield Reaper*, 22 July 1976, 1.

75. *Richfield Reaper*, 15 July 1992, 1–A, 2–A.

76. *Richfield Reaper*, 10 March 1993, 3.

77. *Richfield Reaper*, 22 July 1992, 2-A.

78. *Richfield Reaper*, 12 August 1992, 1–A.

79. *Richfield Reaper*, 12 August 1992, 2–A.

80. Thomas R. Dunlap, *Saving America's Wildlife: Ecology and the American Mind, 1850–1990* (Princeton, NJ: Princeton University Press, 1988), x.

81. *Richfield Reaper*, 22 July 1992, 5-B.

82. *Statistical Abstract of Utah, 1996* (Salt Lake City: Bureau of Economic and Business Research, University of Utah, 1996), 497.

83. Ibid., 489; and *Statistical Abstract of Utah, 1993* (Salt Lake City: Bureau of Economic and Business Research, University of Utah, 1993), 455.

84. *Statistical Abstract of Utah, 1979* (Salt Lake City: Bureau of Economic and Business Research, University of Utah, 1979), xv–16; *Statistical Abstract of Utah, 1996*, 301; 1992 Census of Agriculture, supplied on computer Internet.

85. *Statistical Abstract of Utah, 1979*, xv–18; *Statistical Abstract of Utah, 1996*, 304.

86. *Statistical Abstract of Utah, 1996*, 404.

87. *Statistical Abstract of Utah, 1979,* xii–5; *Statistical Abstract of Utah, 1996,* 435; USA Counties—Sevier County, Utah, 1997 Internet census data.

88. Figures are taken from *Statistical Abstract of Utah,* various years.

89. *Richfield Reaper,* 4 November 1992, 1–A.

90. *Richfield Reaper,* 14 April 1993, 3–B.

91. See *Utah High Schools Activities Association Handbook, 1997–98* (Salt Lake City: Utah High School Activities Association, Inc., n.d.)

92. Ibid., 3–A.

93. *Richfield Reaper,* 14 April 1993, 2.

94. Ibid.

95. Dean L. May, *Utah: A People's History* (Salt Lake City: University of Utah Press, 1987), 191.

96. *Richfield Reaper,* 2 June 1993, 5–A.

97. Ibid.

## *Sevier County Officers*

### *County Commissioners*

**1865**

James Wareham, Peter Rasmussen, James Crawford

**1866**

Peter Rasmussen, Jens K. Peterson, Fred K. Olsen

**1867**

Nels Mortensen

**1871**

Nels Mortensen, Abraham Shaw, Stephen Farnsworth

**1872**

Archibald Buchanan, Moses Gifford, Josiah Martin

**1874**

Jens C. Anderson, Albert K. Thurber

1876

Thomas Cooper

1878

A. K. Thurber, A.T. Oldroyd

1879

Edward S. Dearsley, John A. Helstrom, J.W. Pierce

1880

Joseph W. Horne

1881

John Johnson

1882

William H. Seegmiller, J.W. Sylvester

1883

B.H. Greenwood, A.D. Thurber

1885

A.D. Thurber, H.M. Payne

1887

B.H. Greenwood, Leo A. Bean, James L. Hansen, A.D. Thurber

1888

A.D. Thurber, James L. Jensen

1890

A.D. Thurber, A.W. Buchanan

1891

A.D. Thurber, Peter Gottfredson

1893

J.W. Phillips, J.C. Jensen, Aug. Nelson

1895

Hans Rasmussen, M.A. Abbott, A.C. Shipp

1897

W.H. Robinson, H.H.Bell, J.A. Ross

1899

H.H. Bell, J.W. Phillips, Hans Tuft

1900

H.H. Bell, J.W. Phillips, Hans Tuft

1901

William Ogden, James L. Jensen, Fred Erickson

1902

William Ogden, James L. Jensen, Fred Erickson

1903

William Ogden, George T. Stevens, Fred Erickson

1905

George T. Stevens, Martin Jensen, H.C. Larsen

1906

George T. Stevens, Martin Jensen, H.C. Larsen

1908

George T. Stevens, J.E. Heppler, E.W. Crane

1910

J.E. Heppler, E.W. Crane, H.C. Larsen

1912

J.E. Heppler, A.W. Buchanan, D.G. Burgess

1914

D.G. Burgess, A.W. Buchanan, Joseph R. Staples

1916

D.G. Burgess, Joseph R. Staples, Chris Peterson

1918

D.G. Burgess, A.D. Nebeker, Austin Yergensen

1920

Andreas K. Hansen, A.D. Nebeker, Frank Herbert

1922

Alma Frandsen, George Peterson, Joseph F. Peterson

1924

Abe Hansen, Joseph F. Peterson, Carl Tuft

1926

Abe Hansen, Carl Tuft, Joseph F. Peterson

1928

Moroni Jensen, Carl Tuft, George A. Staples

1930

Moroni Jensen, George A. Staples, Delbert C. Burgess

1932

Moroni Jensen, Edwin Sorensen, George A. Staples

1934

Edwin Sorensen, W.W. Sylvester, Chariton Seegmiller

1936

Edwin Sorensen, Chariton Seegmiller, Delbert Hansen

1938

Chariton Seegmiller, Delbert Hansen, W.W. Sylvester

1940

Delbert Hansen, W.W. Sylvester, Ray H. Buchanan

1942

W.W. Sylvester, Ray H. Buchanan, James I. Rex
(James I. Rex died while in office and R. C. Willardson was
appointed to fill his term.)

1944

Ray H. Buchanan, W. Lloyd Johnson, Lawrence W. Jones

1946

W. Lloyd Johnson, Lawrence W. Jones, Ray H. Buchanan

1948

W. Lloyd Johnson, J. LeRue Ogden, Edwin Sorensen

1950

J. LeRue Ogden, Edwin Sorensen, Lawrence W. Jones

1952

Edwin Sorensen, Lawrence W. Jones, Kendrick Harward

1954

Lawrence W. Jones, Kendrick Harward, Blaine C. Curtis

1956

Kendrick Harward, Blaine C. Curtis, Heber Christiansen

1958

Blaine C. Curtis, Virge N. Brown, Kendrick Harward

1960

Blaine C. Curtis, Kendrick Harward, Virge N. Brown

1962

Blaine C. Curtis, Kendrick Harward, Virge N. Brown

1964

Blaine C. Curtis, Virge N. Brown, Arnel T. Dastrup

1966

Virge N. Brown, Arnel T. Dastrup, Stanley W. Burgess

1968

Virge N. Brown, Dean C. Nielsen, Arnel T. Dastrup

1970

Dean C. Nielsen, Ernest Lee, Elmo Herring

1972

Dean C. Nielsen, David Urie, Ivan Mills

1974

Elmo Herring, Ernest Lee, Dean C. Nielsen

1976

Dean C. Nielsen, Ivan Mills, Elmo Herring

1978

Ivan Mills, Elmo Herring, Ted Sorensen

1980

Elmo Herring, J. Elmer Collings, T. Merlin Ashman

1982

J. Elmer Collings, Elmo Herring, T. Merlin Ashman

1984

J. Elmer Collings, T. Merlin Ashman, Keith Hooper

1986

T. Merlin Ashman, Keith Hooper, Jerry Nice

1988

T. Merlin Ashman, Jerry Nice, Jay F. Gardner

1992

T. Merlin Ashman, Jerry Nice, Gene Mendenhall

1994

Tex R. Olsen, Peggy Mason, Ralph Okerlund

*County Clerk-Auditor*

1866: Jens C.A. Weibye
1867: John Wilson
1871: Austin Farnsworth
1874: William Morrison
1883: J.A. Helstrom
1890: Andrew Heppler
1893: J.E. Heppler
1895: S.G. Clark
1899: H.N. Hayes
1901: J.G. Jorgensen

1905: Parley Magleby
1911: Ed Ross
1915: George M. Hunt
1917: Wallace Sorensen
1918: S.G. Clark
1919: George M. Jones
1923: E.E. Thurston
1930: Wendell Anderson
1934: Wendell Anderson
1938: Marion Bird
1942: Arthur C. Lundgren
1946: J.L. Despain
1950: J.L. Despain
1954: J.L. Despain
1956: Weldon Richardson
1958: Weldon Richardson
1962: DeVon Poulson
1966: DeVon Poulson
1970: DeVon Poulson
1974: DeVon Poulson
1978: DeVon Poulson
1982: DeVon Poulson
1986: DeVon Poulson
1990: Steven Wall
1994: Steven Wall

## County Assessor

1865: W.G. Baker
1871: James M. Peterson
1877: W.G. Baker
1878: Chris Poulsen
1879: W.H. Clark
1888: F.A. Baker
1890: W.H. Robinson
1892: Hans Tuft
1895: Charles Anderson
1897: J.A. Smith

1899: J.E. Sorensen
1901: A.K. Hansen
1903: H.N. Hayes
1905: P.C. Scorup
1907: A. Parker
1911: George A. Christensen
1915: George A. Christensen
1917: Andrew Hansen
1921: R. Rickenbach
1923: L. L. Dastrup
1925: William Sorensen
1930: Soren Sorensen
1934: Cliff M. Powell
1938: Cliff M. Powell
1942: Cliff M. Powell
1946: Cliff M. Powell
1950: Cliff M. Powell
1954: Cliff M. Powell
1958: Milo Jensen
1962: Milo Jensen
1966: Jesse G. Allan
1970: Jesse G. Allan
1974: Stanford Fillmore
1978: Stanford Fillmore
1982: Stanford Fillmore
1986: Pam Henderson
1990: Pam Henderson
1994: Pam Henderson

## County Attorney

1867: Robert W. Glenn
1871: Alonzo Farnsworth
1879: J.W. Pierce
1882: George T. Bean
1890: I.J. Stewart
1892: George T. Bean
1893: W. McCarty

1896: J.B. Jennings
1897: E.W. McDaniels
1899: J.H. Erickson
1903: H.N. Hayes
1905: I.J. Stewart
1907: J.C. Jorgensen
1911: H.N. Hayes
1913: N.J. Bates
1917: Oluf Mickelson
1921: H.E. Beal
1925: Ferd Erickson
1928: T.A. Hunt
1930: T.A. Hunt
1934: Carvel Mattsson
1936: Carvel Mattsson
1938: Carvel Mattsson
1940: T.A. Hunt
1942: D.C. Winget
1944: D.C. Winget
1946: D.C. Winget
1950: D.C. Winget
1954: Tex R. Olsen
1958: Tex R. Olsen
1962: Tex R. Olsen
1966: Tex R. Olsen
1970: K.L. McIff
1974: K.L. McIff
1978: Don Rulon Brown
1982: Don Rulon Brown
1986: Don Rulon Brown
1990: Don Rulon Brown
1994: Don Rulon Brown

## County Recorder

1877: A. M. Farnsworth
1888: Andrew Heppler
1890: S.G. Clark

1892: J.A. Helstrom
1894: J.M. Lauritzen
1897: Maud S. Layton
1899: Eliza Ross
1901: Alveretta Olsen
1905: Lydia Cowley
1909: Viola Burr
1911: May Baker
1913: Matilda Dalton
1915: Clara R. Gray
1919: Mary Bowman
1923: Mary Bowman
1925: Dora B. Jensen
1930: Dora B. Jensen
1934: Hazel Swindle
1938: Hazel Swindle
1942: Hazel Swindle
1946: Hazel Swindle
1950: Hazel Swindle
1954: Hazel Swindle
1958: Henrietta Thalman
1962: Florence Baker
1966: Florence Baker
1970: R. Leon Olcott
1974: Bessie Curtis
1978: Bessie Curtis
1982: Bessie Curtis
1986: Dorothy Vee Henrie
1990: Dorothy Vee Henrie
1994: Dorothy Vee Henrie

## County Sheriff

1866: Nathaniel Hanchett
1871: George Oglivie
1877: —— McBride
1879: W. H. Clark
1889: John W. Coons

1893: John W. Coons
1897: John W. Coons
1899: James L. Jensen
1901: W.H. Clark
1905: M.A. Abbott
1907: M.A. Abbott
1911: A.N. Lawson
1915: C.E. Leavitt
1917: W.S. Greenwood
1921: A.J. Fillmore
1923: A.J. Fillmore
1925: Vern M. Fairbanks
1930: Vern M. Fairbanks
1934: Vern M. Fairbanks
1938: Clarence Smith
1942: Clarence Smith
1946: Clarence Smith
1950: Clarence Smith
1954: Rex L. Huntsman
1958: Rex L. Huntsman
1962: Rex L. Huntsman
1966: Rex L. Huntsman
1970: Rex L. Huntsman
1974: Rex L. Huntsman
1978: Rex L. Huntsman
1982: Billy Weaver
1986: John L. Meacham
1990: John L. Meacham
1994: John L. Meacham

## County Treasurer

1874: William H. Seegmiller
1876: Esk C. Peterson
1878: William H. Seegmiller
1880: W.G. Baker
1884: H.J. Hansen
1888: James M. Peterson

1895: H.J. Hansen
1901: Hans Rasmussen
1907: S.G. Clark
1911: C.W. Powell
1915: E.C. Christiansen
1919: Lou Goldbranson
1921: E.C. Christiansen
1930: E.C. Christiansen
1934: Lynn C. Nielson
1938: Lynn C. Nielson
1942: Lynn C. Nielson
1946: Adelbert Wells
1950: Adelbert Wells
1954: Ben M. Ainsworth
1958: Ben M. Ainsworth
1962: Ben M. Ainsworth
1966: Ben M. Ainsworth
1970: R. Leon Olcott
1974: R. Leon Olcott
1978: Leda Jensen
1982: Leda Jensen
1986: Leda Jensen
1990: Leda Jensen
1994: Leda Jensen

*Selected Bibliography*

The following readily available sources provide basic historical information on Sevier County's past. For more detailed subject references see the notes at the end of each chapter.


Alexander, Thomas G. *The Rise of Multiple-Use Management in the Intermountain West: A History of Region 4 of the Forest Service.* Washington, D.C.: United States Department of Agriculture, 1987.

Arrington, Leonard J. *Great Basin Kingdom: An Economic History of the Latter-day Saints.* Cambridge: Harvard University Press, 1958.

———. "Taming the Turbulent Sevier: A Story of Mormon Desert Conquest." *Western Humanities Review* 4 (Autumn 1951): 393–406.

Arrington, Leonard J., Feramorz Y. Fox, and Dean L. May. *Building the City of God: Community and Cooperation Among the Mormons.* Urbana and Chicago: University of Illinois Press, 1992.

Berry, Michael S. *Time, Space and Transition in Anasazi Prehistory.* Salt Lake City: University of Utah Press, 1982.

Bunte, Pamela A., and Robert J. Franklin, *From the Sands to the Mountain: Change and Persistence in a Southern Paiute Community.* Lincoln: University of Nebraska Press, 1987.

Dastrup, Jeanne. "The Sigurd Story." Paper, 1971; copy at Utah State Historical Society Library.

Dutton, Clarence E. *Report on the Geology of the High Plateaus of Utah.* Washington, D.C.: United States Geological Service, 1880.

Gardner, Frank D. and Charles A. Jensen. *Soil Survey in Sevier Valley, Utah.* Washington, D.C.: U.S. Department of Agriculture, 1900. Copy at the Utah State Historical Society Library, Salt Lake City.

Geary, Edward A. *The Proper Edge of the Sky: The High Plateau County of Utah.* Salt Lake City: University of Utah Press, 1992.

Haymond, Jay M. "The Sevier River of Utah." In *Rolling Rivers: An Encyclopedia of America's Rivers,* edited by Richard A. Bartlett. New York: McGraw-Hill Book Company, 1984.

Holt, Ronald L., *Beneath the Red Cliffs: An Ethnohistory of the Utah Paiutes.* Albuquerque: University of New Mexico Press, 1992.

Houghton, Samuel G. *A Trace of Desert Waters: The Great Basin Story.* Salt Lake City: Howe Brothers, 1986.

Jackson, Richard H. "Utah's Harsh Lands: Hearth of Greatness." *Utah Historical Quarterly* 49 (Winter 1981): 4–25.

Jacobson, Pearl F., comp. and ed. *Golden Sheaves from a Rich Field: A Centennial History of Richfield, Utah.* Richfield, Utah: Richfield Reaper Publishing Company, 1964.

Leigh, Rufus Wood. "Naming of the Green, Sevier and Virgin Rivers." *Utah Historical Quarterly* 29 (April 1961): 137–47.

Madsen, David B. *Exploring the Fremont.* Salt Lake City: Utah Museum of Natural History, 1989.

Morgan, Dale L. *Jedediah Smith and the Opening of the West.* Lincoln: University of Nebraska Press, 1967.

Murdock, Wilford, and Mildred Murdock. *Monroe, Utah: Its First One Hundred Years, 1864–1964.* Monroe, Utah: Monroe Centennial Committee, 1964.

Peterson, Charles S. *Utah: A History.* New York: W.W. Norton & Company, 1977.

Powell, Allan Kent, ed. *Utah History Encyclopedia.* Salt Lake City: University of Utah Press, 1994.

Powell, John Wesley. *Lands of the Arid Region of the United States With a More Detailed Account of the Lands of Utah.* Washington, D.C.: Government Printing Office, 1879.

Richardson, G.B. *Underground Water in Sanpete and Central Sevier River*

*Valleys, Utah.* Washington, D.C.: Government Printing Office, 1907. Copy at Utah State Historical Society Library.

Salisbury, F.B. "The Big Rock Candy Mountain." *Utah Science* 46 (Winter 1985): 112–18.

Sorensen, Iva Lee, and Kaye S. Bybee, comps. *Founded on Faith—A History of Glenwood, 1864–1984.* Glenwood, Utah: Daughters of Utah Pioneers, 1984.

Stegner, Wallace E. *Clarence Edward Dutton: An Appraisal.* Salt Lake City: University of Utah Press, 1936.

Stokes, William Lee. *Geology of Utah.* Salt Lake City: Utah Museum of Natural History and Utah Geological and Mineral Survey, 1986.

Sturgis, Cynthia Jane. "The Mormon Village in Transition: Richfield, Utah, as a Case Study, 1910–1930." Master's thesis, University of Utah, 1978.

U.S. Bureau of the Census. *County and City Data Book, 1972.* Washington, D.C.: U.S. Department of Commerce, 1973.

U.S. Bureau of the Census. *United States Census of Agriculture.* Various years. Washington, D.C.: U.S. Department of Commerce.

*Utah High Schools Activities Association Handbook, 1997–98.* Salt Lake City: Utah High Schools Activities Association, 1997.

Utah State Department of Agriculture. *Utah Agricultural Statistical Report,* various years. Salt Lake City: Utah State Department of Agriculture.

*Utah Statistical Abstract,* various years. Salt Lake City: Bureau of Economic and Business Research, University of Utah.

Van Wagoner, Richard S. *Mormon Polygamy: A History.* 2nd ed. Salt Lake City: Signature Books, 1989.

Warnock, Irvin L., comp. and ed. *Thru the Years: Sevier County Centennial History.* Springville, Utah: Art City Publishing Co. 1947.

Warnock, President and Mrs. Irvin L. *Memories of the Sevier Stake Church of Jesus Christ of Latter-day Saints: Diamond Jubilee Memorial Volume, 1874–1949,* Springville, Utah: Art City Publishing Co., 1969.

Young, Revo M. *Ten Penny Nails: Pioneering Sevier Valley,* n.p., n.d.

*Index*